DIABLO II™

OFFICIAL STRATEGY GUIDE

By Bart Farkas

BLIZZARD
ENTERTAINMENT

////||BRADYGAMES
TAKE YOUR GAME FURTHER™

DIABLO™ II OFFICIAL STRATEGY GUIDE
©2000 Macmillan USA, Inc.

LEGAL STUFF

Brady Publishing
An Imprint of
Macmillan USA, Inc.
201 W. 103rd St.
Indianapolis, IN 46290

ISBN: 1-56686-891-2
LIBRARY OF CONGRESS No.: 99-72855

Printing Code: The rightmost double-digit number is the year of the book's printing; the rightmost single-digit number is the number of the book's printing. For example, 00-1 shows that the first printing of the book occurred in 2000.

03 02 01 00   4 3 2 1

BRADYGAMES STAFF

Editor-In-Chief
H. Leigh Davis

Licensing Manager
David Waybright

Licensing Assistant
Mike Degler

Creative Director
Robin Lasek

Marketing Manager
Janet Eshenour

Marketing Assistant
Tricia Reynolds

CREDITS

Project Editor
David B. Bartley

Screenshot Editor
Michael Owen

Book Designer
Dan Caparo

Production Designers
Lisa England
Bob Klunder
Jane Washburne

Author Acknowledgements

Because of the team effort that's required to put a book like this together, there are plenty of people to thank, so I thought I'd first extend one huge "thank you" to everyone, then list each person who contributed and show what area they were responsible for helping with. Here goes:

Blizzard North

These gentlemen were all part of the design and production of the game, and together and individually provided me with invaluable information. Matt deserves a special thank you for spearheading my trip to Blizzard North and ferrying information to me in large quantities.

Matt Householder

Matt Schaefer

Erik Schaefer

Dave Brevik

Jason Regier

Blizzard Irvine

This is where all of the Quality Assurance for *Diablo II* occurs. The many people in QA, as well as other portions of Blizzard Irvine, all deserve a huge round of thanks. Special thanks go out to John Lagrave, the QA manager for his Herculean efforts to satisfy my every whimsical and trivial *Diablo II*-related question. Also special thanks need to go out to Geoff Frazier for his contributions past and present. Lastly, there's a pile of behind-the-scenes Blizzard employees who have art and other elements that appear in this book, and to them I would also like to say "gracias!" That said, thanks to:

Bill Roper – Senior Producer

Master Blaster (John Lagrave) – Deity of QA

Peter Underwood—Strategies, tips, art

Christian Arretche—Monsters and screenshots

Matt Morris—Monsters

3

Joe Frayne—Tips

Derek "The Kurgan" Simmons—Skill strategies and tips

Carlos Guerrero—Quests, skill strategies, tips

Mark Kern—General information

Diana Smallwood—Tips

Katt Jean—Tips

Conner Brandt —Tips, screenshots

Justin Parker—Quests, strategies

Roger Eberhart—Items

Jason Hutchins—Skills, skills, and more skills

Ian Welke—Strategies

Andy Bond—Screenshots, tips

Dave Fried—Strategies, Mac stuff

Geoff Fraizer—Difficulty Level tips, art

Eric Dodds—Difficulty Level tips

Brian Love—Strategies, Mac stuff

BradyGAMES

The entire staff at BradyGAMES was most excellent to work with. You guys really know and love games, and that's something any *Diablo* fan can appreciate. I'd like to thank you all for your support and help.

DEDICATION

For Cori and Adam

Contents

Introduction 7

Chapter 1: The Basics 9

Chapter 2: The Characters 17

Necromancer 21
Poison and Bone 21
Curses 28
Summoning and Control 34

Amazon 42
Bow and Crossbow 42
Passive and Magic 49
Javelin and Spear 54

Paladin 62
Combat 62
Offensive Auras 68
Defensive Auras 73

Sorceress 80
Fire 80
Lightning 86
Cold 91

Barbarian 98
Combat Skills 98
Combat Masteries 104
Warcries 107

Diablo II Tome of Knowledge 113

Character Skill Trees 114
Adventure Images 124
Horadric Cube Recipes 128

Chapter 3: The Quests 129

Act I: The Sightless Eye 131
Den of Evil 132
Sisters' Burial Ground 133

Cairn Stones 134

Forgotten Tower 136

Tools of the Trade 137

Sisters to the Slaughter 138

ACT II: THE SECRET OF VIZJEREI **140**

Radament's Lair 141

The Horadric Staff 142

Tainted Sun 143

The Arcane Sanctuary 144

The Summoner 145

The Seven Tombs 145

ACT III: THE INFERNAL GATE **147**

The Golden Bird 147

The Blade of the Old Religion 148

Khalim's Will 148

Lam Esen's Tome 150

The Blackened Temple 151

The Guardian 151

ACT IV: THE HARROWING **153**

The Fallen Angel 153

The Hellforge 154

Terror's End 155

CHAPTER 4: THE LISTS **157**

BESTIARY **158**

Standard Monsters 158

Champions & Super Unique Monsters 174

WEAPONS AND ARMOR **179**

CHAPTER 5: MULTIPLAYER **195**

BATTLE.NET **197**

MULTIPLAYER TACTICS **200**

APPENDIX: CHARACTER SKILL TABLES **203**

INDEX **219**

Introduction

In 1996 the original *Diablo* was released to the world and immediately (like al Blizzard games), it reshaped the computer gaming landscape. *Diablo* was a real-time role-playing game that had compelling gameplay—something that had previously been unheard of. Not only was it a great single-player game, it also offered a unique way of playing with other gamers from all over the world with its revolutionary Battle.net system. After *Diablo*'s release, all similar games were destined to be compared to it, and in most cases the efforts were not even worthy of comparison. Even to this day, *Diablo* is still staggeringly popular on Battle.net, and now after over three long years of waiting, *Diablo II* bursts onto the shelves (and millions of hard drives) with everything that a sequel should possess—fabulous movies, an engrossing story, spine-tingling special effects, gut-wrenching battles, and gameplay that will make *Diablo II* the king of this genre for years to come.

What makes *Diablo II* such a fantastic game is the loving attention to detail that Blizzard put into balancing the gameplay so that each of the 150 character skills would have value in the game. Indeed, the largest chapter of this book (Chapter 2: The Characters) contains details on all 150 skills and how to use them in both single and multiplayer action (when applicable). The complexity of the five character classes and their skill sets is astounding, and is the primary reason why *Diablo II* will be replayable hundreds of times.

This book draws on the wisdom and experience of the entire Blizzard crew that helped to create and test *Diablo II*. Many long hours were spent on-site at both Blizzard's San Mateo and Irvine offices consulting with the resident 'experts' who specialize in each of the game's various aspects.

In creating this book, we attempted to make it as useful to the reader as possible; there-fore, there was a heavy emphasis placed on each of the skills, and the basic flow of each of the quests. The Bestiary will give you what you need to know about all of the hideous monsters you'll meet in *Diablo II*—including the Bosses and Unique monsters. The Weapons & Armor section will explain how weapons are created, improved (socketed items), and even has the details for such highly sought-after information as the unique Item Sets! For those interested in Battle.net play, there is a chapter dedicated to getting the most out of the multiplayer experience. Finally, check out The Basics chapter for the low-down on the potions, scrolls, difficulty levels, and even the effects of each of the Shrines that you'll encounter in the world of *Diablo II*.

Let this book be a reference to guide you whenever you have a question or are having difficulty. After all, *Diablo II* is so rich, complex, and huge that there will certainly be times when even the most independent of gamers will need to grab a hint or two from this guide!

Chapter 1
THE BASICS

The Diablo Story

In the first game, Diablo spent two centuries slowly working to corrupt the Soulstone that imprisoned him. In time, he was able to extend his influence into the surrounding area and corrupt both King Leoric and his archbishop, Lazarus. The King proved too strong to fully control, so the Demon took possession of his son, Prince Albrecht. Diablo then began to shape an outpost of Hell within the catacombs that ran beneath the town of Tristram. By spreading terror into the surrounding countryside, the Demon was able to attract many heroes who came to cleanse the land of evil. By the time the strongest of these heroes reached this goal, though, he had become fully influenced by the will of Diablo. In his twisted state, this adventurer believed that the only way to fully control the Demon was to plunge the shard of the Soulstone into his own head. This, of course, was exactly what Diablo had planned as the Demon now had an even stronger body to use in the completion of his ultimate plan.

Now, in *Diablo II*, Diablo has headed east to the desert outside of the city of Lut Gholein, intent on freeing his brother, Baal. The possessed body of the fallen hero has taken on an increasingly Demonic appearance. For this reason, the Demon brought with him a mortal companion to go amongst the people of the city, listening for information, and securing what mundane necessities the Lord of Terror still required. Diablo soon found himself pursued by ever greater mortal heroes as he raged across the lands to wake his brothers.

It's from this point that you begin *Diablo II*, choosing a character from one of five different classes: Amazon, Barbarian, Necromancer, Paladin, or Sorceress. After your character has been chosen, you will work your way through four Acts and 21 quests while en route to destroy Diablo. Along the way you'll go through many sets of armor and weapons. You'll also meet hideous monsters, valued allies, and evil overlords. Only those that are true of heart will be able to make it through the game to defeat *Diablo II*, but then, only those that are true of heart would accept the challenge!

MAJOR CHARACTERS

These are the major characters in the *Diablo II* storyline, as outlined by the game's designers at Blizzard North. This is not a detailed listing of each character's motivations and personality. Instead, it is merely meant to tell you a little about each character so that you can identify where they 'fall' in the storyline as you work your way through the game.

Andariel: *Known as the Maiden of Anguish, she is one of the Lesser Evils.*

Diablo: *Youngest of the Prime Evils and the Lord of Terror.*

Duriel: *The Prince of Pain and one of the Lesser Evils.*

Izual: *The Angel who bore the runeblade "Azure Wrath" in an assault on the Hell Forge. He was eventually corrupted and first gave the demons information about the Soulstone. He now serves as a lieutenant in Hell.*

Mephisto: *The last of the Prime Evils and the Lord of Hatred.*

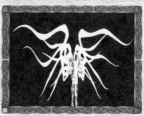

Tyreal: *An Archangel in the ranks of Heaven, he has always been especially concerned for the welfare of humanity. He has also dealt extensively with the Soulstone and Mazulere over the ages. It was he who forged the angelic runeblade "Azure Wrath" that Izual used in his tragic attack on the Hell Forge.*

Baal: *One of the Prime Evils and the Lord of Destruction.*

Tal Rasha: *A Horadrim mage who was in the group pursuing Baal. He voluntarily imprisoned himself to supplement the power of the Soulstone that contained Baal. Tal Rasha was eventually corrupted and revealed the secret of Mazulere to the three Prime Evils.*

Jehred Cain: *The Horadric leader that pursued and eventually captured Diablo.*

Basics

This section reviews much of the information you may already have learned in the manual or from playing the game; however, there are several bits of advice that even experienced *Diablo* gamers might find useful… so read on, brave warrior.

INVENTORY

Your inventory is a limited space that houses everything from potions and scrolls to weapons and armor that you pick up as you work your way through the game. The items that you pick up as you kill monsters can either be used, sold, or stored. Selling items is a great way to obtain gold, especially if you sell a Unique or magically enhanced weapon that you otherwise wouldn't want to use. Of course, the Inventory is a finite space, meaning that it will quickly fill up with items, and then you won't be able to pick up new items that you find. Frequent trips back to town via Town Portals or Waypoints is highly recommended because all of those average items that you sell will eventually add up to one very expensive and powerful item!

Since your inventory fills up so quickly, it would be nice to have another storage place for your extra items, and thankfully there is—your Private Stash. This is a permanent storage chest that appears in each of the four towns and allows you to store some extra treasures. Although your Private Stash is limited in space, it is also protected from others, even if you die! Probably the best advice is to sell or trade what you don't need and keep only the really cool items (like if you're trying to put a special set together) in your Private Stash for later use.

TIP

Once you have obtained the Horadric Cube, you can keep it in your main Inventory. Although it takes up four squares, the Horadric Cube has 12 squares inside it, so you can actually gain eight storage spaces by keeping items inside the Horadric Cube! Be warned, though, that items in the right combination can be altered if you hit the Transmute button, so be careful when using this storage technique.

NOTE......

When you die in Hardcore Mode, you lose everything in your stash!

HORADRIC CUBE RECIPES

The Horadric Cube is a powerful artifact that has the ability to transmute items into other objects. While some of these are vital to solving the mysteries of *Diablo II*, others are simply very useful. Some of these combinations (also called recipes) are well known, but many have been lost to the sands of time. Check out the last page of this guide's *Diablo II Tome of Knowledge* to discover a few of these secret recipes.

'MOUSING' OVER

If you ever want to know something about any item in *Diablo II*, you need only move your mouse cursor over the item (or button) in question and a handy dialogue box will pop up containing all the information you'll want to know about it. Unidentified Items are the exception to this rule. These items will have descriptions that appear in red and you won't be able to equip them.

ARMOR & WEAPONS

This is a no-brainer. If you have armor in your inventory that could be equipped (put on your body) to improve your defense rating, equip it! You never know when a few extra points of defense will mean the difference between a close call and a gruesome death, so always equip the best set of armor and weapons that you have in your inventory. It's also a good idea to keep your armor and weapons in good repair; if the durability of an item falls to zero, that item becomes useless and cannot be wielded until it is repaired.

Managing your Inventory and making sure that you are well equipped are two critical components to success.

THE BELT

The Belt is critical to your success because you can store potions and or scrolls for quick and easy access. You are automatically given four slots to hold items, but if you wear a larger belt or sash you will likely have more spots available. The number keys of 1, 2, 3, and 4 activate the potion or scroll that's in the corresponding belt slot. If you are using a larger belt with slots above, the potion or scroll that was above will automatically slide down into the location you just accessed.

By pressing one of the four number keys (1-4), you can quickly and automatically use potions and scrolls—without having to worry about moving your mouse then right-clicking on an item (not to mention opening your Inventory). You can place Scrolls, Mana Potions, Health Potions, Antidote Potions, Rejuvenation Potions, and Stamina Potions on your belt in any spot. Throwing potions are the only exception to the potion/scroll rule—they cannot be placed in your belt and must be equipped in your hand to use instead.

SCROLLS

There are two kinds of standard scrolls in *Diablo II*, Town Portal Scrolls and Identify Item Scrolls. Both of these can be purchased individually or in books called Tomes. For the purposes of saving space in your inventory, picking up a Tome is very handy because you can save literally 18 inventory slots by filling an Identify Item Tome with 20 scrolls! Here's a little more insight into each of the two scrolls:

Identify Item: This scroll permanently shows you the magical properties of one item. An item that would sell for 100 gold pieces before identification might sell for several thousand gold pieces after it has been exposed as a highly magical item.

Town Portal: When activated, a Town Portal scroll opens a doorway back to the town in the current Act. The importance of this scroll cannot be overstated; not only does it provide a quick and easy way to get back to town to store loot or sell items you've acquired during your conquests, but it also allows you to escape from nasty situations. In Chapter 3: The Quests we will sometimes suggest that you open a Town Portal before you face a particularly tough enemy. Doing this will expedite your escape if your situation becomes desperate.

POTIONS

Potions are literally the lifeblood of your character in *Diablo II*. The two that you will use most frequently are Healing potions and Mana potions, which their names imply, replenish your health and mana. There are, however, other potions in *Diablo II* that are worth looking into, because you'll more than likely find the need to use them all from time to time. Here's a list of the potions and what they do:

Healing Potions: These potions replenish your health and come in five flavors—Minor, Light, Healing, Greater, and Super Healing. Each of these potions does more healing than its predecessor, but only the Minor healing potion can be purchased in normal mode—the others must be found within the game. The better healing potions can be purchased in Nightmare and Hell games.

Mana Potions: Mana potions replenish the energy that courses through each character's body. Even though characters regenerate mana on their own, sometimes it's necessary to augment this natural replenishment with a Mana potion. These potions also come in five varieties of increasing strength: Minor, Light, Mana, Greater, and Super Mana.

Antidote Potion: This potion will cure poison instantly. However, you may want to stock up on these potions if you're facing a great number of poison-spewing enemies because they only cure poison, they don't protect against it.

Rejuvenation Potion: This potion instantly refills one-third of both your mana and health at the same time!

Full Rejuvenation Potion: This potion instantly tops off both your mana and health. When you have lots of mana and health points at higher levels this can be a huge benefit.

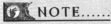

TIP..........

In multiplayer games, Town Portals are sometimes used in numbers, one or two screens apart, so that you can run and escape from difficult situations even if one of the Town Portals is surrounded by enemies.

NOTE......

It is important to remember that a player can have only one Town Portal open at a time.

BASICS

Stamina Potion: Simply put, this potion restores your stamina instantly. It is essentia if you must engage in excessive running.

Thawing Potion: There's nothing worse than getting frozen in a tough battle. If this hap pens, you can use this potion to instantly thaw your character out and continue fighting

Oil Potion: This potion (which must be thrown) causes an explosion and resulting fir that heavily damages enemies.

Exploding Potion: This potion (which must be thrown) causes an explosion that doe damage within a small radius. It is highly effective when thrown into a tightly-packe group of enemies.

Rancid Gas Potion: This potion (which must be thrown) causes poison damage on an enemy near it when it detonates.

Choking Gas Potion: This is a more damaging version of the Rancid Gas Potion.

Strangling Gas Potion: This is the 'big-daddy' of the Gas Potions, and will deal a larg area of poison damage that lasts a considerable amount of time.

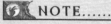

NOTE......

When you use a Healing potion, the effects of it take time to improve your health, so don't wait too long to use a potion; it may not respond fast enough to replenish your health in time to stave off an enemy's attack.

SHRINES

Throughout *Diablo II* you will find Shrines and Wells that will aid in your journeys by tem porarily increasing statistics, granting abilities or rejuvenating your character. These Shrine and Wells are randomly placed, so don't assume that you'll be coming up against monster that will attack with fire simply because you've come across a Resist Fire Shrine! Here's breakdown of each of the Shrines you'll encounter in *Diablo II* and whether it will recharg after it has been used:

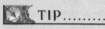

TIP..........

The Horadric Cube can help provide you with a steady supply of Rejuvenation Potions. See the last page of this guide's Diablo II Tome of Knowledge for details.

Refill Shrine (Recharges): Fully refills both your health and your mana.

Health Shrine (Recharges): Fully refills your health.

Mana Shrine (Recharges): Fully refills your mana.

Mana Recharge Shrine (Recharges): Increases the rate at which your mana refills by 50%.

Armor Shrine (Recharges): Boosts your armor by 100%.

Combat Shrine (Recharges): Increases your To Hit by 200%, and your maximum dam age by 200%.

Resist Fire Shrine (Recharges): Increases your resistance to fire by 75%.

Resist Cold Shrine (Recharges): Increases your resistance to cold by 75%.

Resist Poison Shrine (Recharges): Increases your resistance to poison by 75%.

Resist Lightning Shrine (Recharges): Increases your resistance to lightning by 75%.

Skill Shrine (Recharges): Increases all skills that you have already developed by two levels. This is a very powerful shrine since you gain +2 to every skill you have learned!

Recharge Shrine (Recharges): Recharges your mana at a rate that's 400% faster than normal.

Stamina Shrine (Recharges): Gives you unlimited Stamina while active.

Experience Shrine (Does Not Recharge): Gives you 50% more experience per kill. This is a very useful Shrine and if you find one, activate it and then go pick a few fights so that you can get your Experience up quickly.

Monster Shrine (Does Not Recharge): When you touch this Shrine, the nearest enemy becomes a Unique monster!

Fire Shrine (Does Not Recharge): Numerous firebolts erupt in a ring of death and damage anything nearby—including monsters, you, and your allies.

Poison Shrine (Does Not Recharge): A double-edged sword, this Shrine poisons you when you touch it, but also emits between five and ten Gas potions.

Exploding Shrine (Does Not Recharge): Similar to the Poison Shrine, this Shrine will cause damage when touched, but will also release a horde of Exploding Potions.

Gem Shrine (Does Not Recharge): Upgrades one gem selected at random from the player's inventory and drops it onto the ground. If there is no gem to upgrade, it drops a random chipped gem.

HARDCORE MODE

Notice the checkbox for making your new character an elite Hardcore variety.

As mentioned in the manual, Hardcore mode is for players who like to live on the edge. When in Hardcore mode you have only one life, and if you die, you die; there's no resurrecting a Hardcore character. With this in mind, your Hardcore character should always have plenty of health or, better yet, rejuvenation potions handy, and you should stick to attacks that keep you out of harm's way. Also, avoid games with heavy lag or people you do not trust! To even become a Hardcore character involves somewhat of a challenge because you must first defeat *Diablo II* on the normal difficulty setting. Once you have completed this enormous task, you'll be given the option to create a Hardcore character.

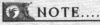
NOTE......

Although death in Hardcore mode is permanent, you can allow another player to get your items and gold by 'looting' your body. The main catch is that this player must be in the game when you die. You must allow looting before you die, however! Keep in mind that being able to loot your body might actually be an incentive for someone to kill you, as well.

As an added bonus, you will also get a special title for your character based on which level of the game you've completed. For Normal difficulty level you get Lord or Lady as a prefix, for Nightmare difficulty level you get Count or Countess, and for the Hell difficulty level you get King or Queen. Considering the challenges involved in defeating *Diablo II* on the Hell difficulty level, a title like King or Queen will be well earned!

DIFFICULTY LEVELS

There are actually two difficulty levels above the default skill level (which this book was written on). However, there are some important things to know about the Nightmare and Hell levels of play. Fortunately, Eric Dodds, Carlos Guerrero, and Geoff Frazier of Blizzard Entertainment have decided to impart their vast knowledge of how to compete in the two upper difficulty levels of *Diablo II* (Nightmare and Hell). Here's what they have to say:

- ❧ It's best to hang out in Act IV for a while, cleaning it out a few times before you move on to the next difficulty level. This will help to make your character(s) stronger and better suited to fight the tougher monsters to come.

- ❧ You get the most experience from monsters no more than five levels lower or higher than your character's level until you reach Level 25. After that, anything goes!

- ❧ Melee classes have trouble hitting monsters that are much above their level, so you may want to postpone going to Nightmare skill level until your character is at level 25 to 30; avoid Hell until you're at level 50. In general, if you find yourself having difficulty hitting monsters, go back to a previous difficulty level for a while.

- ❧ The monsters in Normal - Act IV go up to level 30, so you should optimally leave Normal difficulty somewhere between level 27 and 32.

- ❧ The monsters in Nightmare – Act IV go up to level 55, so you should optimally leave Nightmare difficulty somewhere between level 45 and 55.

- ❧ You can move on to the next Act earlier, but since the experience loss for death is higher in each successive difficulty level, you want to make sure you are ready to go to the next difficulty level. Take your time and build your levels.

- ❧ You can hang out in a difficulty level longer than it would normally be valuable for you to do so by playing in games with lots of players, thus upping the experience reward for killing monsters. It should also be noted, however, that the monsters also become more difficult when there are more players in the game.

- ❧ In the higher difficulty levels you can find exceptional items (better versions of the items found in normal difficulty). These are the items you want Charsi to imbue when you complete the Horadric Malus quest on higher difficulty levels.

Chapter 2
THE CHARACTERS

The *Diablo II* environment allows you to embark on your quest using one of five character classes: the Barbarian, Sorceress, Necromancer, Amazon, or the Paladin. As you might expect, each of these characters has their own strengths and weaknesses, but further to their innate abilities are the three skill sets that each character can improve upon. Each set of skills can be enhanced as the character matures and gains experience within *Diablo II*, but the ability to improve skills is limited. This limitation means that you can fully develop only one skill line, with the other skill lines partially developed or ignored, leaving the door open for significant variation between character's abilities by game's end.

This feature is what makes the character development in *Diablo II* so very impressive. You can have two Amazons that start the game at the same time, but based on the choices each player makes with regard to skill assignments, these two characters can end up having considerably different skill sets by the end of the game. For example, one may have mastered every skill in the Bow and Crossbow skill set while the other has become adept at Healing and Movement skills giving her very different abilities, such as Decoy (the ability to duplicate herself).

This chapter will touch on the basic traits, strengths, and weaknesses of each of the five character classes. More importantly, it will also delve into the intricacies of the skill sets for each character, giving strategies and information about each skill.

Choosing a Character Class

Before examining which skills to develop and in what order, you must first decide which of the five characters you will guide through the complex and challenging world of *Diablo II*. Which character you choose will depend on a number of factors including your preferred style of fighting, the amount of magical abilities you want to have, skills that can be developed (they're different for every character) and of course, personal preference (gender, looks, attitude). In order to help you make your decision, here is a brief description of the style of combat for each of the five character classes:

Amazon— The Amazon is a powerful and versatile character who excels at using magic spells, magic missiles, arrows, and other methods of combat that cause damage from afar. In short, the Amazon likes to stand back and shoot, making her the "fire and forget" character. If you don't want to be repairing armor damaged from constantly taking hits, the Amazon is a good choice. That said, although she usually handles missile weapons, the Amazon is very strong and can fight in hack-and-slash battles surprisingly well when necessary. This extra toughness makes her a popular character.

Barbarian— The Barbarian is the master of hack-and-slash, hand-to hand attacks. He's the bloodthirsty warrior who literally lives to face death in intimate combat situations. He likes to fight with large swords, shields, whirling blades, and sizable armor—and even has a few special moves that can help him to do damage from afar. The Barbarian is a character for those of you who like a straight-up fight with lots of up-close and personal combat, and with ultra-cool moves like Leap Attack, there are some things a Barbarian can do that other character classes can only dream of.

Necromancer— Like the Amazon, the Necromancer prefers to fight from afar but can engage in heavy combat if need be. As his name implies, the Necromancer can raise undead to do his battle for him. The undead minions that have been summoned by the Necromancer will fight to the 'death' for their new master, while he follows behind them and picks up the bounty of their efforts.

Blizzard employees often call the Necromancer 'The General' because of his ability to raise up an army of undead Skeletons, revived enemies, and elemental Golems to do his bidding. Despite the Necromancer's ability to create his own personal army, he's a capable fighter in his own right, and properly equipped will give any group of monsters a run for their money in melee combat.

Paladin— The Paladin can best be described as self-reliant. He can fight in heavy battles or attack from afar, but he also has abilities that allow him to heal himself. These healing skills usually mean that the Paladin does not have to go back to town as often as the other characters to heal his wounds.

Many of the Paladin's skills are best utilized in multiplayer action. His Auras, although effective in single player, really shine when they can work to add benefits to the party that's traveling with the Paladin. A Paladin is an absolute 'must' in a multiplayer party, but can certainly hold his own in the single player version of the game as both a capable fighter and a user of magic.

Sorceress— The Sorceress is a frail being, always attempting to keep as far away from combat as possible. She is all about magic. Equipped with the fire, ice, and lightning attacks, she is indeed an incredibly powerful mage who will use her devastating magic to take out monsters in bunches. This is the character you'll want to take if you enjoy casting fantastic magical attacks rather than getting involved in the minutia of hack-and-slash combat characters.

Character Development

One of the great things about *Diablo II* is that the 150 different skills (30 for each of five characters) make character skill development an important part of the game. You choices in this regard can create dramatically different characters with only a few different skill choices. For example, a Necromancer that puts all of his skill points into Raise Skeletons, Skeleton Mages, and Skeleton Mastery will be very different (and require different strategies) than a Necromancer who specializes in Curses and Poison and Bone skills.

In the entire course of a single-player game, you are likely to get in the neighborhood of about 35 skill points to distribute. This may sound like a lot, but when you consider that each skill can take *20* skill points, you will obviously only be able to use a few skill in any one game. This means that *Diablo II* has nearly infinite replayability, even as single player game! The permutations and combinations of skill mixes is huge, and a such we suggest that you pick the skills you think will benefit you most, then build them up and experiment with their use. This chapter contains detailed information about each of the skills for each character class. In addition to mere descriptions of the skills we've provided strategies for how to use and combine the skills to your advantage.

NOTE......

As you put skill points into specific skills, you will get various benefits in that particular skill area. To learn just what the next level of a skill will give you, move your mouse cursor over the skill icon. This will display the current skill status, as well as details regarding the next level.

Wherever relevant, we've included information about the skills as they pertain to multiplayer action or single-player action, or indeed, certain locations within *Diablo II*. Much of the information for this chapter came from the Blizzard Quality Assurance team, most of whom are listed in the acknowledgements of this book. A large chunk of information was also supplied by Jason Hutchins, Senior QA Analyst.

The Skill Tree screens show you at what level your skills are, as well as what the next skill level offers you.

The Necromancer

The Necromancer is a dark spell caster whose incantations are geared toward the raising of the dead and the summoning and control of various creatures for his purposes. Although his goals are often aligned with those of the forces of light, some believe that these ends cannot justify his foul means. Long hours of study in dank mausoleums have made his skin pale and corpselike, while his figure has more in common with a skeleton than a man. Some shun him for his peculiar looks and ways, but none doubts the power of the Necromancer, which is the stuff of nightmares.

NECROMANCER SKILLS

There are three skill sets that the Necromancer can develop as he moves forward in *Diablo II*. As with the other characters, the skills that are developed will substantially affect the Necromancer's abilities throughout the game. The three skill sets are Curses, Poison and Bone, and Summoning and Control. There is good reason to invest at least some skill points in each of the skill areas, but ultimately you'll have to make a decision as to which kinds of abilities you want your Necromancer to have. Should he have a powerful Golem, or should Skeletons do his bidding? Read on to find out the pros and cons of each skill.

POISON AND BONE

The Poison and Bone skill set incorporates various magical attacks that are associated with, quite literally, poison and bone. These skills/spells serve a variety of purpose—including defense (Bone Armor), attack (Teeth), trap (Bone Prison), and Corpse Explosion, which is a powerful skill that does damage to nearby enemies according to how many hit points the corpse had (before its death).

TEETH (LEVEL 1)

This fires multiple magic teeth from another realm. As you add points to this skill, Teeth increases the number of 'teeth' that are released and the amount of damage that each tooth does. The advantage of Teeth is that it inflicts 'blow through' damage—it goes through the first target and will then hit another target (or targets) behind the first. For these reasons, Teeth is best used against rooms full of enemies, especially at higher skill levels where the amount of damage it inflicts is substantial.

Teeth is a magical missile-type skill that is useful early on for the Necromancer.

MANA COST									
LEVEL 1	LEVEL 2	LEVEL 3	LEVEL 4	LEVEL 5	LEVEL 6	LEVEL 7	LEVEL 8	LEVEL 9	LEVEL 10
3	3.5	4	4.5	5	5.5	6	6.6	7	7.5
LEVEL 11	LEVEL 12	LEVEL 13	LEVEL 14	LEVEL 15	LEVEL 16	LEVEL 17	LEVEL 18	LEVEL 19	LEVEL 20
8	8.5	9	9.5	10	10.5	11	11.5	12	12

DAMAGE									
LEVEL 1	LEVEL 2	LEVEL 3	LEVEL 4	LEVEL 5	LEVEL 6	LEVEL 7	LEVEL 8	LEVEL 9	LEVEL 10
2-4	3-5	4-6	5-7	6-8	7-9	8-10	9-11	10-12	11-13
LEVEL 11	LEVEL 12	LEVEL 13	LEVEL 14	LEVEL 15	LEVEL 16	LEVEL 17	LEVEL 18	LEVEL 19	LEVEL 20
12-14	13-15	14-16	15-17	16-18	17-19	18-20	19-21	20-22	21-23

NUMBER OF TEETH									
LEVEL 1	LEVEL 2	LEVEL 3	LEVEL 4	LEVEL 5	LEVEL 6	LEVEL 7	LEVEL 8	LEVEL 9	LEVEL 10
2	3	4	5	6	7	8	9	10	11
LEVEL 11	LEVEL 12	LEVEL 13	LEVEL 14	LEVEL 15	LEVEL 16	LEVEL 17	LEVEL 18	LEVEL 19	LEVEL 20
12	13	14	15	16	17	18	19	20	21

BONE ARMOR (LEVEL 1)

TIP

If you're going to be using it for melee combat, assign a hot key to Bone Armor so you can recast it frequently. This skill effectively absorbs the enemy's attack damage, but it won't last long against the toughest monsters or large groups of foes.

Invoking this skill creates a protective shield of rotating bone that absorbs the damage enemies inflict on your character. As you put skill points into Bone Armor, you begin to see significant gains in the amount of damage this skill can absorb, making it a valuable tool when fighting with groups of enemies. Bone Armor is especially important if you choose not to use a lot of summoning to aid in your quest through *Diablo II*.

DAMAGE SHIELD									
LEVEL 1	LEVEL 2	LEVEL 3	LEVEL 4	LEVEL 5	LEVEL 6	LEVEL 7	LEVEL 8	LEVEL 9	LEVEL 10
20	30	40	50	60	70	80	90	100	110
LEVEL 11	LEVEL 12	LEVEL 13	LEVEL 14	LEVEL 15	LEVEL 16	LEVEL 17	LEVEL 18	LEVEL 19	LEVEL 20
120	130	140	150	160	170	180	190	200	210

CHAPTER 2: THE CHARACTERS

MANA COST

LEVEL 1	LEVEL 2	LEVEL 3	LEVEL 4	LEVEL 5	LEVEL 6	LEVEL 7	LEVEL 8	LEVEL 9	LEVEL 10
11	12	13	14	15	16	17	18	19	20
LEVEL 11	LEVEL 12	LEVEL 13	LEVEL 14	LEVEL 15	LEVEL 16	LEVEL 17	LEVEL 18	LEVEL 19	LEVEL 20
21	22	23	24	25	26	27	28	29	30

POISON DAGGER (LEVEL 6)

With a weapon of the dagger class in hand, the use of this spell poisons the target you hit. The bonus of this is that you will not only do damage to the enemy with the dagger attack, but the poison will continue to work and do damage for a certain number of seconds (depending on skill level). After you've put five or six skill points into Poison Dagger, it can become a 'fire and forget' type of weapon—you will need only walk up to the enemy, hit them once with the Poison Dagger, then move away and let the Poison do its work. The more skill points you invest in Poison Dagger, the longer the poison lasts and, more importantly, the greater damage it does. The mana cost for Poison Dagger is almost insignificant, so as long as you have a dagger handy (which is mandatory for this skill), you'll be able to inflict plenty of damage on your enemies after landing only one hit.

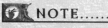

NOTE......

Poison Dagger is only for hand-to-hand (melee) combat, and does not have an effect with a dagger that is thrown.

POISON DAMAGE

LEVEL 1	LEVEL 2	LEVEL 3	LEVEL 4	LEVEL 5	LEVEL 6	LEVEL 7	LEVEL 8	LEVEL 9	LEVEL 10
7-15	10-20	14-26	18-33	23-40	29-48	35-56	41-65	49-75	57-85
LEVEL 11	LEVEL 12	LEVEL 13	LEVEL 14	LEVEL 15	LEVEL 16	LEVEL 17	LEVEL 18	LEVEL 19	LEVEL 20
65-95	74-106	84-118	94-131	105-144	116-157	128-171	141-186	154-201	168-217

DURATION (IN SECONDS)

LEVEL 1	LEVEL 2	LEVEL 3	LEVEL 4	LEVEL 5	LEVEL 6	LEVEL 7	LEVEL 8	LEVEL 9	LEVEL 10
4	5	6	7	8	9	10	11	12	13
LEVEL 11	LEVEL 12	LEVEL 13	LEVEL 14	LEVEL 15	LEVEL 16	LEVEL 17	LEVEL 18	LEVEL 19	LEVEL 20
14	15	16	17	18	19	20	21	22	23

AR BONUS (%)

LEVEL 1	LEVEL 2	LEVEL 3	LEVEL 4	LEVEL 5	LEVEL 6	LEVEL 7	LEVEL 8	LEVEL 9	LEVEL 10
15	25	35	45	55	65	75	85	95	105
LEVEL 11	LEVEL 12	LEVEL 13	LEVEL 14	LEVEL 15	LEVEL 16	LEVEL 17	LEVEL 18	LEVEL 19	LEVEL 20
115	125	135	145	155	165	175	185	195	205

MANA COST

LEVEL 1	LEVEL 2	LEVEL 3	LEVEL 4	LEVEL 5	LEVEL 6	LEVEL 7	LEVEL 8	LEVEL 9	LEVEL 10
3	3.2	3.5	3.7	4.0	4.2	4.5	4.7	5.0	5.2
LEVEL 11	LEVEL 12	LEVEL 13	LEVEL 14	LEVEL 15	LEVEL 16	LEVEL 17	LEVEL 18	LEVEL 19	LEVEL 20
5.5	5.7	6.0	6.2	6.5	6.7	7.0	7.2	7.5	7.7

CORPSE EXPLOSION (LEVEL 6)

TIP..........

Multiplayer Tip: Corpse Explosion is particularly effective in large multiplayer games, because the enemies become more powerful when there are more players in a game. Since Corpse Explosion does damage according to the hit points of the monster corpse it's used on, it becomes considerably more powerful in these situations.

This skill gives you the ability to turn an enemy corpse into a bomb! Once an enemy is dead, you need only target the spell and the enemy's body will violently explode, damaging (or killing) all nearby enemies. As you put skill points into Corpse Explosion, the radius of the explosion increases, thus making it an excellent area of effect skill. An exploding corpse will do damage equal to between 60-100 percent of its hit points (before it died), making this skill one of the most powerful in the Necromancer's arsenal!

Corpse Explosion is one the most important skills for the Necromancer because it does damage that's linked to the hi points of the corpse it explodes

Corpse Explosion is often used when the Necromancer comes up against a large group of enemies. The Necromancer will kill just one of the enemies, and then invoke the Corpse Explosion either killing or heavily damaging any nearby enemies. It's so powerful that Blizzard QA has deemed this Necromancer skill a 'must.'

MANA COST

LEVEL 1	LEVEL 2	LEVEL 3	LEVEL 4	LEVEL 5	LEVEL 6	LEVEL 7	LEVEL 8	LEVEL 9	LEVEL 10
15	16	17	18	19	20	21	22	23	24
LEVEL 11	LEVEL 12	LEVEL 13	LEVEL 14	LEVEL 15	LEVEL 16	LEVEL 17	LEVEL 18	LEVEL 19	LEVEL 20
25	26	27	28	29	30	31	32	33	34

RADIUS (YARDS)

LEVEL 1	LEVEL 2	LEVEL 3	LEVEL 4	LEVEL 5	LEVEL 6	LEVEL 7	LEVEL 8	LEVEL 9	LEVEL 10
2.8	3.3	4	4.6	5.3	6	6.6	7.3	8	8.6
LEVEL 11	LEVEL 12	LEVEL 13	LEVEL 14	LEVEL 15	LEVEL 16	LEVEL 17	LEVEL 18	LEVEL 19	LEVEL 20
9.3	10	10.6	11.3	12	12.6	13.3	14	14.6	15.3

BONE PRISON (LEVEL 24; DURATION = 48 SEC.)

When invoked, this unique skill raises a ring of bone around the target. This ring is designed to prevent the target from getting at you (or moving anywhere for that matter but it will also prevent *you* from getting to the enemy, which can make it difficult to take them out. The Bone Prison is best used to trap an enemy just long enough for you to escape (if running is your choice). Basically, Bone Prison is not unlike Bone Wall except that it forms a circle around the enemy rather than forming a wall.

MANA COST

LEVEL 1	LEVEL 2	LEVEL 3	LEVEL 4	LEVEL 5	LEVEL 6	LEVEL 7	LEVEL 8	LEVEL 9	LEVEL 10
27	25	23	21	19	17	15	13	11	9
LEVEL 11	LEVEL 12	LEVEL 13	LEVEL 14	LEVEL 15	LEVEL 16	LEVEL 17	LEVEL 18	LEVEL 19	LEVEL 20
7	5	3	1	1	1	1	1	1	1

HIT POINTS

LEVEL 1	LEVEL 2	LEVEL 3	LEVEL 4	LEVEL 5	LEVEL 6	LEVEL 7	LEVEL 8	LEVEL 9	LEVEL 10
19	23	28	33	38	42	47	52	57	61
LEVEL 11	LEVEL 12	LEVEL 13	LEVEL 14	LEVEL 15	LEVEL 16	LEVEL 17	LEVEL 18	LEVEL 19	LEVEL 20
66	71	76	80	85	90	95	99	104	109

Bone Wall (Level 12; Mana Cost = 17; Duration = 48 sec.)

This skill creates a barrier of bone that shoots up as a length of wall. The 'bone wall' that's created by this skill prevents any enemies from passing through it, although the wall only last for just over 45 seconds and the number of hit points they have is limited by the amount of skill points that you have put into the skill. For example, a level 1 Bone Wall has under 20 hit points, so an enemy from Act II isn't going to take more than a few seconds to break through the wall and come after you! Because Bone Wall doesn't actively harm the enemy, it has limited use, so you shouldn't put too many of your valuable skill points into it.

Bone Wall can give you a chance to get away from a persistent enemy by creating a physical barrier.

TIP

Bone Wall is best used as a temporary measure that will buy you time if you have a large group of enemies following you. For example, if you enter a room that's full of monsters and your health is low, you may want to back out and throw up several Bone Walls to slow the enemy down while you retreat.

HIT POINTS

LEVEL 1	LEVEL 2	LEVEL 3	LEVEL 4	LEVEL 5	LEVEL 6	LEVEL 7	LEVEL 8	LEVEL 9	LEVEL 10
19	23	28	33	38	42	47	52	57	61
LEVEL 11	LEVEL 12	LEVEL 13	LEVEL 14	LEVEL 15	LEVEL 16	LEVEL 17	LEVEL 18	LEVEL 19	LEVEL 20
66	71	76	80	85	90	95	99	104	109

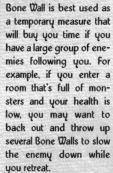

THE NECROMANCER

POISON EXPLOSION (LEVEL 18; MANA COST = 8)

This skill is basically Corpse Explosion, except that it does poison damage. It's a very powerful spell and does a whopping amount of damage to nearby enemies. The bonus of Poison is that it continues to do damage over time—not only when it first hits, but as long as the enemy remains poisoned, as well. There's a reason why this skill is not accessible until your character is at level 18, and it's because Poison Explosion is a 'must have' skill that'll go a long way to helping you complete *Diablo II*.

Like Corpse Explosion, Poison Explosion is best used against tightly grouped packs of enemies. When the corpse explodes, it will leave every nearby enemy taking heaps of poison damage with every passing second. Poison Explosion is also highly effective when used on a Corpse that's in a small room or narrow corridor; in short, it's similar to hurling a strangling or choking gas potion into a confined area.

POISON DAMAGE

LEVEL 1	LEVEL 2	LEVEL 3	LEVEL 4	LEVEL 5	LEVEL 6	LEVEL 7	LEVEL 8	LEVEL 9	LEVEL 10
25-50	30-60	35-70	40-80	45-90	50-100	55-110	60-120	65-130	70-140
LEVEL 11	LEVEL 12	LEVEL 13	LEVEL 14	LEVEL 15	LEVEL 16	LEVEL 17	LEVEL 18	LEVEL 19	LEVEL 20
75-150	80-160	85-170	90-180	95-190	100-200	105-210	110-220	115-230	120-240

DURATION (SECONDS)

LEVEL 1	LEVEL 2	LEVEL 3	LEVEL 4	LEVEL 5	LEVEL 6	LEVEL 7	LEVEL 8	LEVEL 9	LEVEL 10
4	4.8	5.6	6.4	7.2	8	8.8	9.6	10.4	11.2
LEVEL 11	LEVEL 12	LEVEL 13	LEVEL 14	LEVEL 15	LEVEL 16	LEVEL 17	LEVEL 18	LEVEL 19	LEVEL 20
12	12.8	13.6	14.4	15.2	16	16.8	17.6	18.4	19.2

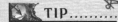
TIP

Bone Spear is a great weapon to use in an underground passage or any area where you're fighting many enemies in a narrow corridor. When in such a situation, your Bone Spear will blow through the targeted enemy and continue on, damaging all enemies behind it!

BONE SPEAR (LEVEL 18)

Bone Spear summons a bone missile of magic that flies forth from the Necromancer's hands and inflicts a solid amount of damage on the enemy it hits. The real advantage to Bone Spear is that it will pass through the enemy at which it is aimed, and then proceed to damage any enemy that it strikes behind your target. This makes Bone Spear very handy for both one-on-one ranged fights, as well as attacking a group of enemies.

DAMAGE

LEVEL 1	LEVEL 2	LEVEL 3	LEVEL 4	LEVEL 5	LEVEL 6	LEVEL 7	LEVEL 8	LEVEL 9	LEVEL 10
16-24	24-32	32-40	40-48	48-56	56-64	64-72	72-80	80-88	88-96
LEVEL 11	LEVEL 12	LEVEL 13	LEVEL 14	LEVEL 15	LEVEL 16	LEVEL 17	LEVEL 18	LEVEL 19	LEVEL 20
96-104	104-112	112-120	120-128	128-136	136-144	144-152	152-160	160-168	168-176

CHAPTER 2: THE CHARACTERS

MANA COST

LEVEL 1	LEVEL 2	LEVEL 3	LEVEL 4	LEVEL 5	LEVEL 6	LEVEL 7	LEVEL 8	LEVEL 9	LEVEL 10
7	7.2	7.5	7.7	8	8.2	8.5	8.7	9	9.2

LEVEL 11	LEVEL 12	LEVEL 13	LEVEL 14	LEVEL 15	LEVEL 16	LEVEL 17	LEVEL 18	LEVEL 19	LEVEL 20
9.5	9.7	10	10.2	10.5	10.7	11	11.2	11.5	11.7

POISON NOVA (LEVEL 30; MANA COST = 25)

This skill sends a ring of poison that explodes outward 360 degrees from the Necromancer. It's a very powerful spell that will poison all nearby enemies when invoked. As skill points are added to it, the Poison Nova inflicts a considerable amount of damage per second to any enemy in its wake. Poison Nova is another skill that deserves serious consideration for any Necromancer because it enables you to begin inflicting any nearby enemies with poison damage at any time. Unfortunately, the Poison Nova has a fairly high mana cost so you can't really use it as a staple skill, but it comes in handy whenever you need to attack several enemies at once. It can also be used to replace Poison Explosion if need be, and it doesn't require a corpse for you to use it!

Poison Nova is a skill that can single-handedly take out large groups of enemies. The power of poison should not be overlooked.

POISON DAMAGE

LEVEL 1	LEVEL 2	LEVEL 3	LEVEL 4	LEVEL 5	LEVEL 6	LEVEL 7	LEVEL 8	LEVEL 9	LEVEL 10
50-75	55-82	60-90	65-97	70-105	75-112	80-120	85-127	90-135	95-142

LEVEL 11	LEVEL 12	LEVEL 13	LEVEL 14	LEVEL 15	LEVEL 16	LEVEL 17	LEVEL 18	LEVEL 19	LEVEL 20
100-150	105-157	110-165	115-172	120-180	125-187	130-195	135-202	190-210	195-217

DURATION (SECONDS)

LEVEL 1	LEVEL 2	LEVEL 3	LEVEL 4	LEVEL 5	LEVEL 6	LEVEL 7	LEVEL 8	LEVEL 9	LEVEL 10
8	8.8	9.6	10.4	11.2	12	12.8	13.6	14.4	15.2

LEVEL 11	LEVEL 12	LEVEL 13	LEVEL 14	LEVEL 15	LEVEL 16	LEVEL 17	LEVEL 18	LEVEL 19	LEVEL 20
16	16.8	17.6	18.4	19.2	20	20.8	21.6	22.4	23.2

⚡ BONE SPIRIT (LEVEL 30)

Bone Spirit releases a spirit (in the form of a shimmering ball) that tracks the target (o finds one), hunts it down, and hits it. It is essentially a high-power seeking missile tha will inflict massive damage to any enemy. This skill isn't available until you hav reached the lofty heights of Level 30, and although it's tempting to pour points into it the fact that it can only be used against a single enemy makes it a very specialized ski that isn't particularly effective against groups of enemies. It does increase dramaticall in damage at a fast pace, however, and will outstrip Bone Spear in damage potentia with the investment of a few skill points. Ultimately, it's probably better to pour you skill points into Bone Spear if you're going to be fighting large groups of monsters with out the help of friends or summoned creatures.

MANA COST									
LEVEL 1	LEVEL 2	LEVEL 3	LEVEL 4	LEVEL 5	LEVEL 6	LEVEL 7	LEVEL 8	LEVEL 9	LEVEL 10
12	12	13	13	14	14	15	15	16	16
LEVEL 11	LEVEL 12	LEVEL 13	LEVEL 14	LEVEL 15	LEVEL 16	LEVEL 17	LEVEL 18	LEVEL 19	LEVEL 20
17	17	18	18	19	19	20	20	21	21

DAMAGE									
LEVEL 1	LEVEL 2	LEVEL 3	LEVEL 4	LEVEL 5	LEVEL 6	LEVEL 7	LEVEL 8	LEVEL 9	LEVEL 10
20-30	36-46	52-62	68-78	84-94	100-110	116-126	132-142	148-158	164-174
LEVEL 11	LEVEL 12	LEVEL 13	LEVEL 14	LEVEL 15	LEVEL 16	LEVEL 17	LEVEL 18	LEVEL 19	LEVEL 20
180-190	196-206	212-222	228-238	244-254	260-270	276-286	292-302	308-318	324-334

CURSES

The Curses are a set of skills that affect the enemy hoards in various ways. As a rule Curses are used in conjunction with other attacks, such as skeletons or golems. In mul tiplayer games Curses work to the benefit of the entire party, not just the Necromance using them. For example, an Amplify Damage curse invoked on a group of tough mon sters will literally make it twice as easy for your group to take out those enemies.

⚡ AMPLIFY DAMAGE (LEVEL 1; MANA COST = 4)

Amplify Damage is a valuable skill because it increases the amount of non-magical damage the cursed unit receives. No matter which level Amplify Damage is at, it will always increase the damage taken by 100 percent. This means that every hit you or one of your minions lands on a cursed unit will do the damage of two hits! As skill points are added to Amplify Damage, the duration and the effect radius increase substantially.

Amplify Damage is a very important skill. Even at level 1, it can make a huge difference in Diablo II.

Assign a hot key to Amplify Damage so you can switch to it at a moment's notice. When you employ this skill on a group of enemies they will all be cursed, taking twice the damage they normally would from each hit your Necromancer or his skeletons/golems land. Because the mana cost for this skill is small, it's an absolute must-have for all Necromancers.

RADIUS (YARDS)

LEVEL 1	LEVEL 2	LEVEL 3	LEVEL 4	LEVEL 5	LEVEL 6	LEVEL 7	LEVEL 8	LEVEL 9	LEVEL 10
2	2.6	3.3	4	4.6	5.3	6	6.6	7.3	8
LEVEL 11	LEVEL 12	LEVEL 13	LEVEL 14	LEVEL 15	LEVEL 16	LEVEL 17	LEVEL 18	LEVEL 19	LEVEL 20
8.6	9.3	10	10.6	11.3	12	12.6	13.3	14	14.6

DURATION (SECONDS)

LEVEL 1	LEVEL 2	LEVEL 3	LEVEL 4	LEVEL 5	LEVEL 6	LEVEL 7	LEVEL 8	LEVEL 9	LEVEL 10
8	11	14	17	20	23	26	29	32	35
LEVEL 11	LEVEL 12	LEVEL 13	LEVEL 14	LEVEL 15	LEVEL 16	LEVEL 17	LEVEL 18	LEVEL 19	LEVEL 20
38	41	44	47	50	53	56	59	62	65

DIM VISION (LEVEL 6; MANA COST = 9)

Dim vision reduces the sight radius of the targeted enemy down to one yard. This literally means that they can barely see past their noses. If you have the ability to launch a ranged attack (with Teeth or with Skeleton Mages), you can sit back and take the cursed enemies out without them ever seeing you! Dim Vision is also often used to blind enemies that rely on ranged attacks (such as Dark Archers) so that they cannot fire their weapons at you or your party.

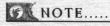

NOTE......

If you must escape, Dim Vision can also provide the cloak of cover you need to get past a particularly difficult enemy, whether you're underpowered or simply too injured to continue the fight. Casting Dim Vision on a tough enemy will blanket them in darkness and give you a chance to get away before the curse wears off.

RADIUS (YARDS)

LEVEL 1	LEVEL 2	LEVEL 3	LEVEL 4	LEVEL 5	LEVEL 6	LEVEL 7	LEVEL 8	LEVEL 9	LEVEL 10
2.6	3.3	4	4.6	5.3	6	6.6	7.3	8	8.6
LEVEL 11	LEVEL 12	LEVEL 13	LEVEL 14	LEVEL 15	LEVEL 16	LEVEL 17	LEVEL 18	LEVEL 19	LEVEL 20
9.3	10	10.6	11.3	12	12.6	13.3	14	14.6	15.3

DURATION (SECONDS)

LEVEL 1	LEVEL 2	LEVEL 3	LEVEL 4	LEVEL 5	LEVEL 6	LEVEL 7	LEVEL 8	LEVEL 9	LEVEL 10
7	9	11	13	15	17	19	21	23	25
LEVEL 11	LEVEL 12	LEVEL 13	LEVEL 14	LEVEL 15	LEVEL 16	LEVEL 17	LEVEL 18	LEVEL 19	LEVEL 20
27	29	31	33	35	37	39	41	43	45

WEAKEN (LEVEL 6; MANA COST = 4)

Weaken reduces the amount of damage the cursed unit can do to you or your minions. When it is used on an enemy (or group of enemies), it reduces the enemy's attack by one third. This skill is best used in a defensive situation where you are surrounded by a great number of enemies and are taking hits from multiple sides. By using Weaken in this crisis, you can reduce the damage you take while you hack through the enemy group.

RADIUS (YARDS)									
LEVEL 1	LEVEL 2	LEVEL 3	LEVEL 4	LEVEL 5	LEVEL 6	LEVEL 7	LEVEL 8	LEVEL 9	LEVEL 10
6	6.6	7.3	8	8.6	9.3	10	10.6	11.3	12
LEVEL 11	LEVEL 12	LEVEL 13	LEVEL 14	LEVEL 15	LEVEL 16	LEVEL 17	LEVEL 18	LEVEL 19	LEVEL 20
12.6	13.3	14	14.6	15.3	16	16.6	17.3	18	18.6

DURATION (SECONDS)									
LEVEL 1	LEVEL 2	LEVEL 3	LEVEL 4	LEVEL 5	LEVEL 6	LEVEL 7	LEVEL 8	LEVEL 9	LEVEL 10
14	16.4	18.8	21.2	23.6	26	28.4	30.8	33.2	35.6
LEVEL 11	LEVEL 12	LEVEL 13	LEVEL 14	LEVEL 15	LEVEL 16	LEVEL 17	LEVEL 18	LEVEL 19	LEVEL 20
38	40.4	42.8	45.2	47.6	50	52.4	54.8	57.2	59.6

IRON MAIDEN (LEVEL 12; MANA COST = 5)

This skill forces the cursed monster to take the damage that it inflicts through its attacks on others. Although Iron Maiden has a fixed radius (4.6 yards) that doesn't change with the addition of skill points, it can still affect multiple enemies with one use if those enemies are nearby your Necromancer. Iron Maiden is a great skill for quickly shortening the life of the enemies it affects because each and every time they land a hit on you, party member, or your minions, they take that much damage back on themselves! In this regard, it truly will hurt them more than it hurts you when they land a blow!

PERCENT DAMAGE RETURNED									
LEVEL 1	LEVEL 2	LEVEL 3	LEVEL 4	LEVEL 5	LEVEL 6	LEVEL 7	LEVEL 8	LEVEL 9	LEVEL 10
200	225	250	275	300	325	350	375	400	425
LEVEL 11	LEVEL 12	LEVEL 13	LEVEL 14	LEVEL 15	LEVEL 16	LEVEL 17	LEVEL 18	LEVEL 19	LEVEL 20
450	475	500	525	550	575	600	625	650	675

DURATION (SECONDS)									
LEVEL 1	LEVEL 2	LEVEL 3	LEVEL 4	LEVEL 5	LEVEL 6	LEVEL 7	LEVEL 8	LEVEL 9	LEVEL 10
12	14.4	16.8	19.2	21.6	24	26.4	28.8	31.2	33.6
LEVEL 11	LEVEL 12	LEVEL 13	LEVEL 14	LEVEL 15	LEVEL 16	LEVEL 17	LEVEL 18	LEVEL 19	LEVEL 20
36	38.4	40.8	43.2	45.6	48	50.4	52.8	55.2	57.6

TERROR (LEVEL 12; MANA COST = 7; RADIUS = 2.6 YARDS)

Terror makes the cursed monsters run away in fear. Although the radius of this skill never changes with the addition of skill points, the duration of the curse extends by one second for each skill point. More than likely, a skill like Terror is not something you'll be using frequently, but when you're in a tight spot and need to force a group of enemies away quickly, this curse will do the job.

 NOTE......

Terror does not work on Unique monsters or Bosses, so don't waste any time attempting to get a powerful monster to run away from you—use your mana for offensive skills instead.

DURATION (SECONDS)

LEVEL 1	LEVEL 2	LEVEL 3	LEVEL 4	LEVEL 5	LEVEL 6	LEVEL 7	LEVEL 8	LEVEL 9	LEVEL 10
8	9	10	11	12	13	14	15	16	17

LEVEL 11	LEVEL 12	LEVEL 13	LEVEL 14	LEVEL 15	LEVEL 16	LEVEL 17	LEVEL 18	LEVEL 19	LEVEL 20
18	19	20	21	22	23	24	25	26	27

CONFUSE (LEVEL 18; MANA COST = 13)

Confuse will affect the enemy by essentially driving them insane and causing them to attack nearby monsters (or you and your team members) randomly. It's important to remember that these attacks are random, and can mean that an enemy that wasn't attacking you before it was cursed may now turn its anger toward your character (in multiplayer). Still, this is a highly effective curse when used on a group of enemies because it will cause them to drop whatever they were doing (most likely chasing you), and attack each other. The chaos that ensues will greatly reduce their collective hit points—they may even kill each other.

Confuse will make monsters attack nearby creatures at random, but that includes you (if you're nearby)!

RADIUS (YARDS)

LEVEL 1	LEVEL 2	LEVEL 3	LEVEL 4	LEVEL 5	LEVEL 6	LEVEL 7	LEVEL 8	LEVEL 9	LEVEL 10
4	4.6	5.3	6	6.6	7.3	8	8.6	9.3	10

LEVEL 11	LEVEL 12	LEVEL 13	LEVEL 14	LEVEL 15	LEVEL 16	LEVEL 17	LEVEL 18	LEVEL 19	LEVEL 20
10.6	11.3	12	12.6	13.3	14	14.6	15.3	16	16.6

DURATION (SECONDS)

LEVEL 1	LEVEL 2	LEVEL 3	LEVEL 4	LEVEL 5	LEVEL 6	LEVEL 7	LEVEL 8	LEVEL 9	LEVEL 10
10	12	14	16	18	20	22	24	26	28

LEVEL 11	LEVEL 12	LEVEL 13	LEVEL 14	LEVEL 15	LEVEL 16	LEVEL 17	LEVEL 18	LEVEL 19	LEVEL 20
30	32	34	36	38	40	42	44	46	48

LIFE TAP (LEVEL 18; MANA COST = 9)

This curse is an effective way to replenish your life. When you curse an enemy with Lif Tap, they give up the life they lose to *you* with every hit you land on them! The amoun of life that you'll steal back from the enemy is always 50 percent of the attack that yo land, so the harder you hit, the more life points that will slide over to your characte Obviously, this is a skill that can change your fortunes quickly if you're running low o life, but it can also be of great benefit to your fellow party members (in multiplayer) wh can also heal from this curse.

NOTE......

When one of your minions (skeletons or golems) hits the enemy, they will not return 50 percent of the enemy's health to you, but they **will** take that health for themselves, thus giving you a way to heal your minions.

RADIUS (YARDS)

LEVEL 1	LEVEL 2	LEVEL 3	LEVEL 4	LEVEL 5	LEVEL 6	LEVEL 7	LEVEL 8	LEVEL 9	LEVEL 10
2.6	3.3	4	4.6	5.3	6	6.6	7.3	8	8.6
LEVEL 11	LEVEL 12	LEVEL 13	LEVEL 14	LEVEL 15	LEVEL 16	LEVEL 17	LEVEL 18	LEVEL 19	LEVEL 20
9.3	10	10.6	11.3	12	12.6	13.3	14	14.6	15.3

DURATION (SECONDS)

LEVEL 1	LEVEL 2	LEVEL 3	LEVEL 4	LEVEL 5	LEVEL 6	LEVEL 7	LEVEL 8	LEVEL 9	LEVEL 10
16	18.4	20.8	23.2	25.6	28	30.4	32.8	35.2	37.6
LEVEL 11	LEVEL 12	LEVEL 13	LEVEL 14	LEVEL 15	LEVEL 16	LEVEL 17	LEVEL 18	LEVEL 19	LEVEL 20
40	42.4	44.8	47.2	49.6	52	54.4	56.8	59.2	61.6

ATTRACT (LEVEL 24; MANA COST = 17; RADIUS = 6 YARDS)

This skill is a highly effective tool for wearing down or eliminating one particularly toug monster. When Attract is used on an enemy, it becomes a target for other enemy force and will therefore be attacked as aggressively as you would be. It should be noted, hov ever, that Attract makes the target one that is of equal interest to the enemies; n greater interest. Therefore, when you use Attract on a particular enemy, the other en mies will attack whoever they are closer to—you (or your party), or the enemy tha you've cursed. Still, if you can use this curse and then run away quickly, the enemi will go after the cursed creature and leave you alone.

DURATION (SECONDS)

LEVEL 1	LEVEL 2	LEVEL 3	LEVEL 4	LEVEL 5	LEVEL 6	LEVEL 7	LEVEL 8	LEVEL 9	LEVEL 10
12	15.6	19.2	22.8	26.4	30	33.6	37.2	40.8	44.4
LEVEL 11	LEVEL 12	LEVEL 13	LEVEL 14	LEVEL 15	LEVEL 16	LEVEL 17	LEVEL 18	LEVEL 19	LEVEL 20
48	51.6	55.2	58.8	62.4	66	69.6	73.2	76.8	80.4

DECREPIFY (LEVEL 24; MANA COST = 11)

Decrepify is a curse that will slow down the enemies it affects. This is one of the few skills in the game that will slow enemies down that doesn't use cold or freezing to accomplish this end. As skill points are added to Decrepify, both the duration and the area of effect of this curse are improved. When used in multiplayer action, this skill is a powerful tool that will slow down enemies long enough for your ranged-weapon party members (or Skeletal Mages) to get in a flurry of shots before the enemy can approach your position.

Aside from cold spells, Decrepify is the only skill that slows the enemies.

RADIUS (YARDS)

LEVEL 1	LEVEL 2	LEVEL 3	LEVEL 4	LEVEL 5	LEVEL 6	LEVEL 7	LEVEL 8	LEVEL 9	LEVEL 10
2.6	3.3	4	4.6	5.3	6	6.6	7.3	8	8.6
LEVEL 11	LEVEL 12	LEVEL 13	LEVEL 14	LEVEL 15	LEVEL 16	LEVEL 17	LEVEL 18	LEVEL 19	LEVEL 20
9.3	10	10.6	11.3	12	12.6	13.3	14	14.6	15.3

DURATION (SECONDS)

LEVEL 1	LEVEL 2	LEVEL 3	LEVEL 4	LEVEL 5	LEVEL 6	LEVEL 7	LEVEL 8	LEVEL 9	LEVEL 10
2	2.2	2.4	2.6	2.8	3	3.2	3.4	3.6	3.8
LEVEL 11	LEVEL 12	LEVEL 13	LEVEL 14	LEVEL 15	LEVEL 16	LEVEL 17	LEVEL 18	LEVEL 19	LEVEL 20
4	4.2	4.4	4.6	4.8	5	5.2	5.4	5.6	5.8

LOWER RESIST (LEVEL 30; MANA COST = 22)

Many of the Necromancer's skills (as well as other character's skills) rely on magic to get the job done. At certain points in the game, however, you'll run into enemies that have a substantial resistance to magic, thus making some of your skills like Teeth and Bone Missile considerably less effective. When Lower Resist is used, the cursed enemies have a reduced resistance to magical attacks, making them easier to deal with. Likewise, other resistances (such as fire) are also lowered, making other skills and minions (such as Fire Golems) more effective. As you add skill points to Lower Resist you'll greatly improve the radius of effect, duration, and even the percentage that the resistance is lowered. Even in its lowest form, Lower Resist will take greater than 30 percent of the enemy's resistance away!

RADIUS (YARDS)

LEVEL 1	LEVEL 2	LEVEL 3	LEVEL 4	LEVEL 5	LEVEL 6	LEVEL 7	LEVEL 8	LEVEL 9	LEVEL 10
4.6	5.3	6	6.6	7.3	8	8.6	9.3	10	10.6
LEVEL 11	LEVEL 12	LEVEL 13	LEVEL 14	LEVEL 15	LEVEL 16	LEVEL 17	LEVEL 18	LEVEL 19	LEVEL 20
11.3	12	12.6	13.3	14	14.6	15.3	16	16.6	17.3

DURATION (SECONDS)

LEVEL 1	LEVEL 2	LEVEL 3	LEVEL 4	LEVEL 5	LEVEL 6	LEVEL 7	LEVEL 8	LEVEL 9	LEVEL 10
20	22	24	26	28	30	32	34	36	38
LEVEL 11	LEVEL 12	LEVEL 13	LEVEL 14	LEVEL 15	LEVEL 16	LEVEL 17	LEVEL 18	LEVEL 19	LEVEL 20
40	42	44	46	48	50	52	54	56	58

LEVEL 1	LEVEL 2	LEVEL 3	LEVEL 4	LEVEL 5	LEVEL 6	LEVEL 7	LEVEL 8	LEVEL 9	LEVEL 10
31	37	41	44	47	49	51	52	54	55

LEVEL 11	LEVEL 12	LEVEL 13	LEVEL 14	LEVEL 15	LEVEL 16	LEVEL 17	LEVEL 18	LEVEL 19	LEVEL 20
56	57	58	59	60	61	61	61	62	62

SUMMONING AND CONTROL

NOTE......

It should be noted that all Skeletons, Golems, and Raised Dead that the Necromancer summons (or controls) will contribute experience to the Necromancer that created them. In short, whatever the Necromancer's minions kill, those experience points pour into the Necromancer's experience pool, which often makes leveling up easier in multiplayer games.

TIP..........

It's ok to use Skeletons early in the game, but once you get into Act III, your Skeletons will begin to have a harder time defeating the enemies and you'll find yourself creating replacement Skeletons very frequently. In the testing department at Blizzard, the testers tend not to rely on Skeletons in higher levels, instead choosing to augment their Skeleton minions with a Golem.

The Necromancer, as his name would imply, has the ability to raise the dead and employ them to do his bidding. The Necromancer's power extends not only over the dead, but also over the elements, which means that he is also capable of summoning Golems from the ground beneath his feet, calling up the fires of hell, or even creating Golem that steals life for your cause.

SKELETON MASTERY (LEVEL 1)

Skeleton Mastery is a very important skill if you have any intention of using Skeleton to help your Necromancer make it through the game. It's a very good idea to put at least a few points into Skeleton Mastery because it dramatically improves the effectiveness of the Skeletons fighting for you (including Skeleton Mages). With each point that you invest in Skeleton Mastery, you will increase your minion's hit points and the damage they inflict; however, in higher levels your Skeletons will have a hard time keeping up with the enemies they'll face.

SKELETON HIT POINTS

LEVEL 1	LEVEL 2	LEVEL 3	LEVEL 4	LEVEL 5	LEVEL 6	LEVEL 7	LEVEL 8	LEVEL 9	LEVEL 10
+7	+14	+21	+28	+35	+42	+49	+56	+63	+70

LEVEL 11	LEVEL 12	LEVEL 13	LEVEL 14	LEVEL 15	LEVEL 16	LEVEL 17	LEVEL 18	LEVEL 19	LEVEL 20
+77	+84	+91	+98	+105	+112	+119	+126	+133	+140

SKELETON DAMAGE

LEVEL 1	LEVEL 2	LEVEL 3	LEVEL 4	LEVEL 5	LEVEL 6	LEVEL 7	LEVEL 8	LEVEL 9	LEVEL 10
+2	+4	+6	+8	+10	+12	+14	+16	+18	+20

LEVEL 11	LEVEL 12	LEVEL 13	LEVEL 14	LEVEL 15	LEVEL 16	LEVEL 17	LEVEL 18	LEVEL 19	LEVEL 20
+22	+24	+26	+28	+30	+32	+34	+36	+38	+40

MONSTER HIT POINTS (%)

LEVEL 1	LEVEL 2	LEVEL 3	LEVEL 4	LEVEL 5	LEVEL 6	LEVEL 7	LEVEL 8	LEVEL 9	LEVEL 10
7	14	21	28	35	42	49	56	63	70

LEVEL 11	LEVEL 12	LEVEL 13	LEVEL 14	LEVEL 15	LEVEL 16	LEVEL 17	LEVEL 18	LEVEL 19	LEVEL 20
77	84	91	98	105	112	119	126	133	140

MONSTER DAMAGE (%)

LEVEL 1	LEVEL 2	LEVEL 3	LEVEL 4	LEVEL 5	LEVEL 6	LEVEL 7	LEVEL 8	LEVEL 9	LEVEL 10
2	4	6	8	10	12	14	16	18	20

LEVEL 11	LEVEL 12	LEVEL 13	LEVEL 14	LEVEL 15	LEVEL 16	LEVEL 17	LEVEL 18	LEVEL 19	LEVEL 20
22	24	26	28	30	32	34	36	38	40

☠ Raise Skeleton (Level 1; Hit Points 21; Damage 1-2)

As the name implies, this skill raises a skeletal warrior that will fight to the death for your Necromancer. Using this skill, the Necromancer can create a small army of Skeletons that will follow him and fight any enemy that gets in their path. When combined with Skeleton Mastery, the Skeletons created using this skill can become very powerful, and indeed they can do the lion's share of the killing for the Necromancer in the first two acts.

Raise Skeleton is a powerful skill that enables you to literally create a small army of Skeletons to do your bidding.

Because one more Skeleton can be raised with every new skill point you put into Raise Skeleton, the temptation is to put in as many points as you can so that you can create a large army of Skeletons to fight for your cause. The problems with this strategy are twofold. First, it's difficult to manage all those skeletons, especially in a tight environment such as an underground cavern. Many Skeletons will get lost or won't be able to quickly follow the Necromancer through the narrow corridors. Secondly, as you progress through the game (into Act III and beyond), you'll find that the relatively weak Skeletons get destroyed quickly by the tougher enemies, and it becomes a challenge to find dead bodies with which to resurrect new Skeletons.

For the above reasons, it's usually best to put a few points into Skeletons and even more into Skeleton Mastery. This tactic will provide you with stronger Skeletons and will still allow you to put points into the Curses and other Summoning skills, such as the Golems.

NUMBER OF SKELETONS ☠

LEVEL 1	LEVEL 2	LEVEL 3	LEVEL 4	LEVEL 5	LEVEL 6	LEVEL 7	LEVEL 8	LEVEL 9	LEVEL 10
1	2	3	4	5	6	7	8	9	10
LEVEL 11	**LEVEL 12**	**LEVEL 13**	**LEVEL 14**	**LEVEL 15**	**LEVEL 16**	**LEVEL 17**	**LEVEL 18**	**LEVEL 19**	**LEVEL 20**
11	12	13	14	15	16	17	18	19	20

MANA COST ☠

LEVEL 1	LEVEL 2	LEVEL 3	LEVEL 4	LEVEL 5	LEVEL 6	LEVEL 7	LEVEL 8	LEVEL 9	LEVEL 10
6	7	8	9	10	11	12	13	14	15
LEVEL 11	**LEVEL 12**	**LEVEL 13**	**LEVEL 14**	**LEVEL 15**	**LEVEL 16**	**LEVEL 17**	**LEVEL 18**	**LEVEL 19**	**LEVEL 20**
16	17	18	19	20	21	22	23	24	25

⚔ 🏛 CLAY GOLEM (LEVEL 6)

> **📖 NOTE......**
>
> The important thing to remember about Golems over Skeletons is that they do not require an enemy corpse in order for the Necromancer to raise them. In certain situations this can be important because there are not always dead enemies nearby for the Necromancer to raise, making a Golem (which can be created out of thin air) very handy indeed.

This skill raises a Golem from the earth to fight for the Necromancer, but unlike the Raise Skeleton skill, you can raise only *one* Clay Golem at a time. One of the great advantages to Clay Golems is that they heal themselves automatically. After a bloody battle, you can sit back and wait while your Golem recovers or simply create another Golem. A level one Golem has an impressive 100 hit points, but a level 20 Clay Golem has over 750 hit points and can do over 35 points of damage with a single hit—and that's without any points in Golem Mastery! For this reason, it's better to move from your Skeletons to a Golem (along with Golem Mastery) as you move to higher levels.

Clay Golems are tough and can do more than just inflict damage to enemies; they can also act as decoys at higher levels.

MANA COST 🏛

LEVEL 1	LEVEL 2	LEVEL 3	LEVEL 4	LEVEL 5	LEVEL 6	LEVEL 7	LEVEL 8	LEVEL 9	LEVEL 10
15	18	21	24	27	30	33	36	39	42
LEVEL 11	LEVEL 12	LEVEL 13	LEVEL 14	LEVEL 15	LEVEL 16	LEVEL 17	LEVEL 18	LEVEL 19	LEVEL 20
45	48	51	54	57	60	63	66	69	72

DAMAGE 🏛

LEVEL 1	LEVEL 2	LEVEL 3	LEVEL 4	LEVEL 5	LEVEL 6	LEVEL 7	LEVEL 8	LEVEL 9	LEVEL 10
2-5	2-6	3-8	4-10	4-12	5-13	6-15	6-17	7-19	8-20
LEVEL 11	LEVEL 12	LEVEL 13	LEVEL 14	LEVEL 15	LEVEL 16	LEVEL 17	LEVEL 18	LEVEL 19	LEVEL 20
9-22	9-24	10-26	11-27	11-29	12-31	13-33	13-34	14-29	15-38

HIT POINTS 🏛

LEVEL 1	LEVEL 2	LEVEL 3	LEVEL 4	LEVEL 5	LEVEL 6	LEVEL 7	LEVEL 8	LEVEL 9	LEVEL 10
100	135	170	205	240	275	310	345	380	415
LEVEL 11	LEVEL 12	LEVEL 13	LEVEL 14	LEVEL 15	LEVEL 16	LEVEL 17	LEVEL 18	LEVEL 19	LEVEL 20
450	485	520	555	590	625	660	695	730	765

⚔ 🏛 GOLEM MASTERY (LEVEL 12)

Boiled down, Golem Mastery can best be described as a skill that increases the healt and speed of Golems. Indeed, if you're going to be using Golems to help you as yo wind your way through *Diablo II*, it will certainly pay to have put some skill points int this area. Some Blizzard employees are fond of putting all of their skill points int Golems and Golem Mastery, thus creating a sort of super-sidekick that can fight wit the toughest of enemies. By the time you have put five points into Golem Master you've doubled your Golem's hit points, so it's well worth the investment.

HIT POINTS (+%) 🏛

LEVEL 1	LEVEL 2	LEVEL 3	LEVEL 4	LEVEL 5	LEVEL 6	LEVEL 7	LEVEL 8	LEVEL 9	LEVEL 10
20	40	60	80	100	120	140	160	180	200
LEVEL 11	LEVEL 12	LEVEL 13	LEVEL 14	LEVEL 15	LEVEL 16	LEVEL 17	LEVEL 18	LEVEL 19	LEVEL 20
220	240	260	280	300	320	340	360	380	400

CHAPTER 2: THE CHARACTERS

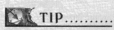

LEVEL 1	LEVEL 2	LEVEL 3	LEVEL 4	LEVEL 5	LEVEL 6	LEVEL 7	LEVEL 8	LEVEL 9	LEVEL 10
8	10	14	17	20	22	23	24	26	27
LEVEL 11	LEVEL 12	LEVEL 13	LEVEL 14	LEVEL 15	LEVEL 16	LEVEL 17	LEVEL 18	LEVEL 19	LEVEL 20
28	29	30	30	31	32	32	32	33	33

#4

RAISE SKELETAL MAGE (LEVEL 12; HIT POINTS = 61)

This skill is similar to Raise Skeleton, except that (as the name implies) it raises a Skeleton Mage to fight for your Necromancer. A Skeleton Mage is a skeleton with a ranged attack (shoots over a distance) that can be one of four classes: Fire, Cold, Poison, or Electrical. Each of these has advantages and disadvantages, but unfortunately you can't choose which kind of Skeleton Mage will appear when you raise it. If you have only one Skeleton Mage, however, you can keep raising one after another until you get the kind you want; the only cost of doing this is mana, along with enemy bodies from which to raise these Mages.

Skeletal Mages give the Necromancer a minion that can use ranged attacks. In combination with Skeletons, Skeletal Mages provide a great one-two punch.

A Skeleton Mage with poison will do poison damage to the enemy, whereas each of the other three classes will do damage according to their class. For example, a cold Skeleton Mage will shoot blasts of cold at the enemies, and each blast of cold will have a chance of freezing the enemy, or even breaking the enemy into chunks of ice! Skeleton Mages are great to have in conjunction with regular Skeletons because they add the ability to attack from afar, rounding out your Necromancer's party.

TIP

A common tactic at Blizzard QA is to put skill points into Skeletons, Skeleton Mages, and Skeleton Mastery so that you can have several Skeletons for melee combat and a pair of Skeleton Mages to stand back and fire from afar. This combination works very well, especially when enough points have been put into Skeleton Mastery, which improves the abilities of **both** the Skeleton Mages and the Skeletons.

NUMBER OF SKELETAL MAGES

LEVEL 1	LEVEL 2	LEVEL 3	LEVEL 4	LEVEL 5	LEVEL 6	LEVEL 7	LEVEL 8	LEVEL 9	LEVEL 10
1	2	3	4	5	6	7	8	9	10
LEVEL 11	LEVEL 12	LEVEL 13	LEVEL 14	LEVEL 15	LEVEL 16	LEVEL 17	LEVEL 18	LEVEL 19	LEVEL 20
11	12	13	14	15	16	17	18	19	20

MANA COST

LEVEL 1	LEVEL 2	LEVEL 3	LEVEL 4	LEVEL 5	LEVEL 6	LEVEL 7	LEVEL 8	LEVEL 9	LEVEL 10
8	9	10	11	12	13	14	15	16	17
LEVEL 11	LEVEL 12	LEVEL 13	LEVEL 14	LEVEL 15	LEVEL 16	LEVEL 17	LEVEL 18	LEVEL 19	LEVEL 20
18	19	20	21	22	23	24	25	26	27

✴ BLOOD GOLEM (LEVEL 18; HIT POINTS = 201)

⚙ NOTE......

You can have only **one** Golem active at a time, meaning you can't have an Iron Golem and a Blood Golem working in tandem. For this reason, it's best not to split your skill points between two kinds of Golems. Choose which type you want to use and stick with it; put points into other Golems only if it means opening up your skill tree.

Blood Golem raises a Golem that's connected to you in health. This means that when the Blood Golem hits an enemy, he'll steal life from the enemy and it will be reflected in *your* health bar (your health will go up). The Blood Golem may sound like it present a win-win situation that steals health with its attacks, but there's a downside as well When the Blood Golem takes a hit, you'll take a hit with it! The key is that the Blood Golem will usually steal more health than he'll lose for you by taking hits. The exception to this occurs when the Blood Golem is surrounded by a large group of enemies and is taking hits fast and furiously while only dishing out a small amount of punishment. When this happens, you'll wish your Blood Golem was somewhere else Fortunately, it can be if you simply re-create a new Blood Golem as you're running away from the action.

MANA COST ✴

LEVEL 1	LEVEL 2	LEVEL 3	LEVEL 4	LEVEL 5	LEVEL 6	LEVEL 7	LEVEL 8	LEVEL 9	LEVEL 10
25	29	33	37	41	45	49	53	57	61
LEVEL 11	LEVEL 12	LEVEL 13	LEVEL 14	LEVEL 15	LEVEL 16	LEVEL 17	LEVEL 18	LEVEL 19	LEVEL 20
65	69	73	77	81	85	89	93	97	101

DAMAGE ✴

LEVEL 1	LEVEL 2	LEVEL 3	LEVEL 4	LEVEL 5	LEVEL 6	LEVEL 7	LEVEL 8	LEVEL 9	LEVEL 10
6-16	8-21	10-27	12-32	14-38	16-44	18-49	20-55	22-60	24-66
LEVEL 11	LEVEL 12	LEVEL 13	LEVEL 14	LEVEL 15	LEVEL 16	LEVEL 17	LEVEL 18	LEVEL 19	LEVEL 20
27-72	29-77	31-83	33-88	35-94	37-100	39-105	41-111	43-116	45-122

HEAL CONVERT DAMAGE ✴

LEVEL 1	LEVEL 2	LEVEL 3	LEVEL 4	LEVEL 5	LEVEL 6	LEVEL 7	LEVEL 8	LEVEL 9	LEVEL 10
31	32	33	34	35	35	35	36	36	36
LEVEL 11	LEVEL 12	LEVEL 13	LEVEL 14	LEVEL 15	LEVEL 16	LEVEL 17	LEVEL 18	LEVEL 19	LEVEL 20
37	37	37	37	37	38	38	38	38	38

✴ ⊕ SUMMON RESIST (LEVEL 24)

Summon Resist is a unique skill that increases the elemental resistance for all of you summoned creatures. This means that any Golems, Raised Dead, or Skeletons that you have in your party will benefit from increased resistance to fire, cold, electrical, and poison attacks. If you are going to progress through the game while using summoned creatures, then it's well worth putting at least one point toward Summon Resist—even a level 1, it dramatically increases your resistance to any elemental attacks. As you progress into Acts III and IV, having some resistance to elemental magic attacks will be a great asset to your summoned creatures.

RESIST ALL (%)

LEVEL 1	LEVEL 2	LEVEL 3	LEVEL 4	LEVEL 5	LEVEL 6	LEVEL 7	LEVEL 8	LEVEL 9	LEVEL 10
28	34	39	44	47	50	52	54	56	57

LEVEL 11	LEVEL 12	LEVEL 13	LEVEL 14	LEVEL 15	LEVEL 16	LEVEL 17	LEVEL 18	LEVEL 19	LEVEL 20
59	60	61	62	62	64	64	65	65	66

IRON GOLEM (LEVEL 24; MANA COST = 35; DAMAGE = 7-19; HIT POINTS = 367)

This skill raises a Golem from a metal item that you throw onto the ground (or an item that's lying on the ground). The cool part about Iron Golem is that it will take on the properties of whatever item you create it from! Therefore, if you create and Iron Golem out of a set of chain mail armor, you'll end up with a Golem that has a very high amount of hit points and defense rating. On the other hand, if you create an Iron Golem out of a sword that has ice damage on top of its normal damage, then the Iron Golem will also have those attack properties. This is an incredibly creative way to create special Golems with unique skills, and it gives you a great motivation to hang on to unique weapons and armor that might otherwise not hold your interest.

TIP

If you find a great weapon early in the game that you can't use (or don't want to use), it may be worth putting it in your Personal Stash so that you can use it later to create a powerful Iron Golem!

THORNS (%)

LEVEL 1	LEVEL 2	LEVEL 3	LEVEL 4	LEVEL 5	LEVEL 6	LEVEL 7	LEVEL 8	LEVEL 9	LEVEL 10
0	150	165	180	195	210	225	240	255	270

LEVEL 11	LEVEL 12	LEVEL 13	LEVEL 14	LEVEL 15	LEVEL 16	LEVEL 17	LEVEL 18	LEVEL 19	LEVEL 20
285	300	315	330	345	360	375	390	405	420

THE NECROMANCER

FIRE GOLEM (LEVEL 30)

This skill creates a Golem of fire that will draw strength from fire attacks. This kind of Golem becomes more valuable later in the game when you must deal with more fire-related attacks (as you get closer to Diablo). With Fire Golems, the more skill points you put into them, the more damage they absorb from fire attacks. It should also be noted, however, that they become more expensive with every skill point you invest.

Fire Golems are excellent against enemies that will use fire against you (like those you'll find in Hell).

MANA COST									
LEVEL 1	LEVEL 2	LEVEL 3	LEVEL 4	LEVEL 5	LEVEL 6	LEVEL 7	LEVEL 8	LEVEL 9	LEVEL 10
50	60	70	80	90	100	110	120	130	140
LEVEL 11	LEVEL 12	LEVEL 13	LEVEL 14	LEVEL 15	LEVEL 16	LEVEL 17	LEVEL 18	LEVEL 19	LEVEL 20
150	160	170	180	190	200	210	220	230	240

DAMAGE									
LEVEL 1	LEVEL 2	LEVEL 3	LEVEL 4	LEVEL 5	LEVEL 6	LEVEL 7	LEVEL 8	LEVEL 9	LEVEL 10
10-27	12-33	15-40	17-47	20-54	22-60	25-67	27-74	30-81	32-87
LEVEL 11	LEVEL 12	LEVEL 13	LEVEL 14	LEVEL 15	LEVEL 16	LEVEL 17	LEVEL 18	LEVEL 19	LEVEL 20
35-99	37-101	40-108	42-114	45-121	47-128	50-135	52-141	55-148	57-155

ABSORBS FIRE DAMAGE TO HP									
LEVEL 1	LEVEL 2	LEVEL 3	LEVEL 4	LEVEL 5	LEVEL 6	LEVEL 7	LEVEL 8	LEVEL 9	LEVEL 10
36	45	52	58	62	66	69	71	74	76
LEVEL 11	LEVEL 12	LEVEL 13	LEVEL 14	LEVEL 15	LEVEL 16	LEVEL 17	LEVEL 18	LEVEL 19	LEVEL 20
78	79	81	82	83	85	85	86	87	88

REVIVE (LEVEL 30)

NOTE......

Remember that as you invest skill points into Revive, the mana cost of reviving goes **down** (which is a good thing), and the hit points and number of monsters you can revive goes **up** (which is also good).

This skill literally resurrects a dead monster to fight for your Necromancer. These res urrected enemies are not like Skeletons or Golems, however, and they won't follow yo as religiously as the other creatures you summon. Revived creatures will fight for you but they are only a shadow of what they were before they died, meaning that at lowe skill levels they have only about 10 percent of the original number of hit points they ha when they were living. However, if you put enough skill points into Revive, you can cre ate revived monsters that are actually *more* powerful than their living counterparts (leve 10 and up). Revived monsters last for only 180 seconds (three minutes) after you cre ate them, so unlike other summoned creatures they will not serve you indefinitely.

There are two other important aspects of Revive that are important to remember. First, Skeleton Mastery points go toward improving revived monsters. Secondly, although you can resurrect tough enemies, you cannot bring bosses back to life to fight for your cause.

MANA COST

LEVEL 1	LEVEL 2	LEVEL 3	LEVEL 4	LEVEL 5	LEVEL 6	LEVEL 7	LEVEL 8	LEVEL 9	LEVEL 10
45	42	39	36	33	30	27	24	21	18
LEVEL 11	LEVEL 12	LEVEL 13	LEVEL 14	LEVEL 15	LEVEL 16	LEVEL 17	LEVEL 18	LEVEL 19	LEVEL 20
15	12	9	6	3	1	1	1	1	1

NUMBER OF MONSTERS

LEVEL 1	LEVEL 2	LEVEL 3	LEVEL 4	LEVEL 5	LEVEL 6	LEVEL 7	LEVEL 8	LEVEL 9	LEVEL 10
1	2	3	4	5	6	7	8	9	10
LEVEL 11	LEVEL 12	LEVEL 13	LEVEL 14	LEVEL 15	LEVEL 16	LEVEL 17	LEVEL 18	LEVEL 19	LEVEL 20
11	12	13	14	15	16	17	18	19	20

HP (ORIGINAL MONSTER (%))

LEVEL 1	LEVEL 2	LEVEL 3	LEVEL 4	LEVEL 5	LEVEL 6	LEVEL 7	LEVEL 8	LEVEL 9	LEVEL 10
200	220	240	260	280	300	320	340	360	380
LEVEL 11	LEVEL 12	LEVEL 13	LEVEL 14	LEVEL 15	LEVEL 16	LEVEL 17	LEVEL 18	LEVEL 19	LEVEL 20
400	420	440	460	480	500	520	540	560	580

The Amazon

This powerful woman warrior belongs to nomadic bands of fighters that roam the are near the South Sea. The Amazon is accustomed to fighting to defend her own, and he lifestyle has made her fiercely independent and able to endure severe hardships in he quest for survival. The Amazon is highly skilled in bowmanship, but is also adept i the use of spears and various throwing weapons. Despite the Amazon's skills a ranged fighting, she is still very dangerous in hand to hand combat, and can fend fo herself impressively.

AMAZON SKILLS

There are three skill sets that the Amazon can develop as she climbs in experience i *Diablo II*. Which skills are developed will ultimately affect her abilities as the ques toward victory progresses. The three skill sets are Bow and Crossbow, Passive an Magic, and Javelin and Spear. The Amazon's large list of passive skills makes her tempting character; this is because passive skills, once you put skill points into then are always "on". By putting skill points into passive skills as well as active skill you will get more mileage out of your skill points. However, there are advantage and disadvantages to every skill choice you make.

BOW AND CROSSBOW

These are all ranged weapons, meaning that they are fired from a distance an keep the Amazon away from the enemy). Seven of the skills in this skill grou are specific weapons, such as the Cold Arrow, the Immolation Arrow, and the Magi Arrow. The other three skills—Strafe, Multiple Shot, and Guided Arrow—are modifie of existing arrow weapons (either from a Crossbow or from a Bow). These don't offer u new distinct missile weapons, but rather they make your existing missile weapon be ter. For example, Multiple Shot sends out several (more when skill points are applie to it) arrows for every *one* arrow you fire. How you apply your points in the Bow an Crossbow category will greatly affect how you fight through the game, so choose to su your style.

MAGIC ARROW (LEVEL 1)

The Magic Arrow skill shoots an arrow created entirely from mana, meaning that you d not need to have any arrows in your quiver to fire. This is a very important skill, especia ly early in the game when you may find yourself running out of arrows, and will help yo to extricate yourself from many sticky situations. It can be used as an emergency backu or used to save conventional arrows whenever you have an excess supply of mana o mana potions. This arrow's damage is the same as a normal arrow. As skill points a added to it, the damage it causes goes up while its mana cost actually goes *down*. At lev 13, the Magic Arrow's cost goes down to ZERO, making it an entirely free weapon.

Although Magic Arrows aren't guided, they never miss their target. Consequently, it is an excellent skill to have if your Dexterity rating is low.

 **TIP..........**

The Magic Arrow skill is best paired with Critical Strike. This is because the Magic Arrow never misses and Critical Strike will often double the damage of the hit. Use a high-powered Bow or Crossbow (which adds to the damage of the Magic Arrow) and you'll have an uber-weapon that can take you through the entire game!

MANA COST

LEVEL 1	LEVEL 2	LEVEL 3	LEVEL 4	LEVEL 5	LEVEL 6	LEVEL 7	LEVEL 8	LEVEL 9	LEVEL 10
1.5	1.3	1.2	1.1	1.0	.8	.7	.6	.5	.3
LEVEL 11	LEVEL 12	LEVEL 13	LEVEL 14	LEVEL 15	LEVEL 16	LEVEL 17	LEVEL 18	LEVEL 19	LEVEL 20
.2	.1	0	0	0	0	0	0	0	0

DAMAGE MODIFIER

LEVEL 1	LEVEL 2	LEVEL 3	LEVEL 4	LEVEL 5	LEVEL 6	LEVEL 7	LEVEL 8	LEVEL 9	LEVEL 10
0	+1	+2	+3	+4	+5	+6	+7	+8	+9
LEVEL 11	LEVEL 12	LEVEL 13	LEVEL 14	LEVEL 15	LEVEL 16	LEVEL 17	LEVEL 18	LEVEL 19	LEVEL 20
+10	+11	+12	+13	+14	+15	+16	+17	+18	+19

FIRE ARROW (LEVEL 1)

When active, Fire Arrow modifies one of your arrows by adding fire to it (you'll need arrows or bolts to make this work). When it hits, the Fire Arrow causes both normal and fire damage, making it much more effective than using a plain arrow. As with all skills, the more skill points you put into Fire Arrow, the more effective it will ultimately be—especially when combined with Critical Strike.

The Fire Arrow gives the Amazon a ranged attack that provides both normal and fire damage.

 **TIP..........**

The Fire Arrow can be used as a kind of "advanced scout" when fired into the darkness of a dungeon. Each Fire Arrow is its own light source, lighting up the area around it as it flies through the air. In this way, it can be a great way to get a peek at what's coming before it emerges from the darkness.

MANA COST

LEVEL 1	LEVEL 2	LEVEL 3	LEVEL 4	LEVEL 5	LEVEL 6	LEVEL 7	LEVEL 8	LEVEL 9	LEVEL 10
3	3.2	3.5	3.7	4	4.2	4.5	4.7	5	5.2
LEVEL 11	LEVEL 12	LEVEL 13	LEVEL 14	LEVEL 15	LEVEL 16	LEVEL 17	LEVEL 18	LEVEL 19	LEVEL 20
5.5	5.7	6	6.2	6.5	6.7	7	7.2	7.5	7.7

FIRE DAMAGE

LEVEL 1	LEVEL 2	LEVEL 3	LEVEL 4	LEVEL 5	LEVEL 6	LEVEL 7	LEVEL 8	LEVEL 9	LEVEL 10
1-4	3-6	5-8	7-10	9-12	11-14	13-16	15-18	17-20	19-22
LEVEL 11	LEVEL 12	LEVEL 13	LEVEL 14	LEVEL 15	LEVEL 16	LEVEL 17	LEVEL 18	LEVEL 19	LEVEL 20
21-24	23-26	25-28	27-30	29-32	31-34	33-36	35-38	37-40	39-42

COLD ARROW (LEVEL 6)

When active, this skill produces an icy blue arrow that smacks its target with a blast c[f] cold, slowing it down for a period of time (depending on the number of skill point[s] invested). The more skill points, the greater the chances that it will actually freeze an[d] shatter the enemy into bits of ice (which subsequently melt). The Cold Arrow is a pow[-] erful ranged weapon because it will usually turn its target blue (make them cold) whe[n] it hits, slowing the enemy down considerably. This is an important tool when you're try[-] ing to keep your distance from an enemy, so that you don't have to get into melee com[-] bat. One tactic that works well is to hit each enemy in a group with a Cold Arrow, caus[-] ing them all to move slowly, then pick them off one at a time while they plod towar[d] you. Like the Fire Arrow, the Cold Arrow is also its own light source, which means tha[t] you can use it to see into the dark when you're stuck in dingy dungeons.

MANA COST

LEVEL 1	LEVEL 2	LEVEL 3	LEVEL 4	LEVEL 5	LEVEL 6	LEVEL 7	LEVEL 8	LEVEL 9	LEVEL 10
3	3.2	3.5	3.7	4	4.2	4.5	4.7	5	5.2
LEVEL 11	LEVEL 12	LEVEL 13	LEVEL 14	LEVEL 15	LEVEL 16	LEVEL 17	LEVEL 18	LEVEL 19	LEVEL 20
5.5	5.7	6	6.2	6.5	6.7	7	7.2	7.5	7.7

COLD DAMAGE

LEVEL 1	LEVEL 2	LEVEL 3	LEVEL 4	LEVEL 5	LEVEL 6	LEVEL 7	LEVEL 8	LEVEL 9	LEVEL 10
3	5	7	9	11	13	15	17	19	21
LEVEL 11	LEVEL 12	LEVEL 13	LEVEL 14	LEVEL 15	LEVEL 16	LEVEL 17	LEVEL 18	LEVEL 19	LEVEL 20
23	25	27	29	31	33	35	37	39	41

COLD LENGTH (SECONDS)

LEVEL 1	LEVEL 2	LEVEL 3	LEVEL 4	LEVEL 5	LEVEL 6	LEVEL 7	LEVEL 8	LEVEL 9	LEVEL 10
4	5.2	6.4	7.6	8.8	10	11.2	12.4	13.6	14.8
LEVEL 11	LEVEL 12	LEVEL 13	LEVEL 14	LEVEL 15	LEVEL 16	LEVEL 17	LEVEL 18	LEVEL 19	LEVEL 20
16	17.2	18.4	19.6	20.8	22	23.2	24.4	25.6	26.8

MULTIPLE SHOT (LEVEL 6)

TIP..........

Combine Multiple Shot with a high attack rating and a magical bow/cross-bow to maximize its effectiveness.

Multiple Shot magically splits one arrow into multiple arrows at a mana cost to you[r] character. As you put more skill points into this skill you'll get more arrows produce[d] with every shot, and the arrows eventually form a 120-degree arc that fans out fro[m] your position when you fire. As you might expect, this can be a highly effective weapon[n] when used against groups of enemies, especially those in wide open spaces. When yo[u] combine Multiple Shot with Critical Strike, a highly level of Dexterity, and a magica[l] bow/crossbow of some sort, this skill can become your bread and butter for dealing wit[h] the enemy hoards you will frequently face in *Diablo II*.

MANA COST

LEVEL 1	LEVEL 2	LEVEL 3	LEVEL 4	LEVEL 5	LEVEL 6	LEVEL 7	LEVEL 8	LEVEL 9	LEVEL 10
4	5	6	7	8	9	10	11	12	13
LEVEL 11	LEVEL 12	LEVEL 13	LEVEL 14	LEVEL 15	LEVEL 16	LEVEL 17	LEVEL 18	LEVEL 19	LEVEL 20
14	15	16	17	18	19	20	21	22	23

CHAPTER 2: THE CHARACTERS

NUMBER OF ARROWS

LEVEL 1	LEVEL 2	LEVEL 3	LEVEL 4	LEVEL 5	LEVEL 6	LEVEL 7	LEVEL 8	LEVEL 9	LEVEL 10
2	3	4	5	6	7	8	9	10	11

LEVEL 11	LEVEL 12	LEVEL 13	LEVEL 14	LEVEL 15	LEVEL 16	LEVEL 17	LEVEL 18	LEVEL 19	LEVEL 20
12	13	14	15	16	17	18	19	20	21

ICE ARROW (LEVEL 18)

The Ice Arrow differs from the Cold Arrow in a specific way—rather than slowing the enemy with cold, it completely freezes the opponent for a time. Indeed, Ice Arrow causes some cold damage while stopping the target in its tracks. The duration of the freeze depends on the number of skill points you've poured into this skill. Once an opponent is frozen, the likelihood that they'll get smashed into chunks of ice on the next hit is reasonably good. For this reason two hits with Ice Arrow often send even the strongest enemies tumbling to the ground as melting hunks of ice. The Ice Arrow can be used in conjunction with the Valkyrie skill, allowing you to stand back and freeze opponents while the Valkyrie hacks them to pieces.

Ice Arrow will freeze enemies in their place—sometimes it will even smash them to bits!

TIP

The Ice Arrow can be a very effective weapon when fighting enemies that can be respawned after they die. This is because an enemy that is turned to ice and then smashed cannot be resurrected from death, making your job of clearing out enemies considerably easier.

MANA COST

LEVEL 1	LEVEL 2	LEVEL 3	LEVEL 4	LEVEL 5	LEVEL 6	LEVEL 7	LEVEL 8	LEVEL 9	LEVEL 10
4	4.2	4.5	4.7	5	5.2	5.5	5.7	6	6.2

LEVEL 11	LEVEL 12	LEVEL 13	LEVEL 14	LEVEL 15	LEVEL 16	LEVEL 17	LEVEL 18	LEVEL 19	LEVEL 20
6.5	6.7	7	7.2	7.5	7.7	8	8.2	8.5	8.7

FREEZE (SECONDS)

LEVEL 1	LEVEL 2	LEVEL 3	LEVEL 4	LEVEL 5	LEVEL 6	LEVEL 7	LEVEL 8	LEVEL 9	LEVEL 10
2	2.2	2.4	2.6	2.8	3	3.2	3.4	3.6	3.8

LEVEL 11	LEVEL 12	LEVEL 13	LEVEL 14	LEVEL 15	LEVEL 16	LEVEL 17	LEVEL 18	LEVEL 19	LEVEL 20
4	4.2	4.4	4.6	4.8	5	5.2	5.4	5.6	5.8

COLD DAMAGE

LEVEL 1	LEVEL 2	LEVEL 3	LEVEL 4	LEVEL 5	LEVEL 6	LEVEL 7	LEVEL 8	LEVEL 9	LEVEL 10
6-10	10-14	14-18	18-22	22-26	26-30	30-34	34-38	38-42	42-46

LEVEL 11	LEVEL 12	LEVEL 13	LEVEL 14	LEVEL 15	LEVEL 16	LEVEL 17	LEVEL 18	LEVEL 19	LEVEL 20
46-50	50-54	54-58	58-62	62-66	66-70	70-74	74-78	78-82	82-86

GUIDED ARROW (LEVEL 18)

The Guided Arrow is the ultimate tracking arrow because it will literally make 90-degre
turns to find its target. In fact, you don't even need to specify a target with the guide
arrow; once you fire it, it will make the necessary turns and adjustments to hit the nea
est enemy (assuming that there is an enemy nearby). A great way to use this skill is to hid
in a corner of a room or at an intersection of a dungeon where the arrow can fly in mult
ple directions, then fire randomly. The Guided Arrows will fly toward the enemies and h
them even if they are in other rooms. Guided Arrow is best used when getting close to th
enemy is something you absolutely don't want to do!

MANA COST

LEVEL 1	LEVEL 2	LEVEL 3	LEVEL 4	LEVEL 5	LEVEL 6	LEVEL 7	LEVEL 8	LEVEL 9	LEVEL 10
7	6.5	6	5.5	5	4.5	4	3.5	3	2.5
LEVEL 11	LEVEL 12	LEVEL 13	LEVEL 14	LEVEL 15	LEVEL 16	LEVEL 17	LEVEL 18	LEVEL 19	LEVEL 20
2	1.5	1	1	1	1	1	1	1	1

DAMAGE MODIFIER (+%)

LEVEL 1	LEVEL 2	LEVEL 3	LEVEL 4	LEVEL 5	LEVEL 6	LEVEL 7	LEVEL 8	LEVEL 9	LEVEL 10
0	5	10	15	20	25	30	35	40	45
LEVEL 11	LEVEL 12	LEVEL 13	LEVEL 14	LEVEL 15	LEVEL 16	LEVEL 17	LEVEL 18	LEVEL 19	LEVEL 20
50	55	60	65	70	75	80	85	90	95

TIP..........

When firing an Exploding
Arrow into a group of
enemies, always aim at the
enemy in the center of the
group.

EXPLODING ARROW (LEVEL 12)

This arrow explodes, causing fire damage around the area of impact. It will do damag
to enemies near the foe you've targeted, making it a great weapon for dealing wit
crowds of bad guys. The higher the skill level, the more damage the arrow will inflic
As you might also expect, it will light up the area it explodes in, thus making it y
another way you can cast some light down a dark corridor or light up a darkened roon

MANA COST

LEVEL 1	LEVEL 2	LEVEL 3	LEVEL 4	LEVEL 5	LEVEL 6	LEVEL 7	LEVEL 8	LEVEL 9	LEVEL 10
5	5.5	6	6.5	7	7.5	8	8.5	9	9.5
LEVEL 11	LEVEL 12	LEVEL 13	LEVEL 14	LEVEL 15	LEVEL 16	LEVEL 17	LEVEL 18	LEVEL 19	LEVEL 20
10	10.5	11	11.5	12	12	13	13	14	14

FIRE DAMAGE

LEVEL 1	LEVEL 2	LEVEL 3	LEVEL 4	LEVEL 5	LEVEL 6	LEVEL 7	LEVEL 8	LEVEL 9	LEVEL 10
2-4	7-9	12-14	17-19	22-24	27-29	32-34	37-39	42-44	47-49
LEVEL 11	LEVEL 12	LEVEL 13	LEVEL 14	LEVEL 15	LEVEL 16	LEVEL 17	LEVEL 18	LEVEL 19	LEVEL 20
52-54	57-59	62-64	67-69	72-74	77-79	82-84	87-89	92-94	97-99

STRAFE (LEVEL 24; MANA COST = 11)

Strafe is a unique skill that fires a missile at each of the targets near your location. As you pour skill points into the Strafe skill, the number of enemies that will be hit by a single shot increases. It's not uncommon to have Strafe up to eight missiles—if eight enemies were onscreen, each of them would take a hit by activating this skill. As with Multiple Shot, this is an important skill for fighting against several enemies, but it's particularly effective when you're fighting in large open areas where foes are approaching you from all sides. Most importantly, this skill works with any missile class weapon—including arrows, bolts, spears and javelins!

MAX. ENEMIES ATTACKED

LEVEL 1	LEVEL 2	LEVEL 3	LEVEL 4	LEVEL 5	LEVEL 6	LEVEL 7	LEVEL 8	LEVEL 9	LEVEL 10
5	7	9	11	13	15	17	19	21	23

LEVEL 11	LEVEL 12	LEVEL 13	LEVEL 14	LEVEL 15	LEVEL 16	LEVEL 17	LEVEL 18	LEVEL 19	LEVEL 20
25	27	29	31	33	35	37	39	41	43

DAMAGE MODIFIER (+%)

LEVEL 1	LEVEL 2	LEVEL 3	LEVEL 4	LEVEL 5	LEVEL 6	LEVEL 7	LEVEL 8	LEVEL 9	LEVEL 10
5	10	15	20	25	30	35	40	45	50

LEVEL 11	LEVEL 12	LEVEL 13	LEVEL 14	LEVEL 15	LEVEL 16	LEVEL 17	LEVEL 18	LEVEL 19	LEVEL 20
55	60	65	70	75	80	85	90	95	100

IMMOLATION ARROW (LEVEL 24)

This is an arrow that creates an area on the ground that ignites and burns for a set amount of time, depending on the level of the skill. Although Immolation Arrow causes an area of fire around the impact point, it also does fire damage when it hits its target. This is an excellent skill to use on groups of tightly packed enemies or in narrow doorways where the enemies will try to file through and attack you. As you add skill points to Immolation Arrow, the explosion damage (initial hit damage), the fire damage, and the duration of the burning all increase dramatically

The Immolation Arrow is like an arrow with a fire bomb on its tip!

with only a one-point-per-level increase in mana cost. Immolation Arrow is a *must* for the Amazon, and best of all, the fire it creates will not hurt you or any members in your party (in single *or* multiplayer).

TIP.........

Although Freezing Arrow becomes very expensive (mana-wise) as you put skill points into it, its attack value and area of effect damage make it an absolutely invaluable tool later in the game when you meet up with multiple powerful and dangerous enemies. If you're going to follow the Bow and Crossbow skill tree, you should strive to put a few points into Freezing Arrow.

MANA COST

LEVEL 1	LEVEL 2	LEVEL 3	LEVEL 4	LEVEL 5	LEVEL 6	LEVEL 7	LEVEL 8	LEVEL 9	LEVEL 10
6	7	8	9	10	11	12	13	14	15
LEVEL 11	LEVEL 12	LEVEL 13	LEVEL 14	LEVEL 15	LEVEL 16	LEVEL 17	LEVEL 18	LEVEL 19	LEVEL 20
16	17	18	19	20	21	22	23	24	25

EXPLOSION DAMAGE

LEVEL 1	LEVEL 2	LEVEL 3	LEVEL 4	LEVEL 5	LEVEL 6	LEVEL 7	LEVEL 8	LEVEL 9	LEVEL 10
4-10	10-16	16-22	22-28	28-34	34-40	40-46	46-52	52-58	58-64
LEVEL 11	LEVEL 12	LEVEL 13	LEVEL 14	LEVEL 15	LEVEL 16	LEVEL 17	LEVEL 18	LEVEL 19	LEVEL 20
64-70	70-76	76-82	82-88	88-94	94-100	100-106	106-112	112-118	118-124

FIRE DURATION (SECONDS)

LEVEL 1	LEVEL 2	LEVEL 3	LEVEL 4	LEVEL 5	LEVEL 6	LEVEL 7	LEVEL 8	LEVEL 9	LEVEL 10
4.6	5.6	6.6	7.6	8.6	9.6	10.6	11.6	12.6	13.6
LEVEL 11	LEVEL 12	LEVEL 13	LEVEL 14	LEVEL 15	LEVEL 16	LEVEL 17	LEVEL 18	LEVEL 19	LEVEL 20
14.6	15.6	16.6	17.6	18.6	19.6	20.6	21.6	22.6	23.6

AVERAGE FIRE DAMAGE

LEVEL 1	LEVEL 2	LEVEL 3	LEVEL 4	LEVEL 5	LEVEL 6	LEVEL 7	LEVEL 8	LEVEL 9	LEVEL 10
8-10	14-16	19-22	25-28	31-33	37-39	43-45	49-51	55-57	60-63
LEVEL 11	LEVEL 12	LEVEL 13	LEVEL 14	LEVEL 15	LEVEL 16	LEVEL 17	LEVEL 18	LEVEL 19	LEVEL 20
66-69	72-75	78-80	84-86	90-92	96-98	101-104	107-110	113-116	119-121

FREEZING ARROW (LEVEL 30; DURATION = 2 SEC.)

This skill launches an arrow with a cold damage area of effect that will not only damage, but also often freeze the enemies it hits—even enemies that are nearby! The result is a very powerful skill that can literally turn the enemy into chunks of ice with a single hit. At the very least, it will freeze the enemies and slow them so that subsequent hits can do enough damage to finish them off.

DAMAGE MODIFIER

LEVEL 1	LEVEL 2	LEVEL 3	LEVEL 4	LEVEL 5	LEVEL 6	LEVEL 7	LEVEL 8	LEVEL 9	LEVEL 10
6-10	12-16	18-22	24-28	30-34	36-40	42-46	48-52	54-58	60-64
LEVEL 11	LEVEL 12	LEVEL 13	LEVEL 14	LEVEL 15	LEVEL 16	LEVEL 17	LEVEL 18	LEVEL 19	LEVEL 20
66-70	72-76	78-82	84-88	90-94	96-100	102-106	108-112	114-118	120-124

MANA COST

LEVEL 1	LEVEL 2	LEVEL 3	LEVEL 4	LEVEL 5	LEVEL 6	LEVEL 7	LEVEL 8	LEVEL 9	LEVEL 10
9	10	11	12	13	14	15	16	17	18
LEVEL 11	LEVEL 12	LEVEL 13	LEVEL 14	LEVEL 15	LEVEL 16	LEVEL 17	LEVEL 18	LEVEL 19	LEVEL 20
19	20	21	22	23	24	25	26	27	28

Passive & Magic

The Passive and Magic skills are the most important of the three skill trees for the Amazon. The passive skills of Dodge, Avoid, and Evade are critical to your survival in higher levels. They give your character a chance to avoid being hit every time an enemy attacks, while the Valkyrie gives you a partner in battle that will not only fight to the death, but will also heal her wounds over time. How you choose to use your skills in this skill tree will greatly affect how you do battle and how effective your other skills will be.

Inner Sight (Level 1; Mana Cost = 5; Radius = 13.3 yards)

This skill places a small light source on all monsters within a radius, which appears as little 'sparkles' dancing above their heads. Because it illuminates the enemies to some degree, this skill allows the Amazon to see dangers in dark places, and can be very handy in dungeons and underground passages. Adding a small amount of light radius to an enemy is a handy feature, but the real benefit of Inner Sight is that it dramatically lowers the enemy's defense rating, making it considerably easier for you to damage them. Essentially, Inner Sight makes the enemy easier to see in dark places and decreases their armor class, which makes your life a heck of a lot easier.

TIP

Multiplayer Tip: It's great to have an Amazon in the group that has a couple of skill points invested in Inner Sight because every member of the party will benefit from the enemy having a substantially reduced defense. In short, it's a great way to make a little mana go a long, long way with your party.

DURATION (SECONDS)

LEVEL 1	LEVEL 2	LEVEL 3	LEVEL 4	LEVEL 5	LEVEL 6	LEVEL 7	LEVEL 8	LEVEL 9	LEVEL 10
8	12	16	20	24	28	32	36	40	44
LEVEL 11	LEVEL 12	LEVEL 13	LEVEL 14	LEVEL 15	LEVEL 16	LEVEL 17	LEVEL 18	LEVEL 19	LEVEL 20
48	52	56	60	64	68	72	76	80	84

ENEMY DEFENSE

LEVEL 1	LEVEL 2	LEVEL 3	LEVEL 4	LEVEL 5	LEVEL 6	LEVEL 7	LEVEL 8	LEVEL 9	LEVEL 10
46	50	54	57	60	62	63	64	66	67
LEVEL 11	LEVEL 12	LEVEL 13	LEVEL 14	LEVEL 15	LEVEL 16	LEVEL 17	LEVEL 18	LEVEL 19	LEVEL 20
68	69	70	70	71	72	72	72	73	73

CRITICAL STRIKE (LEVEL 1)

Critical strike creates a chance that you will do double physical damage when yo attack an enemy with either ranged or thrust attacks. As you add points to this skill, th chances that you'll do double damage go up. In fact, by the time Critical Strike is a level 10, you will have a better than a 50 percent chance of getting a double-damage h (with every weapon you use). Since Critical Strike is a passive skill, you need neve worry about activating it because it's always on. This allows you to concentrate on figh ing, knowing that many of your hits will carry substantially more weight.

2X DAMAGE CHANCE (%)

LEVEL 1	LEVEL 2	LEVEL 3	LEVEL 4	LEVEL 5	LEVEL 6	LEVEL 7	LEVEL	LEVEL 9	LEVEL 10
16	25	32	38	42	46	49	51	54	56
LEVEL 11	LEVEL 12	LEVEL 13	LEVEL 14	LEVEL 15	LEVEL 16	LEVEL 17	LEVEL 18	LEVEL 19	LEVEL 20
58	59	61	62	63	65	65	66	67	68

DODGE (LEVEL 6)

This skill ensures a chance that the Amazon will move out of the way of a hand-to-hand enemy attack. Dodge works only when the Amazon is not moving, but it may make the difference between life and death for your character when you're in a heavy duty fight. If an enemy swings at you and a hit is imminent, your Dodge skill kicks in and you'll still have a chance to step out of the way from that attack. The more points you put into Dodge, the harder it will be for the enemy to hit you; if you put points into Dodge up to level 12, the enemy will have less than a 50 percent chance of hitting you.

Dodge will give the Amazon (passively) a greater chance dodging out of the way wher an enemy attacks in hand-to hand combat.

DODGE MELEE CHANCE (%)

LEVEL 1	LEVEL 2	LEVEL 3	LEVEL 4	LEVEL 5	LEVEL 6	LEVEL 7	LEVEL 8	LEVEL 9	LEVEL 10
18	24	29	34	37	40	42	44	46	47
LEVEL 11	LEVEL 12	LEVEL 13	LEVEL 14	LEVEL 15	LEVEL 16	LEVEL 17	LEVEL 18	LEVEL 19	LEVEL 20
49	50	51	52	52	54	54	55	55	56

SLOW MISSILES (LEVEL 12; MANA COST = 5; RADIUS = 13.3 YARDS)

This is an active skill that, when used, slows nearby enemies' missiles by one-third. Th skill comes in very handy when you're facing groups of enemies that are firing proje tile weapons, as it gives you time to step out of the way of oncoming attacks. As yc pour skill points into Slow Missiles, the length of time that the skill is active increas substantially—by level 10 you can get more than a minute's worth of effect. The Slo Missiles skill is best used when you're in open areas and multiple enemies are firi ranged weapons at you. In conjunction with Avoid, this skill makes it very difficult fc enemies to damage you with ranged attacks.

DURATION (SECONDS)

LEVEL 1	LEVEL 2	LEVEL 3	LEVEL 4	LEVEL 5	LEVEL 6	LEVEL 7	LEVEL 8	LEVEL 9	LEVEL 10
12	18	24	30	36	42	48	54	60	66

LEVEL 11	LEVEL 12	LEVEL 13	LEVEL 14	LEVEL 15	LEVEL 16	LEVEL 17	LEVEL 18	LEVEL 19	LEVEL 20
72	78	84	90	96	102	108	114	120	126

AVOID (LEVEL 12)

Avoid is similar to Dodge, except that it works for ranged attacks. This means that if an enemy throws or shoots a ranged weapon at you, and it is going to hit you, Avoid will increase your chances of stepping out of the way of the enemy attack. As you might expect, having points in both Avoid and Dodge (as well as Evade) will help to make the Amazon a very difficult target for your opponents to hit.

CHANCE TO DODGE MISSILE

LEVEL 1	LEVEL 2	LEVEL 3	LEVEL 4	LEVEL 5	LEVEL 6	LEVEL 7	LEVEL 8	LEVEL 9	LEVEL 10
24	31	36	41	45	48	50	52	54	55

LEVEL 11	LEVEL 12	LEVEL 13	LEVEL 14	LEVEL 15	LEVEL 16	LEVEL 17	LEVEL 18	LEVEL 19	LEVEL 20
57	58	60	61	61	63	63	64	64	65

TIP

When you get into Act III and Act IV of Diablo II the enemy packs a much harder punch, making every chance you have to avoid one of their hits very important. For this reason, anyone using the Amazon should have at least one point in each of Dodge, Avoid, and Evade.

PENETRATE (LEVEL 18)

Penetrate gives your Amazon an increased attack rating with her ranged attacks. This skill is very powerful because your attacks (such as arrow or spear attacks) carry an increased attack rating between 35-225 percent, depending on how many skill points have been added to it. If you have chosen to follow the Javelin and Spear skill tree, then putting points into the passive Penetrate skill is critical. The development of this passive skill along with Critical Strike is an awesome combination. If you develop these two skills, then you'll not only have the chance of your ranged weapons doing double damage with Critical Strike, but you'll also be able to increase the attack rating *on top* of that with Penetrate.

TIP

Many Blizzard QA testers use a combination of Penetrate, Critical Strike, and Evade/Avoid/Dodge to make their characters powerful enough to dispatch any foe in the game.

RANGED ATTACKS AR (+%)

LEVEL 1	LEVEL 2	LEVEL 3	LEVEL 4	LEVEL 5	LEVEL 6	LEVEL 7	LEVEL 8	LEVEL 9	LEVEL 10
35	45	55	65	75	85	95	105	115	125

LEVEL 11	LEVEL 12	LEVEL 13	LEVEL 14	LEVEL 15	LEVEL 16	LEVEL 17	LEVEL 18	LEVEL 19	LEVEL 20
135	145	155	165	175	185	195	205	215	225

DECOY (LEVEL 24)

Decoy is a great way to get an enemy off your back because the Decoy will place another equally attractive target beside you for your foes to attack.

This skill creates a duplicate copy of your Amazon Although the decoy that's created does not fight in you stead, it *will* draw fire from enemies, as it appears to b you! Even in multiplayer the Decoy that's created whe you use this skill will look like you to your enemies, mak ing it an effective tool in both single player, cooperativ multiplayer, and player vs. player. Ultimately, the Decoy best used when you get into a situation where you're bein overwhelmed by enemies; invoking the Decoy at this poin will be useful in distracting enemies while you attack ther from your position. The downside to the Decoy is that will not last very long (10 seconds for a level 1 Decoy). However, as you add skill poin to this skill you may access the Decoy for nearly two minutes at a time.

DURATION (SECONDS)

LEVEL 1	LEVEL 2	LEVEL 3	LEVEL 4	LEVEL 5	LEVEL 6	LEVEL 7	LEVEL 8	LEVEL 9	LEVEL 10
10	15	20	25	30	35	40	45	50	55
LEVEL 11	LEVEL 12	LEVEL 13	LEVEL 14	LEVEL 15	LEVEL 16	LEVEL 17	LEVEL 18	LEVEL 19	LEVEL 20
60	65	70	75	80	85	90	95	100	105

MANA COST

LEVEL 1	LEVEL 2	LEVEL 3	LEVEL 4	LEVEL 5	LEVEL 6	LEVEL 7	LEVEL 8	LEVEL 9	LEVEL 10
19	18	17	16	15	14	13	12	11	10
LEVEL 11	LEVEL 12	LEVEL 13	LEVEL 14	LEVEL 15	LEVEL 16	LEVEL 17	LEVEL 18	LEVEL 19	LEVEL 20
9	8	7	6	5	4	3	2	1	1

EVADE (LEVEL 24)

Evade is a particularly valuable skill because it gives your Amazon a chance to escap any attack while moving. This differs from Avoid and Dodge. Those skills apply on when your character is standing still, whereas Evade works when your character is o *the run*. For this reason you can see why combining Evade, Avoid, and Dodge can mak it very difficult for enemies to land a hit. Evade is highly effective once you get to lev 12 because it provides a 50 percent chance that the enemy will not land their attack. level 18, Evade gives a chance for your character to avoid area of effect spells/attack which means that in some instances clouds of poison or areas of burning ground ca be negotiated without taking a hit!

CHANCE TO DODGE ANY ATTACK

LEVEL 1	LEVEL 2	LEVEL 3	LEVEL 4	LEVEL 5	LEVEL 6	LEVEL 7	LEVEL 8	LEVEL 9	LEVEL 10
18	24	29	34	37	40	42	44	46	47
LEVEL 11	LEVEL 12	LEVEL 13	LEVEL 14	LEVEL 15	LEVEL 16	LEVEL 17	LEVEL 18	LEVEL 19	LEVEL 20
49	50	51	52	52	54	54	55	55	56

VALKYRIE (LEVEL 30; MANA COST = 25)

This is one of the Amazon's most powerful skills. Indeed, the Valkyrie is a very formidable ally to have fighting by your side. When invoked this skill summons a magical Valkyrie warrior to fight for your cause. Even at level 1 Valkyrie has over 350 hit points and packs a substantial punch as an offensive force. As you pour points into the Valkyrie she gains a great deal of strength. For example, a level 5 Valkyrie has over 650 hit points and also has 100 percent modifiers on attack, defense, and damage bonuses!

The Valkyrie is perhaps the Amazon's best skill. When created, the Valkyrie is very tough and fights fiercely in your name.

TIP

A high-level Valkyrie, a Decoy, and a quality mercenary hired in town can give you a fair-sized company battle through in the higher levels of Diablo II.

HIT POINTS

LEVEL 1	LEVEL 2	LEVEL 3	LEVEL 4	LEVEL 5	LEVEL 6	LEVEL 7	LEVEL 8	LEVEL 9	LEVEL 10
377	453	528	604	679	755	830	906	981	1057

LEVEL 11	LEVEL 12	LEVEL 13	LEVEL 14	LEVEL 15	LEVEL 16	LEVEL 17	LEVEL 18	LEVEL 19	LEVEL 20
1132	1208	1283	1359	1434	1510	1585	1661	1736	1812

DAMAGE (%)

LEVEL 1	LEVEL 2	LEVEL 3	LEVEL 4	LEVEL 5	LEVEL 6	LEVEL 7	LEVEL 8	LEVEL 9	LEVEL 10
0	25	50	75	100	125	150	175	200	225

LEVEL 11	LEVEL 12	LEVEL 13	LEVEL 14	LEVEL 15	LEVEL 16	LEVEL 17	LEVEL 18	LEVEL 19	LEVEL 20
250	275	300	325	350	375	400	425	450	475

ATTACK (%)

LEVEL 1	LEVEL 2	LEVEL 3	LEVEL 4	LEVEL 5	LEVEL 6	LEVEL 7	LEVEL 8	LEVEL 9	LEVEL 10
0	25	50	75	100	125	150	175	200	225

LEVEL 11	LEVEL 12	LEVEL 13	LEVEL 14	LEVEL 15	LEVEL 16	LEVEL 17	LEVEL 18	LEVEL 19	LEVEL 20
250	275	300	325	350	375	400	425	450	475

DEFENSE BONUS (%)

LEVEL 1	LEVEL 2	LEVEL 3	LEVEL 4	LEVEL 5	LEVEL 6	LEVEL 7	LEVEL 8	LEVEL 9	LEVEL 10
0	25	50	75	100	125	150	175	200	225

LEVEL 11	LEVEL 12	LEVEL 13	LEVEL 14	LEVEL 15	LEVEL 16	LEVEL 17	LEVEL 18	LEVEL 19	LEVEL 20
250	275	300	325	350	375	400	425	450	475

PIERCE (LEVEL 30)

This is a passive skill that gives the Amazon a chance that any ranged weapon you us‹ be it a spear or an arrow, will hit its target and then continue through toward the ne: target. As with Penetrate, this skill is important if you choose to fight the enemy from distance at all times. Pierce, however, requires 15 skill points before it reaches a 40 pe cent chance of passing through an enemy, so it's not always a worthwhile use of you skill points just to slightly improve your chance of piercing an enemy.

PASS THROUGH CHANCE (%)

LEVEL 1	LEVEL 2	LEVEL 3	LEVEL 4	LEVEL 5	LEVEL 6	LEVEL 7	LEVEL 8	LEVEL 9	LEVEL 10
16	20	24	27	30	32	33	34	36	37

LEVEL 11	LEVEL 12	LEVEL 13	LEVEL 14	LEVEL 15	LEVEL 16	LEVEL 17	LEVEL 18	LEVEL 19	LEVEL 20
38	39	40	40	41	42	42	42	43	43

JAVELIN AND SPEAR

This group of skills enhances the abilities of the Javelin and Spear class of weapon Each skill in this tree in some way improves upon the Javelin/Spear attacks, or mo specifically, they improve upon weapons that use a thrusting or throwing attack. Th higher level skills such as Fend and Lightning Fury provide an excellent power punc while the skills such as Power Strike and Plague Javelin help to provide a backbone ‹ skills that will serve you well as your Amazon progresses through *Diablo II*.

JAB (LEVEL 1)

Jab delivers multiple hits in a single attack, and is an essential requisite if you choose ‹ follow this arm of the skill tree. By perforating the enemy multiple times within the span ‹ a normal attack, you can sometimes finish the creature off in one fell swoop, rather tha having to attempt to hit it multiple times. The downside to the Jab skill is that each su cessive hit is slightly less powerful, and not every jab is guaranteed to hit. However, as yc add points to the Jab skill it quickly becomes more effective in terms of attack rating ar the amount of damage it inflicts on the enemy.

TIP..........

The damage inflicted on the enemy when using Jab is actually lower in the first few levels of Jab. Indeed, it's not until you get up to level 7 Jab that you start to see an increase in the damage modifier (meaning that you must put skill points into Jab for it to be most effective).

ATTACK RATING BONUS

LEVEL 1	LEVEL 2	LEVEL 3	LEVEL 4	LEVEL 5	LEVEL 6	LEVEL 7	LEVEL 8	LEVEL 9	LEVEL 10
+10	+15	+20	+25	+30	+35	+40	+45	+50	+55

LEVEL 11	LEVEL 12	LEVEL 13	LEVEL 14	LEVEL 15	LEVEL 16	LEVEL 17	LEVEL 18	LEVEL 19	LEVEL 20
+60	+65	+70	+75	+80	+85	+90	+95	+100	+105

DAMAGE MODIFIER (%)

LEVEL 1	LEVEL 2	LEVEL 3	LEVEL 4	LEVEL 5	LEVEL 6	LEVEL 7	LEVEL 8	LEVEL 9	LEVEL 10
-15	-12	-9	-6	-3	0	+3	+6	+9	+12

LEVEL 11	LEVEL 12	LEVEL 13	LEVEL 14	LEVEL 15	LEVEL 16	LEVEL 17	LEVEL 18	LEVEL 19	LEVEL 20
+15	+18	+21	+24	+27	+30	+33	+36	+39	+42

MANA COST

LEVEL 1	LEVEL 2	LEVEL 3	LEVEL 4	LEVEL 5	LEVEL 6	LEVEL 7	LEVEL 8	LEVEL 9	LEVEL 10
2	2.2	2.5	2.7	3	3.2	3.5	3.7	4	4.2
LEVEL 11	**LEVEL 12**	**LEVEL 13**	**LEVEL 14**	**LEVEL 15**	**LEVEL 16**	**LEVEL 17**	**LEVEL 18**	**LEVEL 19**	**LEVEL 20**
4.5	4.7	5	5.2	5.5	5.7	6	6.2	6.5	6.7

POWER STRIKE (LEVEL 6)

The Power Strike is a straight-forward skill that simply adds lightning damage to an attack. Adding a different type of damage to an attack is always good because it improves both the damage done and the attack strength for thrusting attacks. Although Power Strike has a mana cost, it is nominal and relatively insignificant compared to the benefit supplied by the spell. This skill is best used when fighting small groups or single enemies because the Lightning damage will only affect a single targeted enemy.

ATTACK MODIFIER

LEVEL 1	LEVEL 2	LEVEL 3	LEVEL 4	LEVEL 5	LEVEL 6	LEVEL 7	LEVEL 8	LEVEL 9	LEVEL 10
10	15	20	25	30	35	40	45	50	55
LEVEL 11	**LEVEL 12**	**LEVEL 13**	**LEVEL 14**	**LEVEL 15**	**LEVEL 16**	**LEVEL 17**	**LEVEL 18**	**LEVEL 19**	**LEVEL 20**
60	65	70	75	80	85	90	95	100	105

DAMAGE

LEVEL 1	LEVEL 2	LEVEL 3	LEVEL 4	LEVEL 5	LEVEL 6	LEVEL 7	LEVEL 8	LEVEL 9	LEVEL 10
1-8	4-11	7-14	10-17	13-20	16-23	19-26	22-29	25-32	28-35
LEVEL 11	**LEVEL 12**	**LEVEL 13**	**LEVEL 14**	**LEVEL 15**	**LEVEL 16**	**LEVEL 17**	**LEVEL 18**	**LEVEL 19**	**LEVEL 20**
31-38	34-41	37-44	40-47	43-50	46-53	49-56	52-59	55-62	58-65

MANA COST

LEVEL 1	LEVEL 2	LEVEL 3	LEVEL 4	LEVEL 5	LEVEL 6	LEVEL 7	LEVEL 8	LEVEL 9	LEVEL 10
2	2.2	2.5	2.7	3	3.2	3.5	3.7	4	4.2
LEVEL 11	**LEVEL 12**	**LEVEL 13**	**LEVEL 14**	**LEVEL 15**	**LEVEL 16**	**LEVEL 17**	**LEVEL 18**	**LEVEL 19**	**LEVEL 20**
4.5	4.7	5	5.2	5.5	5.7	6	6.2	6.5	6.7

Poison Javelin leaves a trail of poison clouds in the area behind it as it flies through the air. For this reason you can use a Javelin throw to block a narrow hallway or valley so that any enemy passing through it will become poisoned. This technique can be very effective, but timing is important since the poison cloud lasts only a few seconds.

POISON JAVELIN (LEVEL 6)

In short, Poison is a great way to damage a group of monsters in a short period of time, so it stands to reason that if you can combine Poison with a Javelin attack you can create some serious carnage. Poison Javelin increases the damage done to an enemy (over and above the normal damage your attacks inflict), but it also poisons the target and any nearby targets. The poison then continues to damage the enemy as long as it lasts; the duration of the poison effect increases with every skill point used for this ability.

A Poison Javelin is best used in areas where there are plenty of enemies.

POISON DAMAGE

LEVEL 1	LEVEL 2	LEVEL 3	LEVEL 4	LEVEL 5	LEVEL 6	LEVEL 7	LEVEL 8	LEVEL 9	LEVEL 10
9-14	14-18	18-23	23-28	28-32	32-39	37-42	42-46	46-51	51-56

LEVEL 11	LEVEL 12	LEVEL 13	LEVEL 14	LEVEL 15	LEVEL 16	LEVEL 17	LEVEL 18	LEVEL 19	LEVEL 20
56-60	60-65	65-70	70-75	75-79	79-84	84-89	89-93	93-98	98-103

MANA COST

LEVEL 1	LEVEL 2	LEVEL 3	LEVEL 4	LEVEL 5	LEVEL 6	LEVEL 7	LEVEL 8	LEVEL 9	LEVEL 10
4	4.2	4.5	4.7	5	5.2	5.5	5.7	6	6.2

LEVEL 11	LEVEL 12	LEVEL 13	LEVEL 14	LEVEL 15	LEVEL 16	LEVEL 17	LEVEL 18	LEVEL 19	LEVEL 20
6.5	6.7	7	7.2	7.5	7.7	8	8.2	8.5	8.7

IMPALE (LEVEL 12; MANA COST = 3)

This skill is a more powerful single attack that, especially at the higher levels, inflicts a much greater amount of damage on the enemy you're attacking. As you put more points into Impale the attack rating goes up considerably, but with a higher cost on the durability of the Javelin you are using. Despite this increased strain on the durability of the particular weapon you are holding when you use Impale, this skill is well worth the mana cost. As with Power Strike, Impale is best used against small groups or single enemies because it can affect only one foe at a time .

ATTACK MODIFIER (%)

LEVEL 1	LEVEL 2	LEVEL 3	LEVEL 4	LEVEL 5	LEVEL 6	LEVEL 7	LEVEL 8	LEVEL 9	LEVEL 10
25	32	39	46	53	60	67	74	81	88
LEVEL 11	LEVEL 12	LEVEL 13	LEVEL 14	LEVEL 15	LEVEL 16	LEVEL 17	LEVEL 18	LEVEL 19	LEVEL 20
95	102	109	116	123	130	137	144	151	158

WEAPON DURABILITY (%)

LEVEL 1	LEVEL 2	LEVEL 3	LEVEL 4	LEVEL 5	LEVEL 6	LEVEL 7	LEVEL 8	LEVEL 9	LEVEL 10
50	51	52	53	54	55	56	57	58	59
LEVEL 11	LEVEL 12	LEVEL 13	LEVEL 14	LEVEL 15	LEVEL 16	LEVEL 17	LEVEL 18	LEVEL 19	LEVEL 20
60	61	62	63	64	65	66	67	68	69

LIGHTNING BOLT (LEVEL 12)

Lightning Bolt turns the Javelin you are throwing into a lightning bolt that does a large amount of damage to the enemy it hits. As Lightning Bolt increases in level, it causes a huge amount of damage, and the mana-cost associated with this skill at those high levels won't break your mana bank (so to speak). Due to the nature of lightning, the bolt that's created is an excellent source of light. As with other similar weapons, you can use the Lightning Bolt to illuminate unexplored or darkened areas, such as caves and tombs. If you're lucky, it may even hit an unsuspecting enemy!

DAMAGE MODIFIER

LEVEL 1	LEVEL 2	LEVEL 3	LEVEL 4	LEVEL 5	LEVEL 6	LEVEL 7	LEVEL 8	LEVEL 9	LEVEL 10
1-40	1-48	1-56	1-64	1-72	1-80	1-88	1-96	1-104	1-112
LEVEL 11	LEVEL 12	LEVEL 13	LEVEL 14	LEVEL 15	LEVEL 16	LEVEL 17	LEVEL 18	LEVEL 19	LEVEL 20
1-120	1-128	1-136	1-144	1-152	1-160	1-168	1-176	1-184	1-192

MANA COST

LEVEL 1	LEVEL 2	LEVEL 3	LEVEL 4	LEVEL 5	LEVEL 6	LEVEL 7	LEVEL 8	LEVEL 9	LEVEL 10
6	6.2	6.5	6.7	7	7.2	7.5	7.7	8	8.2
LEVEL 11	LEVEL 12	LEVEL 13	LEVEL 14	LEVEL 15	LEVEL 16	LEVEL 17	LEVEL 18	LEVEL 19	LEVEL 20
8.5	8.7	9	9.2	9.5	9.7	10	10.2	10.5	10.7

CHARGED STRIKE (LEVEL 18)

This skill provides a lightning attack that also releases charged bolts that move away from your position, doing damage to whatever enemies they encounter. These bolts are not guided, so there's no guarantee that they'll hit any enemy; however, when you're in close combat and fighting against a group of enemies, using Charged Strike can inflict the kind of damage that'll make your job much easier. The first few levels of this skill see a substantial increase in the effectiveness of Charged Strike, so if you choose to put one point into it, you should be prepared to add at least a few more to make it effective in the later levels of *Diablo II*.

Charged Strike packs an electrical punch that will wreak havoc on enemies.

DAMAGE MODIFIER

LEVEL 1	LEVEL 2	LEVEL 3	LEVEL 4	LEVEL 5	LEVEL 6	LEVEL 7	LEVEL 8	LEVEL 9	LEVEL 10
1-15	6-20	11-25	16-30	21-35	26-40	31-45	36-50	41-55	46-60
LEVEL 11	LEVEL 12	LEVEL 13	LEVEL 14	LEVEL 15	LEVEL 16	LEVEL 17	LEVEL 18	LEVEL 19	LEVEL 20
51-65	56-70	61-75	66-80	71-85	76-90	81-95	86-100	91-105	96-110

MANA COST

LEVEL 1	LEVEL 2	LEVEL 3	LEVEL 4	LEVEL 5	LEVEL 6	LEVEL 7	LEVEL 8	LEVEL 9	LEVEL 10
4	4.2	4.5	4.7	5	5.2	5.5	5.7	6	6.2
LEVEL 11	LEVEL 12	LEVEL 13	LEVEL 14	LEVEL 15	LEVEL 16	LEVEL 17	LEVEL 18	LEVEL 19	LEVEL 20
6.5	6.7	7	7.2	7.5	7.7	8	8.2	8.5	8.7

PLAGUE JAVELIN (LEVEL 18)

This weapon is very similar to Poison Javelin, but it also creates an expanding cloud of poison around the target it hits. Like the Poison Javelin, this skill leaves a trail of poison that can be used as a deadly barrier in crowded areas or narrow passageways, but the Plague Javelin also inflicts an area of damage when it impacts the enemy. This explosion of poison means that firing a Plague Javelin into a group of enemies will leave *all* of them poisoned as their final breaths leave their wracked bodies.

POISON DAMAGE

LEVEL 1	LEVEL 2	LEVEL 3	LEVEL 4	LEVEL 5	LEVEL 6	LEVEL 7	LEVEL 8	LEVEL 9	LEVEL 10
9-14	14-18	18-23	23-28	28-32	32-39	37-42	42-46	46-51	51-56
LEVEL 11	LEVEL 12	LEVEL 13	LEVEL 14	LEVEL 15	LEVEL 16	LEVEL 17	LEVEL 18	LEVEL 19	LEVEL 20
56-60	60-65	65-70	70-75	75-79	79-84	84-89	89-93	93-98	98-103

CHAPTER 2: THE CHARACTERS

MANA COST

LEVEL 1	LEVEL 2	LEVEL 3	LEVEL 4	LEVEL 5	LEVEL 6	LEVEL 7	LEVEL 8	LEVEL 9	LEVEL 10
7	8	9	10	11	12	13	14	15	16

LEVEL 11	LEVEL 12	LEVEL 13	LEVEL 14	LEVEL 15	LEVEL 16	LEVEL 17	LEVEL 18	LEVEL 19	LEVEL 20
17	18	19	20	21	22	23	24	25	26

FEND (LEVEL 24; MANA COST = 5)

This skill is for hand-to-hand combat only and is very effective when you are surrounded by a group of foul creatures. Fend attacks multiple adjacent targets quickly, hitting *every* adjacent enemy! With a few skill points in Fend you can take down a feverish group of enemies in a few hits, because each time you strike each adjacent enemy takes a hit. As skill points are added to Fend, it becomes increasingly effective as both the Attack and Damage modifiers increase dramatically.

ATTACK MODIFIER (+%)

LEVEL 1	LEVEL 2	LEVEL 3	LEVEL 4	LEVEL 5	LEVEL 6	LEVEL 7	LEVEL 8	LEVEL 9	LEVEL 10
10	15	20	25	30	35	40	45	50	55

LEVEL 11	LEVEL 12	LEVEL 13	LEVEL 14	LEVEL 15	LEVEL 16	LEVEL 17	LEVEL 18	LEVEL 19	LEVEL 20
60	65	70	75	80	85	90	95	100	105

DAMAGE MODIFIER (+%)

LEVEL 1	LEVEL 2	LEVEL 3	LEVEL 4	LEVEL 5	LEVEL 6	LEVEL 7	LEVEL 8	LEVEL 9	LEVEL 10
25	28	31	34	37	40	43	46	49	52

LEVEL 11	LEVEL 12	LEVEL 13	LEVEL 14	LEVEL 15	LEVEL 16	LEVEL 17	LEVEL 18	LEVEL 19	LEVEL 20
55	58	61	64	67	70	73	76	79	82

TIP..........

Assign a hot key to the Fend skill so you can use it if you suddenly become surrounded by a group of enemies. A few uses of Fend can thin out the enemy ranks very quickly and, at the very least, open up a pathway for your escape.

It's important to note that with both Lightning Strike and Lightning Fury the initial hit is weaker than the chain lightning hits that follow. It's not uncommon for the enemy you hit first to remain standing while those behind him fall at the hands of the sparks. For this reason it isn't always the best idea to hit the toughest enemy first when using these skills.

LIGHTNING STRIKE (LEVEL 30)

This skill turns your Javelin into a lightning bolt as soon as it makes contact with the enemy. When you hit your foe, Lightning Strike will release chain lightning that travels from enemy to enemy within range. This skill is very similar to Lightning Fury, except that it's not nearly as powerful and it requires you to be adjacent to the enemy in order to start the chain of lightning. This is an excellent skill to master if you enjoy getting into melee combat with your Amazon, but if you prefer to fight from afar, put your points into Lightning Fury.

LIGHTNING BOLT DAMAGE

LEVEL 1	LEVEL 2	LEVEL 3	LEVEL 4	LEVEL 5	LEVEL 6	LEVEL 7	LEVEL 8	LEVEL 9	LEVEL 10
1-14	1-16	1-18	1-20	1-22	1-24	1-26	1-28	1-30	1-32
LEVEL 11	LEVEL 12	LEVEL 13	LEVEL 14	LEVEL 15	LEVEL 16	LEVEL 17	LEVEL 18	LEVEL 19	LEVEL 20
1-34	1-36	1-38	1-40	1-42	1-44	1-46	1-48	1-50	1-52

NUMBER OF BOLTS

LEVEL 1	LEVEL 2	LEVEL 3	LEVEL 4	LEVEL 5	LEVEL 6	LEVEL 7	LEVEL 8	LEVEL 9	LEVEL 10
2	3	4	5	6	7	8	9	10	11
LEVEL 11	LEVEL 12	LEVEL 13	LEVEL 14	LEVEL 15	LEVEL 16	LEVEL 17	LEVEL 18	LEVEL 19	LEVEL 20
12	13	14	15	16	17	18	19	20	21

LIGHTNING DAMAGE

LEVEL 1	LEVEL 2	LEVEL 3	LEVEL 4	LEVEL 5	LEVEL 6	LEVEL 7	LEVEL 8	LEVEL 9	LEVEL 10
5-25	15-35	25-45	35-55	45-65	55-75	65-85	75-95	85-105	95-115
LEVEL 11	LEVEL 12	LEVEL 13	LEVEL 14	LEVEL 15	LEVEL 16	LEVEL 17	LEVEL 18	LEVEL 19	LEVEL 20
105-125	115-135	125-145	135-155	145-165	155-175	165-185	175-195	185-205	195-215

MANA COST

LEVEL 1	LEVEL 2	LEVEL 3	LEVEL 4	LEVEL 5	LEVEL 6	LEVEL 7	LEVEL 8	LEVEL 9	LEVEL 10
9	9.5	10	10.5	11	11.5	12	12	13	13
LEVEL 11	LEVEL 12	LEVEL 13	LEVEL 14	LEVEL 15	LEVEL 16	LEVEL 17	LEVEL 18	LEVEL 19	LEVEL 20
14	14	15	15	16	16	17	17	18	18

LIGHTNING FURY (LEVEL 30)

There's a reason that Lightning Fury is a Level 30 skill—it's powerful!

Lightning Fury is a skill that turns your Javelin into a chained lightning bolt as soon as it leaves your hands. The result is a single thrown Javelin that can take down or seriously injure an entire group of enemies, depending on the level of the skill and the strength of your enemies. This is a ranged skill and is best used that way, although you can certainly use it in melee combat if necessary. Ideally, you'll want to stay out of harm's way, fire Lightning Strike at the 'lead' enemy, and then sit back and watch the tentacles of electricity rip through the enemy ranks. Lightning Fury can be used in the same way a grenade is lobbed into an enemy area. If you fire a Lightning Fury at an enemy who's the first of many behind him, the resulting chain lightning will rip through every enemy within range and possibly even clear out the room for you!

TIP

A clever trick with Lightning Fury is to bounce it off a wall when attacking enemies. This can be effective because the lightning attacks that spread out after the bounce are more powerful than the original attack.

LIGHTNING BOLT DAMAGE

LEVEL 1	LEVEL 2	LEVEL 3	LEVEL 4	LEVEL 5	LEVEL 6	LEVEL 7	LEVEL 8	LEVEL 9	LEVEL 10
1-40	1-44	1-48	1-52	1-56	1-60	1-64	1-68	1-72	1-76

LEVEL 11	LEVEL 12	LEVEL 13	LEVEL 14	LEVEL 15	LEVEL 16	LEVEL 17	LEVEL 18	LEVEL 19	LEVEL 20
1-80	1-84	1-88	1-92	1-96	1-100	1-104	1-108	1-112	1-116

NUMBER OF BOLTS

LEVEL 1	LEVEL 2	LEVEL 3	LEVEL 4	LEVEL 5	LEVEL 6	LEVEL 7	LEVEL 8	LEVEL 9	LEVEL 10
2	3	4	5	6	7	8	9	10	11

LEVEL 11	LEVEL 12	LEVEL 13	LEVEL 14	LEVEL 15	LEVEL 16	LEVEL 17	LEVEL 18	LEVEL 19	LEVEL 20
12	13	14	15	16	17	18	19	20	21

LIGHTNING DAMAGE

LEVEL 1	LEVEL 2	LEVEL 3	LEVEL 4	LEVEL 5	LEVEL 6	LEVEL 7	LEVEL 8	LEVEL 9	LEVEL 10
1-40	11-50	21-60	31-70	41-80	51-90	61-100	71-110	81-120	91-130

LEVEL 11	LEVEL 12	LEVEL 13	LEVEL 14	LEVEL 15	LEVEL 16	LEVEL 17	LEVEL 18	LEVEL 19	LEVEL 20
101-190	111-150	121-160	131-170	141-180	151-190	161-200	171-210	181-220	191-230

MANA COST

LEVEL 1	LEVEL 2	LEVEL 3	LEVEL 4	LEVEL 5	LEVEL 6	LEVEL 7	LEVEL 8	LEVEL 9	LEVEL 10
10	10.5	11	11.5	12	12	13	13	14	14

LEVEL 11	LEVEL 12	LEVEL 13	LEVEL 14	LEVEL 15	LEVEL 16	LEVEL 17	LEVEL 18	LEVEL 19	LEVEL 20
15	15	16	16	17	17	18	18	19	19

The Paladin

The Paladin is a battle-ready warrior for whom faith is a shield; he fights for what he believes to be right. Furthermore, his steadfastness gives him powers to do good upon friends, and wreak cruel justice upon foes. There are those who call the Paladin an overwrought zealot, but others recognize in him the strength and goodness of the Light. The Paladin is a crusading believer in all that is good, just, and holy. He stands tall and intimidate with a deep, commanding voice that sounds appropriate coming from either the pulpit or the battlefield.

PALADIN SKILLS

There are three skill sets that the Paladin can develop as he progresses in *Diablo II*. As with the other characters, which skills are developed in each area will ultimately affect the Paladin's abilities in the game. The three skill sets are Combat, Offensive Auras, and Defensive Auras.

COMBAT

As the name implies, this set of skills aids the Paladin in his ability to engage in combat against the evil forces he will face. From multi-faceted attacks such as Smite (which not only damages, but also knocks back and stuns), to melee enhancing skills like Zeal, this line contains important skills that the Paladin must use in order to be successful.

If you have a life-stealing weapon that will replenish lost life with every hit, the Sacrifice becomes a very practical and powerful skill. However, if you do not have such a weapon or item, it would behoove you to keep health potions on hand at all times you're going to use this skill.

SACRIFICE (LEVEL 1)

This is an odd skill because it gives you the ability to do more damage to the enemy by improving your attack rating; but it does so at the cost of 8 percent to your health. The upside of Sacrifice is that it greatly increases the damage you do, and the cost is always only 8 percent of your life, regardless of your level of Sacrifice. Still, the cost of draining some of your own life in order to do damage must always be weighed against the benefits of having a more powerful attack.

ATTACK RATING MODIFIER (+%)

LEVEL 1	LEVEL 2	LEVEL 3	LEVEL 4	LEVEL 5	LEVEL 6	LEVEL 7	LEVEL 8	LEVEL 9	LEVEL 10
20	25	30	35	40	45	50	55	60	65
LEVEL 11	LEVEL 12	LEVEL 13	LEVEL 14	LEVEL 15	LEVEL 16	LEVEL 17	LEVEL 18	LEVEL 19	LEVEL 20
70	75	80	85	90	95	100	105	110	115

DAMAGE (+%)

LEVEL 1	LEVEL 2	LEVEL 3	LEVEL 4	LEVEL 5	LEVEL 6	LEVEL 7	LEVEL 8	LEVEL 9	LEVEL 10
180	192	204	216	228	240	252	264	276	288
LEVEL 11	LEVEL 12	LEVEL 13	LEVEL 14	LEVEL 15	LEVEL 16	LEVEL 17	LEVEL 18	LEVEL 19	LEVEL 20
300	312	324	336	348	360	372	384	396	408

SMITE (LEVEL 1; MANA COST = 2)

Smite is best described as a shield bash. When this skill is used, it knocks back and damages the enemy. The real benefit, however, is in its ability to stun the enemy. When you Smite an enemy, they become stunned for a short time (increasing as more skill points are spent on this skill), and during this time they cannot move, attack, cast spells, or use abilities. By the time Smite reaches level 15, you're doing a crushing amount of damage (225 percent more) and the enemy is being stunned for a full three seconds, which means that you can continue to hit them without fear of retaliation.

Smite not only knocks the enemy back, but it also stuns them and does damage, as well.

TIP..........

You can take even a tough enemy out by simply continually using Smite on them. Every time you use Smite, the enemy will be knocked back, stunning them for a brief period of time. If you Smite them repeatedly, you can push them back against a wall and simply continue to Smite them or trade a sword attack with a Smite attack until they are dead. Using this technique will prevent your foe from fighting back because they will be perpetually stunned.

DAMAGE MODIFIER (+%)

LEVEL 1	LEVEL 2	LEVEL 3	LEVEL 4	LEVEL 5	LEVEL 6	LEVEL 7	LEVEL 8	LEVEL 9	LEVEL 10
15	30	45	60	75	90	105	120	135	150
LEVEL 11	LEVEL 12	LEVEL 13	LEVEL 14	LEVEL 15	LEVEL 16	LEVEL 17	LEVEL 18	LEVEL 19	LEVEL 20
165	180	195	210	225	240	255	270	285	300

STUN (SECONDS)

LEVEL 1	LEVEL 2	LEVEL 3	LEVEL 4	LEVEL 5	LEVEL 6	LEVEL 7	LEVEL 8	LEVEL 9	LEVEL 10
0.6	0.8	1.0	1.2	1.4	1.6	1.8	2.0	2.2	2.4
LEVEL 11	LEVEL 12	LEVEL 13	LEVEL 14	LEVEL 15	LEVEL 16	LEVEL 17	LEVEL 18	LEVEL 19	LEVEL 20
2.6	2.8	3.0	3.2	3.4	3.6	3.8	4.0	4.2	4.4

HOLY BOLT (LEVEL 6)

Holy Bolt is a powerful bolt of divine energy that damages undead monsters, often to the point of destroying them in one shot. However, as an attack this is really *only* effective against the undead. If you have skill points in Holy Bolt, but are not fighting the undead, you can still use Holy Bolt to heal members of your party by shooting them with it! This is a very unique skill because it can be used as both a weapon and an instrument of healing. For this reason, it's worth having a skill point or two invested in Holy Bolt.

MAGIC DAMAGE

LEVEL 1	LEVEL 2	LEVEL 3	LEVEL 4	LEVEL 5	LEVEL 6	LEVEL 7	LEVEL 8	LEVEL 9	LEVEL 10
8-16	14-22	20-28	26-34	32-40	38-46	44-52	50-58	56-64	62-70

LEVEL 11	LEVEL 12	LEVEL 13	LEVEL 14	LEVEL 15	LEVEL 16	LEVEL 17	LEVEL 18	LEVEL 19	LEVEL 20
68-76	74-82	80-88	86-94	92-100	98-106	104-112	110-118	116-124	122-130

HEALING

LEVEL 1	LEVEL 2	LEVEL 3	LEVEL 4	LEVEL 5	LEVEL 6	LEVEL 7	LEVEL 8	LEVEL 9	LEVEL 10
1-6	3-8	5-10	7-12	9-14	11-16	13-18	15-20	17-22	19-24

LEVEL 11	LEVEL 12	LEVEL 13	LEVEL 14	LEVEL 15	LEVEL 16	LEVEL 17	LEVEL 18	LEVEL 19	LEVEL 20
21-26	23-28	25-30	27-32	29-34	31-36	33-38	35-40	37-42	39-44

MANA COST

LEVEL 1	LEVEL 2	LEVEL 3	LEVEL 4	LEVEL 5	LEVEL 6	LEVEL 7	LEVEL 8	LEVEL 9	LEVEL 10
4	4.2	4.5	4.7	5	5.2	5.5	5.7	6	6.2

LEVEL 11	LEVEL 12	LEVEL 13	LEVEL 14	LEVEL 15	LEVEL 16	LEVEL 17	LEVEL 18	LEVEL 19	LEVEL 20
6.5	6.7	7	7.2	7.5	7.7	8	8.2	8.5	8.7

ZEAL (LEVEL 12; MANA COST = 2)

This skill is extremely effective when you are in a situation where you are surrounded because it enables you to quickly strike multiple adjacent enemies with one attack. As you add points to this skill you'll be able to land more hits with a more powerful attack, making this a valuable tool in close quarters fighting with a group of enemies. Zeal can also be used to make a weapon with a very slow attack speed, such as a spear, much faster so that you can do the large amount of damage that a slow weapon offers at a vastly improved rate of speed.

ATTACK MODIFIER (+%)

LEVEL 1	LEVEL 2	LEVEL 3	LEVEL 4	LEVEL 5	LEVEL 6	LEVEL 7	LEVEL 8	LEVEL 9	LEVEL 10
10	15	20	25	30	35	40	45	50	55

LEVEL 11	LEVEL 12	LEVEL 13	LEVEL 14	LEVEL 15	LEVEL 16	LEVEL 17	LEVEL 18	LEVEL 19	LEVEL 20
60	65	70	75	80	85	90	95	100	105

NUMBER OF HITS

LEVEL 1	LEVEL 2	LEVEL 3	LEVEL 4	LEVEL 5	LEVEL 6	LEVEL 7	LEVEL 8	LEVEL 9	LEVEL 10
2	3	4	5	6	7	8	9	10	11

LEVEL 11	LEVEL 12	LEVEL 13	LEVEL 14	LEVEL 15	LEVEL 16	LEVEL 17	LEVEL 18	LEVEL 19	LEVEL 20
12	13	14	15	16	17	18	19	20	21

CHARGE (LEVEL 12: MANA COST = 9)

This is a skill that's related to Smite since it uses a shield bash to hit the enemy. Charge, however, also substantially increases the amount of damage the smash does and closes ground on the enemy by making your Paladin run up to the enemy and then hit it with a hard shield smash. The enemy is not stunned as with Smite, but the attack is often powerful enough to take an enemy out in one or two Charges. This is a good skill to use to close distance on an enemy quickly and surprise them.

DAMAGE MODIFIER (+%)

LEVEL 1	LEVEL 2	LEVEL 3	LEVEL 4	LEVEL 5	LEVEL 6	LEVEL 7	LEVEL 8	LEVEL 9	LEVEL 10
100	125	150	175	200	225	250	275	300	325
LEVEL 11	LEVEL 12	LEVEL 13	LEVEL 14	LEVEL 15	LEVEL 16	LEVEL 17	LEVEL 18	LEVEL 19	LEVEL 20
350	375	400	425	450	475	500	525	550	575

VENGEANCE (LEVEL 18; MANA COST = 4)

This is a very unique skill that not only does standard damage, but also adds fire, lightning, and cold damage to the attack. This is an important skill because it will deal a wicked blow to an enemy that has no resistances, but it will also be effective against monsters that have specific resistances. For example, if an enemy has resistance to fire, then the Vengeance attack will still hit them with standard attack, cold attack, and electrical attack. This is a skill well worth employing at any time, and when a few skill points have been invested in it, the enemies you hit will be slowed by cold for several seconds as well.

MANA COST

LEVEL 1	LEVEL 2	LEVEL 3	LEVEL 4	LEVEL 5	LEVEL 6	LEVEL 7	LEVEL 8	LEVEL 9	LEVEL 10
4	4.5	5	5.5	6	6.5	7	7.5	8	8.5
LEVEL 11	LEVEL 12	LEVEL 13	LEVEL 14	LEVEL 15	LEVEL 16	LEVEL 17	LEVEL 18	LEVEL 19	LEVEL 20
9	9.5	10	10.5	11	11.5	12	12	13	13

COLD LENGTH

LEVEL 1	LEVEL 2	LEVEL 3	LEVEL 4	LEVEL 5	LEVEL 6	LEVEL 7	LEVEL 8	LEVEL 9	LEVEL 10
1.2	1.8	2.4	3.0	3.6	4.2	4.8	5.4	6.0	6.6
LEVEL 11	LEVEL 12	LEVEL 13	LEVEL 14	LEVEL 15	LEVEL 16	LEVEL 17	LEVEL 18	LEVEL 19	LEVEL 20
7.2	7.8	8.4	9.0	9.6	10.2	10.8	11.4	12.0	12.6

ELEMENTAL DAMAGE (+%)

LEVEL 1	LEVEL 2	LEVEL 3	LEVEL 4	LEVEL 5	LEVEL 6	LEVEL 7	LEVEL 8	LEVEL 9	LEVEL 10
35	40	45	50	55	60	65	70	75	80
LEVEL 11	LEVEL 12	LEVEL 13	LEVEL 14	LEVEL 15	LEVEL 16	LEVEL 17	LEVEL 18	LEVEL 19	LEVEL 20
85	90	95	100	105	110	115	120	125	130

⚔ BLESSED HAMMER (LEVEL 12)

The Blessed Hammer creates a spinning mallet that spirals outward, damaging any enemies it encounters, while doing double damage to undead creatures. This is not a targeted weapon, but when it hits an undead creature it will do a heap of damage, often killing the undead in one hit. As skill points are added to Blessed Hammer it gains a great deal of attack strength, but since its mana cost also increases and it can be difficult to use in close quarters, it is not a skill in which points should be heavily invested.

DAMAGE MODIFIER (+%) ⚔

LEVEL 1	LEVEL 2	LEVEL 3	LEVEL 4	LEVEL 5	LEVEL 6	LEVEL 7	LEVEL 8	LEVEL 9	LEVEL 10
12-16	20-24	28-32	36-40	44-48	52-56	60-64	68-72	76-80	84-88
LEVEL 11	LEVEL 12	LEVEL 13	LEVEL 14	LEVEL 15	LEVEL 16	LEVEL 17	LEVEL 18	LEVEL 19	LEVEL 20
92-96	100-104	108-112	116-120	124-128	132-136	140-144	148-152	156-160	164-168

MANA COST ⚔

LEVEL 1	LEVEL 2	LEVEL 3	LEVEL 4	LEVEL 5	LEVEL 6	LEVEL 7	LEVEL 8	LEVEL 9	LEVEL 10
5	5.2	5.5	5.7	6	6.2	6.5	6.7	7	7.2
LEVEL 11	LEVEL 12	LEVEL 13	LEVEL 14	LEVEL 15	LEVEL 16	LEVEL 17	LEVEL 18	LEVEL 19	LEVEL 20
7.5	7.7	8	8.2	8.5	8.7	9	9.2	9.5	9.7

⚔ CONVERSION (LEVEL 24; MANA COST = 4)

NOTE......

You can convert multiple enemies to fight for you at the same time, but you must convert them one at a time. Hence, you won't ever be able to achieve the numbers of followers that the Necromancer summons with Revive.

This skill gives a chance that you'll convert a monster to fight for your Paladin, but only for a short period of time. The duration of this effect is extended when more skill points are invested in the skill, along with the chance of successful conversion. This skill works with your normal melee weapon attack, with the enemy being damaged by each hit. However, there's a chance that your attack will also convert the enemy to your side; if this happens, a small symbol will appear over the head of the enemy and they'll become your ally for the prescribed amount of time.

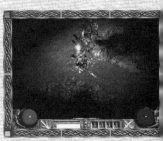

Conversion temporarily makes your enemy an ally.

CHANCE TO CONVERT (%) ⚔

LEVEL 1	LEVEL 2	LEVEL 3	LEVEL 4	LEVEL 5	LEVEL 6	LEVEL 7	LEVEL 8	LEVEL 9	LEVEL 10
11	20	27	33	37	41	44	46	49	51
LEVEL 11	LEVEL 12	LEVEL 13	LEVEL 14	LEVEL 15	LEVEL 16	LEVEL 17	LEVEL 18	LEVEL 19	LEVEL 20
53	54	56	57	58	60	60	61	62	63

DURATION (SECONDS) ⚔

LEVEL 1	LEVEL 2	LEVEL 3	LEVEL 4	LEVEL 5	LEVEL 6	LEVEL 7	LEVEL 8	LEVEL 9	LEVEL 10
20	30	40	50	60	70	80	90	100	110
LEVEL 11	LEVEL 12	LEVEL 13	LEVEL 14	LEVEL 15	LEVEL 16	LEVEL 17	LEVEL 18	LEVEL 19	LEVEL 20
120	130	140	150	160	170	180	190	200	210

HOLY SHIELD (LEVEL 24; MANA COST = 35)

Holy Shield magically enhances your shield to absorb damage while increasing your chance to block an enemy's attack. The drawback is that it takes a whopping 35 mana, and, in the first few levels, doesn't provide a huge benefit to your Paladin. However, once Holy Shield gets up to level 10, it becomes a substantial defensive skill that lasts for a full two minutes and gives almost a 200 percent defensive improvement.

DURATION (SECONDS)

LEVEL 1	LEVEL 2	LEVEL 3	LEVEL 4	LEVEL 5	LEVEL 6	LEVEL 7	LEVEL 8	LEVEL 9	LEVEL 10
30	40	50	60	70	80	90	100	110	120

LEVEL 11	LEVEL 12	LEVEL 13	LEVEL 14	LEVEL 15	LEVEL 16	LEVEL 17	LEVEL 18	LEVEL 19	LEVEL 20
130	140	150	160	170	180	190	200	210	220

DEFENSE MODIFIER (+%)

LEVEL 1	LEVEL 2	LEVEL 3	LEVEL 4	LEVEL 5	LEVEL 6	LEVEL 7	LEVEL 8	LEVEL 9	LEVEL 10
25	40	55	70	85	100	115	130	145	160

LEVEL 11	LEVEL 12	LEVEL 13	LEVEL 14	LEVEL 15	LEVEL 16	LEVEL 17	LEVEL 18	LEVEL 19	LEVEL 20
175	190	205	220	235	250	265	280	295	310

CHANCE TO BLOCK (+%)

LEVEL 1	LEVEL 2	LEVEL 3	LEVEL 4	LEVEL 5	LEVEL 6	LEVEL 7	LEVEL 8	LEVEL 9	LEVEL 10
8	10	12	13	15	16	16	17	18	18

LEVEL 11	LEVEL 12	LEVEL 13	LEVEL 14	LEVEL 15	LEVEL 16	LEVEL 17	LEVEL 18	LEVEL 19	LEVEL 20
19	19	20	20	20	21	21	21	21	21

FIST OF THE HEAVENS (LEVEL 30)

This is a skill that not only does a substantial amount of damage with a lightning bolt, but it also releases Holy Bolts after the initial hit. These Holy Bolts then go about doing their own damage to any nearby undead, or, if you have party members nearby, the Holy Bolts will heal them! This is a high-level skill that carries a steep mana cost, but when you've invested 10+ skill points into it, you'll be able to take some tough enemies down in one or two shots. This skill is a must-have when fighting against any group of undead because of the radiating Holy Bolts that will extend from the initial lightning strike area.

HOLY BOLT DAMAGE

LEVEL 1	LEVEL 2	LEVEL 3	LEVEL 4	LEVEL 5	LEVEL 6	LEVEL 7	LEVEL 8	LEVEL 9	LEVEL 10
1-16	1-22	1-28	1-34	1-40	1-46	1-52	1-58	1-64	1-70

LEVEL 11	LEVEL 12	LEVEL 13	LEVEL 14	LEVEL 15	LEVEL 16	LEVEL 17	LEVEL 18	LEVEL 19	LEVEL 20
1-76	1-82	1-88	1-94	1-100	1-106	1-112	1-118	1-124	1-130

LIGHTNING DAMAGE

LEVEL 1	LEVEL 2	LEVEL 3	LEVEL 4	LEVEL 5	LEVEL 6	LEVEL 7	LEVEL 8	LEVEL 9	LEVEL 10
1-90	9-98	17-56	25-64	33-72	41-80	49-88	57-96	65-104	73-112

LEVEL 11	LEVEL 12	LEVEL 13	LEVEL 14	LEVEL 15	LEVEL 16	LEVEL 17	LEVEL 18	LEVEL 19	LEVEL 20
81-120	89-128	97-136	105-144	113-152	121-160	129-168	137-176	145-184	153-192

MANA COST

LEVEL 1	LEVEL 2	LEVEL 3	LEVEL 4	LEVEL 5	LEVEL 6	LEVEL 7	LEVEL 8	LEVEL 9	LEVEL 10
25	27	29	31	33	35	37	39	41	43

LEVEL 11	LEVEL 12	LEVEL 13	LEVEL 14	LEVEL 15	LEVEL 16	LEVEL 17	LEVEL 18	LEVEL 19	LEVEL 20
45	47	49	51	53	55	57	59	61	63

OFFENSIVE AURAS

This set of skills is aimed at improving existing combat skills, but also provides som unique attributes that will wreak havoc with the enemies. For example, Holy Fire w periodically hit any nearby enemies with a blast of fire, while Thorns will return dar age to the monster that's inflicting it on you! Where the Offensive Auras really shin however, is in multiplayer action. A multiplayer team without a Paladin versed in the skills will be at a considerable disadvantage.

MIGHT (LEVEL 1)

This aura increases the amount of damage caused by your character and friendly unit Might, like all auras, is best used when it can help an entire party rather just yo Paladin; however, it is still a very powerful aura by itself. Indeed, at level 7 it is alread doubling the attack value of any hits you land on an enemy monster.

TIP..........

Activate Might when playing in a tight group during a fight with tough monsters in Multiplayer. This aura will increase your offensive power (as a group) enough to alter the outcome of a close battle in your favor.

RADIUS (YARDS)

LEVEL 1	LEVEL 2	LEVEL 3	LEVEL 4	LEVEL 5	LEVEL 6	LEVEL 7	LEVEL 8	LEVEL 9	LEVEL 10
7.3	8.6	10	11.3	12.6	14	15.3	16.6	18	19.3

LEVEL 11	LEVEL 12	LEVEL 13	LEVEL 14	LEVEL 15	LEVEL 16	LEVEL 17	LEVEL 18	LEVEL 19	LEVEL 20
20.6	22	23.3	24.6	26	27.3	28.6	30	31.3	32.6

DAMAGE MODIFIER (+%)

LEVEL 1	LEVEL 2	LEVEL 3	LEVEL 4	LEVEL 5	LEVEL 6	LEVEL 7	LEVEL 8	LEVEL 9	LEVEL 10
40	50	60	70	80	90	100	110	120	130

LEVEL 11	LEVEL 12	LEVEL 13	LEVEL 14	LEVEL 15	LEVEL 16	LEVEL 17	LEVEL 18	LEVEL 19	LEVEL 20
140	150	160	170	180	190	200	210	220	230

HOLY FIRE (LEVEL 6)

This aura is a very powerful skill that, when active, period-ally blasts unfriendly units with a hit of fire! The amount f damage that it will do on the nearby enemies varies with-a range for the level of the skill. By putting more skill oints into Holy Fire, you will not only increase the amount f damage that you inflict on nearby enemies, but also ncrease the radius of effect. A great way to use this skill is run into an area with a large group of enemies, drink own a stamina potion, then simply run around and avoid the enemies while the Holy re hits them every few seconds. This technique comes in very handy when your armor damaged or you are near death, but still need to kill off a group of enemies.

When active, this skill launches a fire attack on all nearby enemies.

NOTE......

Once you reach Act III, Holy Fire will not be effective enough to use consistently—the damage it inflicts may not take out the tougher enemies you'll face.

RADIUS (YARDS)

LEVEL 1	LEVEL 2	LEVEL 3	LEVEL 4	LEVEL 5	LEVEL 6	LEVEL 7	LEVEL 8	LEVEL 9	LEVEL 10
4	4.6	5.3	6	6.6	7.3	8	8.6	9.3	10
LEVEL 11	LEVEL 12	LEVEL 13	LEVEL 14	LEVEL 15	LEVEL 16	LEVEL 17	LEVEL 18	LEVEL 19	LEVEL 20
10.6	11.3	12	12.6	13.3	14	14.6	15.3	16	16.6

FIRE DAMAGE

LEVEL 1	LEVEL 2	LEVEL 3	LEVEL 4	LEVEL 5	LEVEL 6	LEVEL 7	LEVEL 8	LEVEL 9	LEVEL 10
1-3	1.5-3.5	2.5-4.5	3-5	4-6	4.5-6.5	5.5-7.5	6-8	7-9	7.5-9.5
LEVEL 11	LEVEL 12	LEVEL 13	LEVEL 14	LEVEL 15	LEVEL 16	LEVEL 17	LEVEL 18	LEVEL 19	LEVEL 20
8.5-10.5	9-11	10-12	10.5-12.5	11.5-13.5	12-14	13-15	13.5-15.5	14.5-16.5	15-17

THORNS (LEVEL 6)

his is (in the opinion of many Blizzard employees) the most powerful aura the Paladin as at his disposal. This aura returns damage to any enemy that inflicts damage on you r any ally that is within the raduis of effect. The key to this skill is just how much dam-ge is returned! Indeed, if an enemy hits you and inflicts 10 points of damage, and you ave Thorns at level 1, the enemy will take a 250 percent hit, or 25 points, back! Marvel t the numbers: Thorns at level 10 will return over 600 percent damage to the enemy! he one downside to Thorns is that it is effective only with melee attacks, and does not pply to damage inflicted by ranged weapons or magical effects.

NOTE......

At higher levels having Thorns on can be enough for enemies to kill themselves with one successful hit against you. For example, at level 10, if an enemy hits with a 10-point attack, it will take a 61-point hit itself.

RADIUS (YARDS)

LEVEL 1	LEVEL 2	LEVEL 3	LEVEL 4	LEVEL 5	LEVEL 6	LEVEL 7	LEVEL 8	LEVEL 9	LEVEL 10
7.3	8.6	10	11.3	12.6	14	15.3	16.6	18	19.3
LEVEL 11	LEVEL 12	LEVEL 13	LEVEL 14	LEVEL 15	LEVEL 16	LEVEL 17	LEVEL 18	LEVEL 19	LEVEL 20
20.6	22	23.3	24.6	26	27.3	28.6	30	31.3	32.6

DAMAGE RETURN (+%)

LEVEL 1	LEVEL 2	LEVEL 3	LEVEL 4	LEVEL 5	LEVEL 6	LEVEL 7	LEVEL 8	LEVEL 9	LEVEL 10
250	290	330	370	410	450	490	530	570	610
LEVEL 11	LEVEL 12	LEVEL 13	LEVEL 14	LEVEL 15	LEVEL 16	LEVEL 17	LEVEL 18	LEVEL 19	LEVEL 20
650	690	730	770	810	850	890	930	970	1010

◎ Blessed Aim (Level 12)

This aura increases your attack rating, while doing the same for all nearby allies. Th[e] bonus to your attack rating increases as you add points to Blessed Aim, and the radi[us] of effect is also improved. Although it can be effective in the single-player game, Blesse[d] Aim is one of the auras that's more important during multiplayer action where it ca[n] help to improve the attack rating of the entire group.

RADIUS (YARDS) ◎

LEVEL 1	LEVEL 2	LEVEL 3	LEVEL 4	LEVEL 5	LEVEL 6	LEVEL 7	LEVEL 8	LEVEL 9	LEVEL 10
7.3	8.6	10	11.3	12.6	14	15.3	16.6	18	19.3

LEVEL 11	LEVEL 12	LEVEL 13	LEVEL 14	LEVEL 15	LEVEL 16	LEVEL 17	LEVEL 18	LEVEL 19	LEVEL 20
20.6	22	23.3	24.6	26	27.3	28.6	30	31.3	32.6

ATTACK MODIFIER (+%) ◎

LEVEL 1	LEVEL 2	LEVEL 3	LEVEL 4	LEVEL 5	LEVEL 6	LEVEL 7	LEVEL 8	LEVEL 9	LEVEL 10
75	90	105	120	135	150	165	180	195	210

LEVEL 11	LEVEL 12	LEVEL 13	LEVEL 14	LEVEL 15	LEVEL 16	LEVEL 17	LEVEL 18	LEVEL 19	LEVEL 20
225	240	255	270	285	300	315	330	345	360

⊘ Concentration (Level 18)

Concentration gives you a chance that your attack will be not be interrupted, and add[s] to the damage your attacks will do. This is an important aura because when you're i[n] a pitched battle, taking many hits from multiple sides, your attacks will get interrupte[d] and you'll find it hard to land a blow on an enemy. Concentration increases the chanc[e] that your attacks will follow through even if you're being interrupted by an enem[y] attack. As skill points are added to Concentration, your chance of being interrupte[d] decreases. Use this skill in tense situations where you need your attacks to find pu[r-] chase on enemy flesh!

UNINTERRUPT CHANCE ⊘

LEVEL 1	LEVEL 2	LEVEL 3	LEVEL 4	LEVEL 5	LEVEL 6	LEVEL 7	LEVEL 8	LEVEL 9	LEVEL 10
20	20	20	20	20	20	20	20	20	20

LEVEL 11	LEVEL 12	LEVEL 13	LEVEL 14	LEVEL 15	LEVEL 16	LEVEL 17	LEVEL 18	LEVEL 19	LEVEL 20
20	20	20	20	20	20	20	20	20	20

DAMAGE (+%) ⊘

LEVEL 1	LEVEL 2	LEVEL 3	LEVEL 4	LEVEL 5	LEVEL 6	LEVEL 7	LEVEL 8	LEVEL 9	LEVEL 10
60	75	90	105	120	135	150	165	180	195

LEVEL 11	LEVEL 12	LEVEL 13	LEVEL 14	LEVEL 15	LEVEL 16	LEVEL 17	LEVEL 18	LEVEL 19	LEVEL 20
210	225	240	255	270	285	300	315	330	345

HOLY FREEZE (LEVEL 18)

Holy Freeze acts somewhat like Holy Fire—it will affect units within its radius every few seconds. However, instead of inflicting cold damage, it merely slows the enemies down. As with all auras, this is a very valuable skill to use in a group situation because it will freeze all nearby enemies, making them slower and ultimately more manageable for other party members to destroy. Also, Holy Freeze is an attack powered by the faith of the Paladin and not elemental magic, so resistances against cold do not protect enemies from this spell.

RADIUS (YARDS)

LEVEL 1	LEVEL 2	LEVEL 3	LEVEL 4	LEVEL 5	LEVEL 6	LEVEL 7	LEVEL 8	LEVEL 9	LEVEL 10
4	4.6	5.3	6	6.6	7.3	8	8.6	9.3	10

LEVEL 11	LEVEL 12	LEVEL 13	LEVEL 14	LEVEL 15	LEVEL 16	LEVEL 17	LEVEL 18	LEVEL 19	LEVEL 20
10.6	11.3	12	12.6	13.3	14	14.6	15.3	16	16.6

SLOWS ENEMIES (%)

LEVEL 1	LEVEL 2	LEVEL 3	LEVEL 4	LEVEL 5	LEVEL 6	LEVEL 7	LEVEL 8	LEVEL 9	LEVEL 10
30	34	37	40	42	44	45	46	48	48

LEVEL 11	LEVEL 12	LEVEL 13	LEVEL 14	LEVEL 15	LEVEL 16	LEVEL 17	LEVEL 18	LEVEL 19	LEVEL 20
49	50	51	51	52	53	53	53	54	54

HOLY SHOCK (LEVEL 24)

Holy Shock hits unfriendly units with a spark of electricity every few seconds. The amount of damage that this aura will inflict on the nearby enemies varies within a range for the level of the skill, but the addition of skill points will increase the amount of damage that you deal on nearby enemies, as well as the radius of effect. You can clear an area filled with a large group of enemies by drinking a stamina potion and then running around while avoiding the enemies as Holy Shock hits them every few seconds. This technique is especially useful when your armor is damaged, your weapon has broken, or you are near death but you still need to kill off a group of enemies.

This skill periodically hits nearby monsters with an electrical spark!

RADIUS (YARDS)

LEVEL 1	LEVEL 2	LEVEL 3	LEVEL 4	LEVEL 5	LEVEL 6	LEVEL 7	LEVEL 8	LEVEL 9	LEVEL 10
3.3	4	4.6	5.3	6	6.6	7.3	8	8.6	9.3

LEVEL 11	LEVEL 12	LEVEL 13	LEVEL 14	LEVEL 15	LEVEL 16	LEVEL 17	LEVEL 18	LEVEL 19	LEVEL 20
10	10.6	11.3	12	12.6	13.3	14	14.6	15.3	16

LIGHTNING DAMAGE

LEVEL 1	LEVEL 2	LEVEL 3	LEVEL 4	LEVEL 5	LEVEL 6	LEVEL 7	LEVEL 8	LEVEL 9	LEVEL 10
1-5	2-6	4-8	5-9	7-11	8-12	10-14	11-15	13-17	14-18

LEVEL 11	LEVEL 12	LEVEL 13	LEVEL 14	LEVEL 15	LEVEL 16	LEVEL 17	LEVEL 18	LEVEL 19	LEVEL 20
16-20	17-21	19-23	20-24	22-26	23-27	25-29	26-30	28-32	29-33

⊙ SANCTUARY (LEVEL 24) ✴

Sanctuary is a special aura that essentially prevents undead monsters from reaching the Paladin. It does substantial damage to the undead and, as a rule, will destroy them before they have a chance to get close enough to cause you damage. This aura is especially useful in places like the Graveyard or the Tombs where the undead thrive. As you add points to Sanctuary, both the damage inflicted on the undead and the radius of effect increases dramatically. However, because many of the tougher monsters you face in *Diablo II* are not undead, it's not advisable to put all of your eggs into this one basket.

RADIUS (YARDS)

LEVEL 1	LEVEL 2	LEVEL 3	LEVEL 4	LEVEL 5	LEVEL 6	LEVEL 7	LEVEL 8	LEVEL 9	LEVEL 10
3.3	4	4.6	5.3	6	6.6	7.3	8	8.6	9.3
LEVEL 11	LEVEL 12	LEVEL 13	LEVEL 14	LEVEL 15	LEVEL 16	LEVEL 17	LEVEL 18	LEVEL 19	LEVEL 20
10	10.6	11.3	12	12.6	13.3	14	14.6	15.3	16

MAGIC DAMAGE

LEVEL 1	LEVEL 2	LEVEL 3	LEVEL 4	LEVEL 5	LEVEL 6	LEVEL 7	LEVEL 8	LEVEL 9	LEVEL 10
8-16	12-20	16-24	20-28	24-32	28-36	32-40	36-44	40-48	44-52
LEVEL 11	LEVEL 12	LEVEL 13	LEVEL 14	LEVEL 15	LEVEL 16	LEVEL 17	LEVEL 18	LEVEL 19	LEVEL 20
48-56	52-60	56-64	60-68	64-72	68-76	72-80	76-84	80-88	84-92

⊜ FANATICISM (LEVEL 30)

Fanaticism boosts the attack rate and power for the Paladin and nearby party members (within a radius of 7.3 yards). This aura moderately increases these attack factors, but after level 2 the amount that the rating increases may not be worth the cost of a skill point to you. This is an excellent aura to use in multiplayer when your party wants to quickly hack through a large group of enemies; the increase in attack rate will allow your party members (and yourself) to strike quicker, do more damage, and keep the enemy from attacking.

RADIUS (YARDS)

LEVEL 1	LEVEL 2	LEVEL 3	LEVEL 4	LEVEL 5	LEVEL 6	LEVEL 7	LEVEL 8	LEVEL 9	LEVEL 10
7.3	7.3	7.3	7.3	7.3	7.3	7.3	7.3	7.3	7.3
LEVEL 11	LEVEL 12	LEVEL 13	LEVEL 14	LEVEL 15	LEVEL 16	LEVEL 17	LEVEL 18	LEVEL 19	LEVEL 20
7.3	7.3	7.3	7.3	7.3	7.3	7.3	7.3	7.3	7.3

ATTACK RATE (+%)

LEVEL 1	LEVEL 2	LEVEL 3	LEVEL 4	LEVEL 5	LEVEL 6	LEVEL 7	LEVEL 8	LEVEL 9	LEVEL 10
14	18	20	23	25	26	27	28	29	30
LEVEL 11	LEVEL 12	LEVEL 13	LEVEL 14	LEVEL 15	LEVEL 16	LEVEL 17	LEVEL 18	LEVEL 19	LEVEL 20
31	31	32	33	33	34	34	34	34	35

ATTACK MODIFIER (+%)

LEVEL 1	LEVEL 2	LEVEL 3	LEVEL 4	LEVEL 5	LEVEL 6	LEVEL 7	LEVEL 8	LEVEL 9	LEVEL 10
40	45	50	55	60	65	70	75	80	85
LEVEL 11	LEVEL 12	LEVEL 13	LEVEL 14	LEVEL 15	LEVEL 16	LEVEL 17	LEVEL 18	LEVEL 19	LEVEL 20
90	95	100	105	110	115	120	125	130	135

CONVICTION (LEVEL 30)

Conviction is an aura that reduces the armor class and maximum resistances of enemies that come within its radius of effect. For example, an enemy within 6 yards of a Paladin with level 1 Conviction active has its defense rating lowered by 49 percent, and its maximum resistances reduced by 26 percent. Because this affects any enemies within the radius, it can benefit other party members in multiplayer if they are fighting close to your position.

RADIUS (YARDS)

LEVEL 1	LEVEL 2	LEVEL 3	LEVEL 4	LEVEL 5	LEVEL 6	LEVEL 7	LEVEL 8	LEVEL 9	LEVEL 10
6	6.6	7.3	8	8.6	9.3	10	10.6	11.3	12

LEVEL 11	LEVEL 12	LEVEL 13	LEVEL 14	LEVEL 15	LEVEL 16	LEVEL 17	LEVEL 18	LEVEL 19	LEVEL 20
12.6	13.3	14	14.6	15.3	16	16.6	17.3	18	18.6

DEFENSE MODIFIER (-%)

LEVEL 1	LEVEL 2	LEVEL 3	LEVEL 4	LEVEL 5	LEVEL 6	LEVEL 7	LEVEL 8	LEVEL 9	LEVEL 10
49	56	61	66	70	73	75	77	79	80

LEVEL 11	LEVEL 12	LEVEL 13	LEVEL 14	LEVEL 15	LEVEL 16	LEVEL 17	LEVEL 18	LEVEL 19	LEVEL 20
82	83	85	86	86	88	88	89	89	90

MAXIMUM RESIST (-%)

LEVEL 1	LEVEL 2	LEVEL 3	LEVEL 4	LEVEL 5	LEVEL 6	LEVEL 7	LEVEL 8	LEVEL 9	LEVEL 10
26	32	36	39	42	44	46	47	49	50

LEVEL 11	LEVEL 12	LEVEL 13	LEVEL 14	LEVEL 15	LEVEL 16	LEVEL 17	LEVEL 18	LEVEL 19	LEVEL 20
51	52	53	54	55	56	56	56	57	57

DEFENSIVE AURAS

This set of skills is aimed at improving existing defensive combat skills. For the Paladin, the Defensive Auras are of great importance in multiplayer games because of their ability to protect/affect other party members. Again, as with the Offensive Auras, the Defensive Auras are great in single-player action, but really shine when they can be applied to a team.

NOTE......

In multiplayer, the Paladin can simply stay behind other party members and leave the Prayer skill active in order to heal everyone as they take hits. This skill underscores the importance of having a Paladin in a multiplayer party.

PRAYER (LEVEL 1)

This is one of the Paladin's most powerful skills because it has the ability to heal you and your nearby allies passively, simply by being active. When it heals you or a member of your party, Prayer takes mana from your reserve, but only when it heals; otherwise it is simply 'on' passively waiting for your health to fall below optimum. When used in a multiplayer party, Prayer is incredibly important, especially at higher levels because it can heal everyone in the party simultaneously.

RADIUS (YARDS)

LEVEL 1	LEVEL 2	LEVEL 3	LEVEL 4	LEVEL 5	LEVEL 6	LEVEL 7	LEVEL 8	LEVEL 9	LEVEL 10
7.3	8.6	10	11.3	12.6	14	15.3	16.6	18	19.3

LEVEL 11	LEVEL 12	LEVEL 13	LEVEL 14	LEVEL 15	LEVEL 16	LEVEL 17	LEVEL 18	LEVEL 19	LEVEL 20
20.6	22	23.3	24.6	26	27.3	28.6	30	31.3	32.6

HEALING

LEVEL 1	LEVEL 2	LEVEL 3	LEVEL 4	LEVEL 5	LEVEL 6	LEVEL 7	LEVEL 8	LEVEL 9	LEVEL 10
2	3	4	5	6	7	8	9	10	11

LEVEL 11	LEVEL 12	LEVEL 13	LEVEL 14	LEVEL 15	LEVEL 16	LEVEL 17	LEVEL 18	LEVEL 19	LEVEL 20
12	13	14	15	16	17	18	19	20	21

MANA COST

LEVEL 1	LEVEL 2	LEVEL 3	LEVEL 4	LEVEL 5	LEVEL 6	LEVEL 7	LEVEL 8	LEVEL 9	LEVEL 10
1	1.1	1.3	1.5	1.7	1.9	2.1	2.3	2.5	2.6

LEVEL 11	LEVEL 12	LEVEL 13	LEVEL 14	LEVEL 15	LEVEL 16	LEVEL 17	LEVEL 18	LEVEL 19	LEVEL 20
2.8	3	3.2	3.4	3.6	3.8	4	4.1	4.3	4.5

RESIST FIRE (LEVEL 1)

This skill increases your resistance to fire, along with any friendly units within the radius of the aura. Once again, this is a great way to protect yourself and your party members in a multiplayer game when you're up against enemies that deal out fire-based damage. Note that this skill doesn't require the expenditure of mana, so it can be left on indefinitely.

RADIUS (YARDS)

LEVEL 1	LEVEL 2	LEVEL 3	LEVEL 4	LEVEL 5	LEVEL 6	LEVEL 7	LEVEL 8	LEVEL 9	LEVEL 10
7.3	8.6	10	11.3	12.6	14	15.3	16.6	18	19.3

LEVEL 11	LEVEL 12	LEVEL 13	LEVEL 14	LEVEL 15	LEVEL 16	LEVEL 17	LEVEL 18	LEVEL 19	LEVEL 20
20.6	22	23.3	24.6	26	27.3	28.6	30	31.3	32.6

RESIST FIRE (+%)

LEVEL 1	LEVEL 2	LEVEL 3	LEVEL 4	LEVEL 5	LEVEL 6	LEVEL 7	LEVEL 8	LEVEL 9	LEVEL 10
54	58	60	63	65	66	67	68	69	70

LEVEL 11	LEVEL 12	LEVEL 13	LEVEL 14	LEVEL 15	LEVEL 16	LEVEL 17	LEVEL 18	LEVEL 19	LEVEL 20
71	71	72	73	73	74	74	74	74	75

DEFIANCE (LEVEL 6)

Defiance boosts your defensive rating substantially when active. It also does the same for party members in the same amount (between 70 and 260 percent, depending on skill level), making it an excellent tool for multiplayer games. As you add points to Defiance, you'll increase the radius of this aura's effect, as well as the amount of defensive boost it affords you and the other allies under its influence.

RADIUS (YARDS)

LEVEL 1	LEVEL 2	LEVEL 3	LEVEL 4	LEVEL 5	LEVEL 6	LEVEL 7	LEVEL 8	LEVEL 9	LEVEL 10
7.3	8.6	10	11.3	12.6	14	15.3	16.6	18	19.3

LEVEL 11	LEVEL 12	LEVEL 13	LEVEL 14	LEVEL 15	LEVEL 16	LEVEL 17	LEVEL 18	LEVEL 19	LEVEL 20
20.6	22	23.3	24.6	26	27.3	28.6	30	31.3	32.6

DEFENSE MODIFIER (+%)

LEVEL 1	LEVEL 2	LEVEL 3	LEVEL 4	LEVEL 5	LEVEL 6	LEVEL 7	LEVEL 8	LEVEL 9	LEVEL 10
70	80	90	100	110	120	130	140	150	160

LEVEL 11	LEVEL 12	LEVEL 13	LEVEL 14	LEVEL 15	LEVEL 16	LEVEL 17	LEVEL 18	LEVEL 19	LEVEL 20
170	180	190	200	210	220	230	240	250	260

RESIST COLD (LEVEL 6)

This skill increases your resistance to cold, along with that of any friendly units within the radius of the aura. Use this aura to help protect yourself and your party members in a multiplayer game when you're up against any enemies that attack with cold. Note that this skill doesn't require the expenditure of mana, so it can be left on indefinitely to provide constant protection.

RADIUS (YARDS)

LEVEL 1	LEVEL 2	LEVEL 3	LEVEL 4	LEVEL 5	LEVEL 6	LEVEL 7	LEVEL 8	LEVEL 9	LEVEL 10
7.3	8.6	10	11.3	12.6	14	15.3	16.6	18	19.3

LEVEL 11	LEVEL 12	LEVEL 13	LEVEL 14	LEVEL 15	LEVEL 16	LEVEL 17	LEVEL 18	LEVEL 19	LEVEL 20
20.6	22	23.3	24.6	26	27.3	28.6	30	31.3	32.6

RESIST COLD

LEVEL 1	LEVEL 2	LEVEL 3	LEVEL 4	LEVEL 5	LEVEL 6	LEVEL 7	LEVEL 8	LEVEL 9	LEVEL 10
54	58	60	63	65	66	67	68	69	70

LEVEL 11	LEVEL 12	LEVEL 13	LEVEL 14	LEVEL 15	LEVEL 16	LEVEL 17	LEVEL 18	LEVEL 19	LEVEL 20
71	71	72	73	73	74	74	74	74	75

Cleansing (Level 12)

Cleansing reduces the amount of time that poison will affect you or any members of your party within the aura's radius of effect. This aura is important in places like the Tombs or the Spider Cave where you're likely to face several enemies that can infect you with a dose of poison. Because poison can be so devastating, especially to a party if they all get poisoned, this aura is a huge asset in multiplayer games.

RADIUS (YARDS)

LEVEL 1	LEVEL 2	LEVEL 3	LEVEL 4	LEVEL 5	LEVEL 6	LEVEL 7	LEVEL 8	LEVEL 9	LEVEL 10
7.3	8.6	10	11.3	12.6	14	15.3	16.6	18	19.3

LEVEL 11	LEVEL 12	LEVEL 13	LEVEL 14	LEVEL 15	LEVEL 16	LEVEL 17	LEVEL 18	LEVEL 19	LEVEL 20
20.6	22	23.3	24.6	26	27.3	28.6	30	31.3	32.6

DURATION REDUCTION

LEVEL 1	LEVEL 2	LEVEL 3	LEVEL 4	LEVEL 5	LEVEL 6	LEVEL 7	LEVEL 8	LEVEL 9	LEVEL 10
39	46	51	56	60	63	65	67	69	70

LEVEL 11	LEVEL 12	LEVEL 13	LEVEL 14	LEVEL 15	LEVEL 16	LEVEL 17	LEVEL 18	LEVEL 19	LEVEL 20
72	73	75	76	76	78	78	79	79	80

Resist Lightning (Level 12)

As with the Resist Fire and Resist Cold auras, Resist Lightning affords you and the nearby members of your party some level of protection from lightning attacks. Of course, when more skill points are added to Resist Lightning, you'll acquire increased radius and resistance ratings, making this a powerful aura when you're taking electrical damage from enemies.

RADIUS (YARDS)

LEVEL 1	LEVEL 2	LEVEL 3	LEVEL 4	LEVEL 5	LEVEL 6	LEVEL 7	LEVEL 8	LEVEL 9	LEVEL 10
7.3	8.6	10	11.3	12.6	14	15.3	16.6	18	19.3

LEVEL 11	LEVEL 12	LEVEL 13	LEVEL 14	LEVEL 15	LEVEL 16	LEVEL 17	LEVEL 18	LEVEL 19	LEVEL 20
20.6	22	23.3	24.6	26	27.3	28.6	30	31.3	32.6

RESIST LIGHTNING

LEVEL 1	LEVEL 2	LEVEL 3	LEVEL 4	LEVEL 5	LEVEL 6	LEVEL 7	LEVEL 8	LEVEL 9	LEVEL 10
54	58	60	63	65	66	67	68	69	70

LEVEL 11	LEVEL 12	LEVEL 13	LEVEL 14	LEVEL 15	LEVEL 16	LEVEL 17	LEVEL 18	LEVEL 19	LEVEL 20
71	71	72	73	73	74	74	74	74	75

VIGOR (LEVEL 18)

This aura boosts the stamina regeneration rate of you and your allies so you are able to more quickly recover from running. Stamina recovery is only one part of the benefits of this aura, however, because it also increases your maximum stamina and walk/run speed! As an added bonus, any nearby allies will also feel the effect of Vigor (depending on how many skill points have been added to this skill). Vigor is best used in situations where you and/or your party members need to be nimble, moving quickly to hit the enemy before running away.

Vigor is a skill that boosts the stamina regeneration rate for both you and your allies.

RADIUS (YARDS)

LEVEL 1	LEVEL 2	LEVEL 3	LEVEL 4	LEVEL 5	LEVEL 6	LEVEL 7	LEVEL 8	LEVEL 9	LEVEL 10
10	12	14	16	18	20	22	24	26	28

LEVEL 11	LEVEL 12	LEVEL 13	LEVEL 14	LEVEL 15	LEVEL 16	LEVEL 17	LEVEL 18	LEVEL 19	LEVEL 20
30	32	34	36	38	40	42	44	46	48

WALK/RUN SPEED (+%)

LEVEL 1	LEVEL 2	LEVEL 3	LEVEL 4	LEVEL 5	LEVEL 6	LEVEL 7	LEVEL 8	LEVEL 9	LEVEL 10
13	18	22	25	28	30	32	33	35	36

LEVEL 11	LEVEL 12	LEVEL 13	LEVEL 14	LEVEL 15	LEVEL 16	LEVEL 17	LEVEL 18	LEVEL 19	LEVEL 20
37	38	39	40	40	41	41	42	42	43

MAX. STAMINA INCREASE (+%)

LEVEL 1	LEVEL 2	LEVEL 3	LEVEL 4	LEVEL 5	LEVEL 6	LEVEL 7	LEVEL 8	LEVEL 9	LEVEL 10
50	75	100	125	150	175	200	225	250	275

LEVEL 11	LEVEL 12	LEVEL 13	LEVEL 14	LEVEL 15	LEVEL 16	LEVEL 17	LEVEL 18	LEVEL 19	LEVEL 20
300	325	350	375	400	425	450	475	500	525

INCR. STAMINA RECOVERY (+%)

LEVEL 1	LEVEL 2	LEVEL 3	LEVEL 4	LEVEL 5	LEVEL 6	LEVEL 7	LEVEL 8	LEVEL 9	LEVEL 10
50	75	100	125	150	175	200	225	250	275

LEVEL 11	LEVEL 12	LEVEL 13	LEVEL 14	LEVEL 15	LEVEL 16	LEVEL 17	LEVEL 18	LEVEL 19	LEVEL 20
300	325	350	375	400	425	450	475	500	525

MEDITATION (LEVEL 24)

This aura increases the mana recovery rate for your Paladin and nearby party members. In the first level, Meditation speeds up mana recovery by 60 percent; however, when you've put 20 skill points into this aura, you can get a mana regeneration rate that's 300 percent faster than normal! In a group of Sorceresses and Necromancers, this ability to regenerate mana quickly is a highly prized skill.

RADIUS (YARDS)

LEVEL 1	LEVEL 2	LEVEL 3	LEVEL 4	LEVEL 5	LEVEL 6	LEVEL 7	LEVEL 8	LEVEL 9	LEVEL 10
7.3	8.6	10	11.3	12.6	14	15.3	16.6	18	19.3
LEVEL 11	LEVEL 12	LEVEL 13	LEVEL 14	LEVEL 15	LEVEL 16	LEVEL 17	LEVEL 18	LEVEL 19	LEVEL 20
20.6	22	23.3	24.6	26	27.3	28.6	30	31.3	32.6

MANA RECOVERY (+%)

LEVEL 1	LEVEL 2	LEVEL 3	LEVEL 4	LEVEL 5	LEVEL 6	LEVEL 7	LEVEL 8	LEVEL 9	LEVEL 10
65	80	95	110	125	140	155	170	185	200
LEVEL 11	LEVEL 12	LEVEL 13	LEVEL 14	LEVEL 15	LEVEL 16	LEVEL 17	LEVEL 18	LEVEL 19	LEVEL 20
215	230	245	260	275	290	305	320	335	350

REDEMPTION (LEVEL 30)

Redemption is one of the most powerful skills in the game. When it is left on, this aura will reclaim the bodies of fallen enemies and turn them into mana for your Paladin! Not only is this a fantastic way to restore mana, but it also works to permanently remove dead monster corpses that could otherwise be resurrected by certain enemies. Redemption is a powerful aura and should be used whenever there is a lack of mana or you need to eliminate fallen enemies from the battlefield.

RADIUS (YARDS)

LEVEL 1	LEVEL 2	LEVEL 3	LEVEL 4	LEVEL 5	LEVEL 6	LEVEL 7	LEVEL 8	LEVEL 9	LEVEL 10
7.3	7.3	7.3	7.3	7.3	7.3	7.3	7.3	7.3	7.3
LEVEL 11	LEVEL 12	LEVEL 13	LEVEL 14	LEVEL 15	LEVEL 16	LEVEL 17	LEVEL 18	LEVEL 19	LEVEL 20
7.3	7.3	7.3	7.3	7.3	7.3	7.3	7.3	7.3	7.3

CHANCE TO REDEEM

LEVEL 1	LEVEL 2	LEVEL 3	LEVEL 4	LEVEL 5	LEVEL 6	LEVEL 7	LEVEL 8	LEVEL 9	LEVEL 10
23	34	42	49	55	59	63	65	69	71
LEVEL 11	LEVEL 12	LEVEL 13	LEVEL 14	LEVEL 15	LEVEL 16	LEVEL 17	LEVEL 18	LEVEL 19	LEVEL 20
73	75	77	79	80	82	82	83	84	85

HP/MANA RECOVERY (PTS)

LEVEL 1	LEVEL 2	LEVEL 3	LEVEL 4	LEVEL 5	LEVEL 6	LEVEL 7	LEVEL 8	LEVEL 9	LEVEL 10
25	30	35	40	45	50	55	60	65	70
LEVEL 11	LEVEL 12	LEVEL 13	LEVEL 14	LEVEL 15	LEVEL 16	LEVEL 17	LEVEL 18	LEVEL 19	LEVEL 20
75	80	85	90	95	100	105	110	115	120

Salvation (Level 30)

This aura protects you and any nearby allies from all enemy elemental damage—including cold, fire, and electrical damage. Each skill point you add to Salvation grants a small bonus to the amount of damage that is diverted from these attacks. Paladin engaged in multiplayer battles will enjoy the dramatic increase in the radius of effect for Salvation. By the time you've invested 10 skill points into this aura, you'll have an effective protection radius of nearly 20 yards, which means that your party member can stray farther from you and still be protected under the effects of this aura.

RADIUS (YARDS)

LEVEL 1	LEVEL 2	LEVEL 3	LEVEL 4	LEVEL 5	LEVEL 6	LEVEL 7	LEVEL 8	LEVEL 9	LEVEL 10
7.3	8.6	10	11.3	12.6	14	15.3	16.6	18	19.3

LEVEL 11	LEVEL 12	LEVEL 13	LEVEL 14	LEVEL 15	LEVEL 16	LEVEL 17	LEVEL 18	LEVEL 19	LEVEL 20
20.6	22	23.3	24.6	26	27.3	28.6	30	31.3	32.6

RESIST ALL

LEVEL 1	LEVEL 2	LEVEL 3	LEVEL 4	LEVEL 5	LEVEL 6	LEVEL 7	LEVEL 8	LEVEL 9	LEVEL 10
54	58	60	63	65	66	67	68	69	70

LEVEL 11	LEVEL 12	LEVEL 13	LEVEL 14	LEVEL 15	LEVEL 16	LEVEL 17	LEVEL 18	LEVEL 19	LEVEL 20
71	71	72	73	73	74	74	74	74	75

The Sorceress

One of the rebellious women who have wrested the secrets of magic use from the mal[e] dominated Mage-Clans of the East, the Sorceress is an expert in mystical creatio[n] *ex nihilo*. Although she lacks hand-to hand comb[at] skills, she does have fierce combative magi[c] for both offense and defense.

Both solitary and reclusive, the Sorceress ac[t] based on motives and ethics that often seem fick[le] and even spiteful. In reality, she understands the strugg[le] between Order and Chaos all too clearly, and uses this balance and fit into her role as a warrior in the battles [of] *Diablo II*.

SORCERESS SKILLS

The three skill sets that the Sorceress can develop are Fire, Lightning, an[d] Cold. As with the other characters, the skills that are developed in each ar[ea] will ultimately affect the abilities the Sorceress ends up mastering in *Diablo*

The Sorceress is the master of magic. So if you're looking for some bon[e] crushing melee combat, the Sorceress is probably not your best choic[e]. However, if you want visually impressive and extremely powerful magi[c], this is the character for you.

FIRE

These spells give the Sorceress command over the powerful realm of fire, and inclu[de] the very effective spells Fire Wall and Blaze. In addition she has Meteor, which ca[n] instantly eliminate almost any tightly grouped pack of enemies.

While all of the fire spells are worthwhile, perhaps the most important is Warmth. Th[is] ability helps to improve the Mana recharge rate for the Sorceress, which is the lifeblo[od] of this spell caster.

FIRE BOLT (LEVEL 1; MANA COST = 2.5)

ire Bolt shoots a bolt of fire that causes fire damage to a ingle enemy. The Sorceress starts the game with a staff hat grants this skill. Fire Bolt increases in power as you ut skill points into it, but its Mana cost stays the same at .5 Mana points.

This is the bread-and-butter spell for the Sorceress that can effectively be used throughout much of the game.

lthough Fire Bolt uses little Mana, it can only hit one nemy and its damage is limited. This means that there are robably other skills in the Fire skill tree that you will want

o explore, especially when you are fighting larger groups of tougher monsters.

DAMAGE

LEVEL 1	LEVEL 2	LEVEL 3	LEVEL 4	LEVEL 5	LEVEL 6	LEVEL 7	LEVEL 8	LEVEL 9	LEVEL 10
3-6	4-7	6-9	7-10	9-12	10-13	12-15	13-15	15-18	16-19
LEVEL 11	LEVEL 12	LEVEL 13	LEVEL 14	LEVEL 15	LEVEL 16	LEVEL 17	LEVEL 18	LEVEL 19	LEVEL 20
18-21	19-22	21-24	22-25	24-27	25-28	27-30	28-31	30-33	31-34

WARMTH (LEVEL 1)

Varmth is a passive skill that increases the Mana recovery rate of the Sorceress. It is mperative that you add points to this skill because the Sorceress requires plenty of Mana to cast her spells.

Varmth increases the Mana recharge rate by a percentage. When you reach Level 7 of Varmth, you'll see a recharge rate that is greater than double the standard recharge ate, which obviously makes this one of the most important skills in the game.

TIP.........

Don't wait to put points into Warmth. The benefits of having at least five points in this skill will hold you in good stead from the very first Act.

MANA RECHARGE RATE (+%)

LEVEL 1	LEVEL 2	LEVEL 3	LEVEL 4	LEVEL 5	LEVEL 6	LEVEL 7	LEVEL 8	LEVEL 9	LEVEL 10
30	42	54	66	78	90	102	114	126	138
LEVEL 11	LEVEL 12	LEVEL 13	LEVEL 14	LEVEL 15	LEVEL 16	LEVEL 17	LEVEL 18	LEVEL 19	LEVEL 20
150	162	174	186	198	210	222	234	246	258

INFERNO (LEVEL 6; MANA COST = 6/SEC.)

nferno resembles a flame-thrower that follows the direction that you move your mouse he front of the Sorceress). The more points that you put into Inferno, the greater the ange of the flame and the more damage it will cause.

fter adding just a few skill points to Inferno, you can increase the damage points *per econd* to around 37-47! This kind of power can cut a path through a line of enemies ery quickly. This is a great spell to employ when you are backed into a corner and urrounded by multiple enemies.

DAMAGE (PER SECOND)

LEVEL 1	LEVEL 2	LEVEL 3	LEVEL 4	LEVEL 5	LEVEL 6	LEVEL 7	LEVEL 8	LEVEL 9	LEVEL 10
12-25	21-34	37-43	40-53	50-62	59-71	68-81	78-90	87-100	96-109
LEVEL 11	**LEVEL 12**	**LEVEL 13**	**LEVEL 14**	**LEVEL 15**	**LEVEL 16**	**LEVEL 17**	**LEVEL 18**	**LEVEL 19**	**LEVEL 20**
106-118	115-128	125-137	139-136	143-146	153-165	162-175	171-184	181-193	190-203

RANGE (YARDS)

LEVEL 1	LEVEL 2	LEVEL 3	LEVEL 4	LEVEL 5	LEVEL 6	LEVEL 7	LEVEL 8	LEVEL 9	LEVEL 10
3.3	3.3	4	4.6	5.3	5.3	6	6.6	7.3	7.3
LEVEL 11	**LEVEL 12**	**LEVEL 13**	**LEVEL 14**	**LEVEL 15**	**LEVEL 16**	**LEVEL 17**	**LEVEL 18**	**LEVEL 19**	**LEVEL 20**
8	8.6	9.3	9.3	10	10.6	11.3	11.3	12	12.6

BLAZE (LEVEL 12; MANACOST = 11)

Perhaps the coolest spell in the game, Blaze leaves a trail of highly damaging flames behind the Sorceress as she moves.

Blaze leaves a wall of fire wherever the Sorceress goes. This wall of fire inflicts a significant amount of damage every second the enemy is inside it, so there are a couple of important uses for this spell.

First, you can use Blaze to enclose a group of enemies by invoking the spell and then running around them in a circle. This forces the enemies to pass over the deadly fire to get at you or, at least, keeps them trapped while you get away or prepare another spell. You can also use Blaze when you're running away from a group of enemies. As you flee, the enemies will chase you and get trapped in the fire that you leave behind. Since Blaze causes a large amount of damage every second, most enemies will succumb in short order.

DAMAGE (PER SECOND)

LEVEL 1	LEVEL 2	LEVEL 3	LEVEL 4	LEVEL 5	LEVEL 6	LEVEL 7	LEVEL 8	LEVEL 9	LEVEL 10
18-37	28-46	37-56	46-65	56-75	65-84	75-93	84-103	93-112	103-121
LEVEL 11	**LEVEL 12**	**LEVEL 13**	**LEVEL 14**	**LEVEL 15**	**LEVEL 16**	**LEVEL 17**	**LEVEL 18**	**LEVEL 19**	**LEVEL 20**
112-131	121-140	131-150	190-159	150-168	159-178	168-187	178-196	187-206	196-215

DURATION (SECONDS)

LEVEL 1	LEVEL 2	LEVEL 3	LEVEL 4	LEVEL 5	LEVEL 6	LEVEL 7	LEVEL 8	LEVEL 9	LEVEL 10
4.6	5.6	6.6	7.6	8.6	9.6	10.6	11.6	12.6	13.6
LEVEL 11	**LEVEL 12**	**LEVEL 13**	**LEVEL 14**	**LEVEL 15**	**LEVEL 16**	**LEVEL 17**	**LEVEL 18**	**LEVEL 19**	**LEVEL 20**
14.6	15.6	16.6	17.6	18.6	19.6	20.6	21.6	22.6	23.6

MANA COST

LEVEL 1	LEVEL 2	LEVEL 3	LEVEL 4	LEVEL 5	LEVEL 6	LEVEL 7	LEVEL 8	LEVEL 9	LEVEL 10
11	11.5	12	12	13	13	14	14	15	15
LEVEL 11	**LEVEL 12**	**LEVEL 13**	**LEVEL 14**	**LEVEL 15**	**LEVEL 16**	**LEVEL 17**	**LEVEL 18**	**LEVEL 19**	**LEVEL 20**
16	16	17	17	18	18	19	19	20	20

FIRE BALL (LEVEL 12; RADIUS = 2 YARDS)

This spell is like a Fire Bolt with a wide area of effect. Fire Ball shoots orb of flame that causes fire damage around the impact point, thus damaging anything within the area.

A ranged spell, Fire Ball is great to use against groups of enemies that are even a short distance away. If you get too close, however, it may prove difficult to invoke the spell with enemies swinging at you. Mana cost for this spell is nominal.

DAMAGE

LEVEL 1	LEVEL 2	LEVEL 3	LEVEL 4	LEVEL 5	LEVEL 6	LEVEL 7	LEVEL 8	LEVEL 9	LEVEL 10
6-14	13-21	20-28	27-35	34-42	41-49	48-56	55-63	62-70	69-77

LEVEL 11	LEVEL 12	LEVEL 13	LEVEL 14	LEVEL 15	LEVEL 16	LEVEL 17	LEVEL 18	LEVEL 19	LEVEL 20
76-84	85-91	90-98	97-105	104-112	111-119	118-126	125-133	132-140	139-147

ENCHANT (LEVEL 18)

Enchant magically enhances a weapon with fire damage, and increases the attack rating. This spell is a necessity during hand-to-hand combat. If you don't take part in a lot of melee combat, it's best to stick with one level of Enchant rather than sinking many points into it.

On the other hand, if you plan to use Enchant on a regular basis, it's definitely worth adding skill points. Invest 20 skill points into Enchant and you'll be able to imbue a weapon with impressive fire damage for nearly 10 minutes.

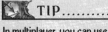

TIP..........

In multiplayer, you can use Enchant to add fire damage to the weapons of your party members.

MANA COST

LEVEL 1	LEVEL 2	LEVEL 3	LEVEL 4	LEVEL 5	LEVEL 6	LEVEL 7	LEVEL 8	LEVEL 9	LEVEL 10
25	30	35	40	45	50	55	60	65	70

LEVEL 11	LEVEL 12	LEVEL 13	LEVEL 14	LEVEL 15	LEVEL 16	LEVEL 17	LEVEL 18	LEVEL 19	LEVEL 20
75	80	85	90	95	100	105	110	115	120

DAMAGE

LEVEL 1	LEVEL 2	LEVEL 3	LEVEL 4	LEVEL 5	LEVEL 6	LEVEL 7	LEVEL 8	LEVEL 9	LEVEL 10
8-10	9-11	10-12	11-13	12-14	13-15	14-16	15-17	16-18	17-19

LEVEL 11	LEVEL 12	LEVEL 13	LEVEL 14	LEVEL 15	LEVEL 16	LEVEL 17	LEVEL 18	LEVEL 19	LEVEL 20
18-20	19-21	20-22	21-23	22-24	23-25	24-26	25-27	26-28	27-29

DURATION (SECONDS)

LEVEL 1	LEVEL 2	LEVEL 3	LEVEL 4	LEVEL 5	LEVEL 6	LEVEL 7	LEVEL 8	LEVEL 9	LEVEL 10
144	168	192	216	240	264	288	312	336	360

LEVEL 11	LEVEL 12	LEVEL 13	LEVEL 14	LEVEL 15	LEVEL 16	LEVEL 17	LEVEL 18	LEVEL 19	LEVEL 20
384	408	432	456	480	504	528	552	576	600

FIRE WALL (LEVEL 18)

This is a classic spell from the original *Diablo*. Fire Wall creates a barrier of flame tha
inflicts a huge amount of damage on any enemies that venture into it. You can use thi
skill for many purposes, including creating a defensive 'grid' of Fire Walls that th
enemy must traverse in order to get at your position.

You can also cast Fire Wall multiple times in rows so that
every square inch of a room is left burning, thus killing anything inside. Also, try standing in a doorway so that nothing
can pass; then cast Fire Wall repeatedly in rows moving
away from your position so that it's impossible for an enemy
to approach you without getting caught in the flames.

Fire Wall is a powerful spell that lasts longer and grows
wider with each level that it attains. It's highly recommended that any Sorceress put as many points into Fire
Wall as possible. Note that at Level 10 Fire Wall causes
200 points of damage *per second*! (See Appendix for Mana
Cost and Radius of Effect.)

*Fire Wall is similar to Blaze,
except that it inflicts considerably more damage. When choos
ing which Fire skill to develop,
put this one at the top of the lis*

DAMAGE (PER SECOND)

LEVEL 1	LEVEL 2	LEVEL 3	LEVEL 4	LEVEL 5	LEVEL 6	LEVEL 7	LEVEL 8	LEVEL 9	LEVEL 10
32-42	51-60	70-79	89-98	107-117	125-135	145-154	164-173	182-192	201-210
LEVEL 11	LEVEL 12	LEVEL 13	LEVEL 14	LEVEL 15	LEVEL 16	LEVEL 17	LEVEL 18	LEVEL 19	LEVEL 20
220-229	239-248	257-267	276-285	295-304	314-323	332-342	351-360	370-379	389-398

DURATION (SECONDS)

LEVEL 1	LEVEL 2	LEVEL 3	LEVEL 4	LEVEL 5	LEVEL 6	LEVEL 7	LEVEL 8	LEVEL 9	LEVEL 10
4.6	5.6	6.6	7.6	8.6	9.6	10.6	11.6	12.6	13.6
LEVEL 11	LEVEL 12	LEVEL 13	LEVEL 14	LEVEL 15	LEVEL 16	LEVEL 17	LEVEL 18	LEVEL 19	LEVEL 20
14.6	15.6	16.6	17.6	18.6	19.6	20.6	21.6	22.6	23.6

METEOR (LEVEL 24; MANA COST = 17)

This spell summons a meteor to drop from the sky a short time after it is invoked, caus
ing massive fire damage and leaving a wide area of scattered flames. It can be used o
enemies in other rooms, on groups, or anywhere you have a line of sight. Meteor ofte
takes the targeted monsters with it, and is often used to clear out rooms or areas wher
the Sorceress would not want to venture without a preliminary Meteor strike. Man
Cost for this spell ranges between 17 and 36.

DAMAGE

LEVEL 1	LEVEL 2	LEVEL 3	LEVEL 4	LEVEL 5	LEVEL 6	LEVEL 7	LEVEL 8	LEVEL 9	LEVEL 10
40-50	52-62	64-74	76-86	88-98	100-110	112-122	124-134	136-146	148-158
LEVEL 11	LEVEL 12	LEVEL 13	LEVEL 14	LEVEL 15	LEVEL 16	LEVEL 17	LEVEL 18	LEVEL 19	LEVEL 20
160-170	172-182	184-194	196-206	208-218	220-230	232-242	244-254	256-266	268-278

FIRE DAMAGE (PER SECOND)

LEVEL 1	LEVEL 2	LEVEL 3	LEVEL 4	LEVEL 5	LEVEL 6	LEVEL 7	LEVEL 8	LEVEL 9	LEVEL 10
16-21	23-28	30-35	37-42	44-49	51-56	58-63	65-70	72-77	79-84

LEVEL 11	LEVEL 12	LEVEL 13	LEVEL 14	LEVEL 15	LEVEL 16	LEVEL 17	LEVEL 18	LEVEL 19	LEVEL 20
86-91	93-98	100-105	107-112	114-119	121-126	128-133	135-140	142-147	150-154

FIRE MASTERY (LEVEL 30)

Fire Mastery is of critical importance because it increases the amount of damage caused by all Sorceress fire spells. Putting just two extra skill points into Fire Mastery will boost the damage bonus from 18 to 43 percent. When you factor that into spells like Fire Wall and Meteor, it means you'll be able to inflict massive damage on the enemy!

FIRE DAMAGE (+%)

LEVEL 1	LEVEL 2	LEVEL 3	LEVEL 4	LEVEL 5	LEVEL 6	LEVEL 7	LEVEL 8	LEVEL 9	LEVEL 10
18	32	43	52	60	66	70	74	79	81

LEVEL 11	LEVEL 12	LEVEL 13	LEVEL 14	LEVEL 15	LEVEL 16	LEVEL 17	LEVEL 18	LEVEL 19	LEVEL 20
85	87	90	92	93	96	97	98	99	100

HYDRA (LEVEL 30)

The Hydra makes a great defensive sentinel.

A sure favorite among those who play as the Sorceress, the Hydra spell creates a multi-headed beast of flame that shoots fire bolts at nearby enemies. It's great to use when you must defend an area from advancing enemies while simultaneously healing your character, dealing with inventory, or simply avoiding combat. Hydras act as sentinels that stand guard and attack any enemy that comes within their range. Although the damage they do is not substantial, a grid of five or six Hydras in a crossfire can handle most enemies. (See Appendix for Mana Costs.)

DAMAGE

LEVEL 1	LEVEL 2	LEVEL 3	LEVEL 4	LEVEL 5	LEVEL 6	LEVEL 7	LEVEL 8	LEVEL 9	LEVEL 10
11-23	15-27	19-31	23-35	27-39	31-43	35-47	39-51	43-55	47-59

LEVEL 11	LEVEL 12	LEVEL 13	LEVEL 14	LEVEL 15	LEVEL 16	LEVEL 17	LEVEL 18	LEVEL 19	LEVEL 20
51-63	55-67	59-71	63-75	67-79	71-83	75-87	79-91	83-95	87-99

DURATION (SECONDS)

LEVEL 1	LEVEL 2	LEVEL 3	LEVEL 4	LEVEL 5	LEVEL 6	LEVEL 7	LEVEL 8	LEVEL 9	LEVEL 10
12	13	14	15	16	17	18	19	20	21

LEVEL 11	LEVEL 12	LEVEL 13	LEVEL 14	LEVEL 15	LEVEL 16	LEVEL 17	LEVEL 18	LEVEL 19	LEVEL 20
22	23	24	25	26	27	28	29	30	31

LIGHTNING

These spells allow the Sorceress to use lightning to destroy her enemies. They als[o] enable her to use the energy of lightning to engage in telekenesis and teleporting. Lik[e] Fire and Cold, Lightning is an important form of elemental damage, so develop this ski[ll] tree in at least a limited way to take advantage of the damage it deals.

CHARGED BOLT (LEVEL 1)

This spell fires multiple, randomly moving bolts of electricity toward the target. Eac[h] bolt does a small amount of electrical damage when it hits an enemy, with more bol[ts] (which do more damage) being released at higher levels. At level 20 you unleash a[n] impressive 22 bolts, but the amount of damage that each bolt does is not substanti[al] enough to make the kind of impact that's necessary later in the game. For this reaso[n] Charged Bolt is best used early in the game—avoid spending skill points on it after th[e] first Act.

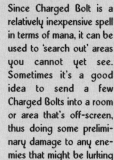

TIP..........

Since Charged Bolt is a relatively inexpensive spell in terms of mana, it can be used to 'search out' areas you cannot yet see. Sometimes it's a good idea to send a few Charged Bolts into a room or area that's off-screen, thus doing some preliminary damage to any enemies that might be lurking ahead.

DAMAGE

LEVEL 1	LEVEL 2	LEVEL 3	LEVEL 4	LEVEL 5	LEVEL 6	LEVEL 7	LEVEL 8	LEVEL 9	LEVEL 10
2-4	2-4	3-5	3-5	4-6	4-6	5-7	5-7	6-8	6-8
LEVEL 11	LEVEL 12	LEVEL 13	LEVEL 14	LEVEL 15	LEVEL 16	LEVEL 17	LEVEL 18	LEVEL 19	LEVEL 20
7-9	7-9	8-10	8-10	9-11	9-11	10-12	10-12	11-13	11-13

NUMBER OF BOLTS

LEVEL 1	LEVEL 2	LEVEL 3	LEVEL 4	LEVEL 5	LEVEL 6	LEVEL 7	LEVEL 8	LEVEL 9	LEVEL 10
3	4	5	6	7	8	9	10	11	12
LEVEL 11	LEVEL 12	LEVEL 13	LEVEL 14	LEVEL 15	LEVEL 16	LEVEL 17	LEVEL 18	LEVEL 19	LEVEL 20
13	14	15	16	17	18	19	20	21	22

MANA COST

LEVEL 1	LEVEL 2	LEVEL 3	LEVEL 4	LEVEL 5	LEVEL 6	LEVEL 7	LEVEL 8	LEVEL 9	LEVEL 10
3	3.5	4	4.5	5	5.5	6	6.5	7	7.5
LEVEL 11	LEVEL 12	LEVEL 13	LEVEL 14	LEVEL 15	LEVEL 16	LEVEL 17	LEVEL 18	LEVEL 19	LEVEL 20
8	8.5	9	9.5	10	10.5	11	11.5	12	12

STATIC FIELD (LEVEL 6; MANA COST = 9)

TIP

If you are so inclined, you can kill enemies with Static Field, but it takes numerous castings to get the enemy's health low enough. It's much better to use the spell a few times and then simply attack the enemy with your staff or wand when it is weakened, rather than wasting precious mana.

This is an incredibly powerful spell because it reduces the enemy's hit points by one-third, no matter how strong your adversary is!

Static Field is very powerful as an initial way to greet any group of enemies because it will cause each target in a radius around your Sorceress to lose one-third of its current hit points. This is especially helpful when you're in a group and are fighting a powerful enemy with a large number of hit points, because two hits with a Static Field will chop that foe's hit points in half. Each successive hit of Static Field causes the target to lose one-third of its current hit points, making it easy to damage your opponent, but less effective for ultimately killing them with this spell alone.

RADIUS (YARDS)

LEVEL 1	LEVEL 2	LEVEL 3	LEVEL 4	LEVEL 5	LEVEL 6	LEVEL 7	LEVEL 8	LEVEL 9	LEVEL 10
3.3	4	4.6	5.3	6	6.6	7.3	8	8.6	9.3

LEVEL 11	LEVEL 12	LEVEL 13	LEVEL 14	LEVEL 15	LEVEL 16	LEVEL 17	LEVEL 18	LEVEL 19	LEVEL 20
10	10.6	11.3	12	12.6	13.3	14	14.6	15.3	16

TELEKINESIS (LEVEL 6)

This skill allows the Sorceress to pick up items, open doors and crates, and attack monsters and players from a distance. The primary use for Telekinesis is for opening crates or stashes from afar to avoid taking any hits or damage from a trap. Telekinesis is also very useful in combat—it is comparable to how the Paladin uses Smite. When cast on an enemy, it will shove the target back, do damage to it, and stun it for a short period of time!

TIP

Telekinesis can be used to pick up objects on the other side of a grating or blocked passage, or to grab a valuable item before it can be reached by anyone else. Also, you can use this spell to activate a town portal from a distance—very effective when there is a pack of monsters between you and your only way out.

MANA COST

LEVEL 1	LEVEL 2	LEVEL 3	LEVEL 4	LEVEL 5	LEVEL 6	LEVEL 7	LEVEL 8	LEVEL 9	LEVEL 10
7	7	7	7	7	7	7	7	7	7

LEVEL 11	LEVEL 12	LEVEL 13	LEVEL 14	LEVEL 15	LEVEL 16	LEVEL 17	LEVEL 18	LEVEL 19	LEVEL 20
7	7	7	7	7	7	7	7	7	7

DAMAGE

LEVEL 1	LEVEL 2	LEVEL 3	LEVEL 4	LEVEL 5	LEVEL 6	LEVEL 7	LEVEL 8	LEVEL 9	LEVEL 10
1-2	2-3	3-4	4-5	5-6	6-7	7-8	8-9	9-10	10-11

LEVEL 11	LEVEL 12	LEVEL 13	LEVEL 14	LEVEL 15	LEVEL 16	LEVEL 17	LEVEL 18	LEVEL 19	LEVEL 20
11-12	12-13	13-14	14-15	15-16	16-17	17-18	18-19	19-20	20-21

THE SORCERESS

☀ NOVA (LEVEL 12)

Nova is an awesome spell that generates an electrical shockwave that spreads out in a[ll]
directions around your Sorceress, causing substantial lightning damage to all target[s]
within its range. It's a superb choice for the first two Acts of *Diablo II*, but it can't com[-]
pete with the higher level monsters and their resistance to elemental damage later in th[e]
game. For this reason, Nova is well worth investing in, but is not the only spell you war[t]
to develop.

MANA COST

LEVEL 1	LEVEL 2	LEVEL 3	LEVEL 4	LEVEL 5	LEVEL 6	LEVEL 7	LEVEL 8	LEVEL 9	LEVEL 10
15	16	17	18	19	20	21	22	23	24
LEVEL 11	LEVEL 12	LEVEL 13	LEVEL 14	LEVEL 15	LEVEL 16	LEVEL 17	LEVEL 18	LEVEL 19	LEVEL 20
25	26	27	28	29	30	31	32	33	34

DAMAGE

LEVEL 1	LEVEL 2	LEVEL 3	LEVEL 4	LEVEL 5	LEVEL 6	LEVEL 7	LEVEL 8	LEVEL 9	LEVEL 10
1-20	8-27	15-34	22-41	29-48	36-55	43-62	50-69	57-76	64-83
LEVEL 11	LEVEL 12	LEVEL 13	LEVEL 14	LEVEL 15	LEVEL 16	LEVEL 17	LEVEL 18	LEVEL 19	LEVEL 20
71-90	78-97	85-104	92-111	99-118	106-125	113-132	120-139	127-146	134-153

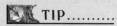

TIP..........

Whenever the enemies are stacked two or three deep, you should use Lightning to blow through them with raw electrical power. This is a spell that deserves its own hot key for easy access.

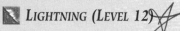

LIGHTNING (LEVEL 12)

Lightning sends out a bolt of pure electrical energy that goes right through all targets[,]
inflicting a healthy dose of damage to each one. As you approach level 20 in this skill[,]
the amount of damage being done is huge, and because it passes through one enem[y]
and onto the next, it offers an excellent means for attacking groups of enemies that ar[e]
stacked in tight hallways or narrow canyons.

MANA COST

LEVEL 1	LEVEL 2	LEVEL 3	LEVEL 4	LEVEL 5	LEVEL 6	LEVEL 7	LEVEL 8	LEVEL 9	LEVEL 10
8	8.5	9	9.5	10	10.5	11	11.5	12	12
LEVEL 11	LEVEL 12	LEVEL 13	LEVEL 14	LEVEL 15	LEVEL 16	LEVEL 17	LEVEL 18	LEVEL 19	LEVEL 20
13	13	14	14	15	15	16	16	17	17

DAMAGE

LEVEL 1	LEVEL 2	LEVEL 3	LEVEL 4	LEVEL 5	LEVEL 6	LEVEL 7	LEVEL 8	LEVEL 9	LEVEL 10
1-40	1-48	1-56	1-64	1-72	1-80	1-88	1-96	1-104	1-112
LEVEL 11	LEVEL 12	LEVEL 13	LEVEL 14	LEVEL 15	LEVEL 16	LEVEL 17	LEVEL 18	LEVEL 19	LEVEL 20
1-120	1-128	1-136	1-144	1-152	1-160	1-168	1-176	1-184	1-192

CHAIN LIGHTNING (LEVEL 18)

Chain Lightning sends out a streak of lightning that will bounce and jump through several targets, doing damage to everything it hits along the way. As skill points are added to Chain Lightning, the amount of damage that its five hits strike grows. Remember that it will even bounce off of walls, so put it to good use when you're in a cramped dungeon!

Chain Lightning is a great spell for taking out large numbers of enemies in a wide area of occupation.

MANA COST

LEVEL 1	LEVEL 2	LEVEL 3	LEVEL 4	LEVEL 5	LEVEL 6	LEVEL 7	LEVEL 8	LEVEL 9	LEVEL 10
9	10	11	12	13	14	15	16	17	18
LEVEL 11	LEVEL 12	LEVEL 13	LEVEL 14	LEVEL 15	LEVEL 16	LEVEL 17	LEVEL 18	LEVEL 19	LEVEL 20
19	20	21	22	23	24	25	26	27	28

DAMAGE

LEVEL 1	LEVEL 2	LEVEL 3	LEVEL 4	LEVEL 5	LEVEL 6	LEVEL 7	LEVEL 8	LEVEL 9	LEVEL 10
1-32	7-38	13-44	19-50	25-56	31-62	37-68	43-74	49-80	55-86
LEVEL 11	LEVEL 12	LEVEL 13	LEVEL 14	LEVEL 15	LEVEL 16	LEVEL 17	LEVEL 18	LEVEL 19	LEVEL 20
61-92	67-98	73-104	79-110	85-116	91-122	97-128	103-134	109-140	115-146

TELEPORT (LEVEL 18)

Teleport instantly moves the Sorceress to the area you've targeted with your mouse. It's a very powerful spell that can get you out of trouble or transport you over vast expanses in the blink of an eye, but it is not without its limitations. For example, you cannot teleport to any area that you would not otherwise be able to walk to, which in areas like the Lost City leaves some ridges off limits. Still, when you're in trouble and you're taking a beating from some persistent monsters, you can often simply teleport to high ground or to the other side of a wall to get your Sorceress out of trouble.

MANA COST

LEVEL 1	LEVEL 2	LEVEL 3	LEVEL 4	LEVEL 5	LEVEL 6	LEVEL 7	LEVEL 8	LEVEL 9	LEVEL 10
24	23	22	21	20	19	18	17	16	15
LEVEL 11	LEVEL 12	LEVEL 13	LEVEL 14	LEVEL 15	LEVEL 16	LEVEL 17	LEVEL 18	LEVEL 19	LEVEL 20
14	13	12	11	10	9	8	7	6	5

⚡ THUNDER STORM (LEVEL 24)

This skill creates a thunderstorm that will periodically hit a nearby enemy with a bolt o[f] lightning. It is much more powerful and effective when you've been able to put a fe[w] skill points into it. The level 1 Thunder Storm has a minimum damage of 1, wherea[s] level 2 has a minimum damage of 11, so just one skill point makes a 1100 percent di[f]ference!

MANA COST ⚡

LEVEL 1	LEVEL 2	LEVEL 3	LEVEL 4	LEVEL 5	LEVEL 6	LEVEL 7	LEVEL 8	LEVEL 9	LEVEL 10
19	19	19	19	19	19	19	19	19	19
LEVEL 11	LEVEL 12	LEVEL 13	LEVEL 14	LEVEL 15	LEVEL 16	LEVEL 17	LEVEL 18	LEVEL 19	LEVEL 20
19	19	19	19	19	19	19	19	19	19

DAMAGE ⚡

LEVEL 1	LEVEL 2	LEVEL 3	LEVEL 4	LEVEL 5	LEVEL 6	LEVEL 7	LEVEL 8	LEVEL 9	LEVEL 10
1-100	11-110	21-120	31-130	41-140	51-150	61-160	71-170	81-180	91-190
LEVEL 11	LEVEL 12	LEVEL 13	LEVEL 14	LEVEL 15	LEVEL 16	LEVEL 17	LEVEL 18	LEVEL 19	LEVEL 20
101-200	111-210	121-220	131-230	141-240	151-250	161-260	171-270	181-280	191-290

DURATION (SECONDS) ⚡

LEVEL 1	LEVEL 2	LEVEL 3	LEVEL 4	LEVEL 5	LEVEL 6	LEVEL 7	LEVEL 8	LEVEL 9	LEVEL 10
32	40	48	56	64	72	80	88	96	104
LEVEL 11	LEVEL 12	LEVEL 13	LEVEL 14	LEVEL 15	LEVEL 16	LEVEL 17	LEVEL 18	LEVEL 19	LEVEL 20
112	120	128	136	144	152	160	168	176	184

◎ ENERGY SHIELD (LEVEL 24; MANA COST = 5)

Energy Shield creates a defensive shield that's based on your mana supply. This shiel[d] absorbs some physical and all magic damage through mana instead of hit points, thu[s] extending your life considerably in hairy situations. You can add to your lifespan b[y] using the Energy Shield and then drinking both life and mana potions to keep your li[fe] and Energy Shield topped off. Use this spell only when you have plenty of mana or ar[e] in desperate need of extra 'life' since your mana will drain quickly as you take hits, leav[ing] you with no way to employ other skills.

DAMAGE ABSORBED (%) ◎

LEVEL 1	LEVEL 2	LEVEL 3	LEVEL 4	LEVEL 5	LEVEL 6	LEVEL 7	LEVEL 8	LEVEL 9	LEVEL 10
15	23	30	35	40	43	46	48	51	52
LEVEL 11	LEVEL 12	LEVEL 13	LEVEL 14	LEVEL 15	LEVEL 16	LEVEL 17	LEVEL 18	LEVEL 19	LEVEL 20
54	56	57	58	59	61	61	62	63	63

DURATION (SECONDS)

LEVEL 1	LEVEL 2	LEVEL 3	LEVEL 4	LEVEL 5	LEVEL 6	LEVEL 7	LEVEL 8	LEVEL 9	LEVEL 10
144	192	240	288	336	384	432	480	528	576

LEVEL 11	LEVEL 12	LEVEL 13	LEVEL 14	LEVEL 15	LEVEL 16	LEVEL 17	LEVEL 18	LEVEL 19	LEVEL 20
624	672	720	768	816	864	912	960	1008	1056

✦ LIGHTNING MASTERY (LEVEL 30)

Lightning Mastery is a passive skill that reduces the mana cost of lightning spells with each point that you put into the mastery. If you are going to develop the Lightning skill tree, it is imperative that you invest skill points in Lightning Mastery because it will ultimately save you hundreds, or even thousands, of mana points over the course of an entire game.

MANA COST (-%)

LEVEL 1	LEVEL 2	LEVEL 3	LEVEL 4	LEVEL 5	LEVEL 6	LEVEL 7	LEVEL 8	LEVEL 9	LEVEL 10
15	23	30	35	40	43	46	48	51	52

LEVEL 11	LEVEL 12	LEVEL 13	LEVEL 14	LEVEL 15	LEVEL 16	LEVEL 17	LEVEL 18	LEVEL 19	LEVEL 20
54	56	57	58	59	61	61	62	63	63

COLD

This skill tree gives the Sorceress control over the realm of cold and ice. Cold is an important element because it naturally slows enemies, but more than that it can sometimes freeze enemies and shatter them into tiny shards of ice that melt away. An enemy that's been destroyed in this manner cannot be resurrected. Like the other elemental damage spells, Cold is an important skill tree to invest in, even if it's in just a limited way.

ICE BOLT (LEVEL 1; MANA COST = 3)

This is the base-level spell that not only inflicts cold damage on the target, but also slows the enemy for a period of time. How much damage is inflicted and how long the enemy is slowed depends on how many skill points you've put into this spell. Invest at least one skill point here because the slowing of enemies can be an important ability later in the game, and of course Ice Bolt is a prerequisite for Ice learning Blast and Glacial Spike.

TIP

Slowing your enemies with cold is something that shouldn't be underestimated. This is an excellent spell to have hot-keyed in the first two Acts of **Diablo II** because it can delay a tough enemy long enough for you to take them out or run away.

DAMAGE

LEVEL 1	LEVEL 2	LEVEL 3	LEVEL 4	LEVEL 5	LEVEL 6	LEVEL 7	LEVEL 8	LEVEL 9	LEVEL 10
3-5	4-6	5-7	6-8	7-9	8-10	9-11	10-12	11-13	12-14

LEVEL 11	LEVEL 12	LEVEL 13	LEVEL 14	LEVEL 15	LEVEL 16	LEVEL 17	LEVEL 18	LEVEL 19	LEVEL 20
13-15	14-16	15-17	16-18	17-19	18-20	19-21	20-22	21-23	22-24

DURATION (SECONDS)

LEVEL 1	LEVEL 2	LEVEL 3	LEVEL 4	LEVEL 5	LEVEL 6	LEVEL 7	LEVEL 8	LEVEL 9	LEVEL 10
6	7.4	8.8	10.2	11.6	13	14.4	15.8	17.2	18.6

LEVEL 11	LEVEL 12	LEVEL 13	LEVEL 14	LEVEL 15	LEVEL 16	LEVEL 17	LEVEL 18	LEVEL 19	LEVEL 20
20	21.4	22.8	24.2	25.6	27	28.4	29.8	31.2	32.6

FROZEN ARMOR (LEVEL 1; MANA COST = 7)

Frozen Armor is a long-lasting defensive spell that will improve your defensive rating while freezing any enemy attacker that lands a hit on your character. The duration of Frozen Armor (two minutes at level 1, and almost six minutes at level 20) is the real bonus because you can simply invoke it and move on. It's most effective when your Sorceress is involved in a great deal of melee fighting.

DEFENSE BONUS (%)

LEVEL 1	LEVEL 2	LEVEL 3	LEVEL 4	LEVEL 5	LEVEL 6	LEVEL 7	LEVEL 8	LEVEL 9	LEVEL 10
30	35	40	45	50	55	60	65	70	75

LEVEL 11	LEVEL 12	LEVEL 13	LEVEL 14	LEVEL 15	LEVEL 16	LEVEL 17	LEVEL 18	LEVEL 19	LEVEL 20
80	85	90	95	100	105	110	115	120	125

DURATION (SECONDS)

LEVEL 1	LEVEL 2	LEVEL 3	LEVEL 4	LEVEL 5	LEVEL 6	LEVEL 7	LEVEL 8	LEVEL 9	LEVEL 10
120	132	144	156	168	180	192	204	216	228

LEVEL 11	LEVEL 12	LEVEL 13	LEVEL 14	LEVEL 15	LEVEL 16	LEVEL 17	LEVEL 18	LEVEL 19	LEVEL 20
240	252	264	276	288	300	312	324	336	348

FREEZE DURATION (SECONDS)

LEVEL 1	LEVEL 2	LEVEL 3	LEVEL 4	LEVEL 5	LEVEL 6	LEVEL 7	LEVEL 8	LEVEL 9	LEVEL 10
1.2	1.3	1.4	1.5	1.6	1.8	1.9	2	2.1	2.2

LEVEL 11	LEVEL 12	LEVEL 13	LEVEL 14	LEVEL 15	LEVEL 16	LEVEL 17	LEVEL 18	LEVEL 19	LEVEL 20
2.4	2.5	2.6	2.7	2.8	3	3.1	3.2	3.3	3.4

FROST NOVA (LEVEL 6)

Frost Nova generates an icy shockwave that spreads out in all directions around your Sorceress, freezing all targets it hits as it travels outward from your position. For this reason, the Frost Nova is an excellent skill to use when you are in an area that's tightly packed with enemies.

The Frost Nova freezes anything it hits.

By putting just two extra skill points into Frost Nova, you can double the length of time that it slows enemies with cold and nearly double the damage it does. Put at least three skill points into Frost Nova for best use in Acts I and II.

MANA COST

LEVEL 1	LEVEL 2	LEVEL 3	LEVEL 4	LEVEL 5	LEVEL 6	LEVEL 7	LEVEL 8	LEVEL 9	LEVEL 10
9	11	13	15	17	19	21	23	25	27

LEVEL 11	LEVEL 12	LEVEL 13	LEVEL 14	LEVEL 15	LEVEL 16	LEVEL 17	LEVEL 18	LEVEL 19	LEVEL 20
29	31	33	35	37	39	41	43	45	47

COLD DAMAGE

LEVEL 1	LEVEL 2	LEVEL 3	LEVEL 4	LEVEL 5	LEVEL 6	LEVEL 7	LEVEL 8	LEVEL 9	LEVEL 10
2-4	4-6	6-8	8-10	10-12	12-14	14-16	16-18	18-20	20-22

LEVEL 11	LEVEL 12	LEVEL 13	LEVEL 14	LEVEL 15	LEVEL 16	LEVEL 17	LEVEL 18	LEVEL 19	LEVEL 20
22-24	24-26	26-28	28-30	30-32	32-34	34-36	36-38	38-40	40-42

DURATION (SECONDS)

LEVEL 1	LEVEL 2	LEVEL 3	LEVEL 4	LEVEL 5	LEVEL 6	LEVEL 7	LEVEL 8	LEVEL 9	LEVEL 10
8	9	10	11	12	13	14	15	16	17

LEVEL 11	LEVEL 12	LEVEL 13	LEVEL 14	LEVEL 15	LEVEL 16	LEVEL 17	LEVEL 18	LEVEL 19	LEVEL 20
18	19	20	21	22	23	24	25	26	27

ICE BLAST (LEVEL 6)

This spell creates a bolt of ice that freezes and damages the enemy target. In short, it's a more powerful version of the Ice Bolt. It's unique quality is that it doesn't just slow the enemies, it freezes them for a short time while dealing significant damage. The amount of damage climbs quickly with just a few skill points invested. Augmenting Ice Blast to level 3 will give you the power to freeze enemies for over three seconds and still do more than 20 points of damage for a relatively small mana cost.

TIP

Remember that a frozen enemy can sometimes be smashed by taking another Ice Blast or by taking a hit from a melee weapon. One bonus of freezing and then smashing your enemies into ice shards is that their destroyed bodies cannot be resurrected by magical enemies.

MANA COST

LEVEL 1	LEVEL 2	LEVEL 3	LEVEL 4	LEVEL 5	LEVEL 6	LEVEL 7	LEVEL 8	LEVEL 9	LEVEL 10
6	6.5	7	7.5	8	8.5	9	9.5	10	10.5

LEVEL 11	LEVEL 12	LEVEL 13	LEVEL 14	LEVEL 15	LEVEL 16	LEVEL 17	LEVEL 18	LEVEL 19	LEVEL 20
11	11.5	12	12	13	13	14	14	15	15

DAMAGE

LEVEL 1	LEVEL 2	LEVEL 3	LEVEL 4	LEVEL 5	LEVEL 6	LEVEL 7	LEVEL 8	LEVEL 9	LEVEL 10
10	17	24	31	38	45	52	59	66	73

LEVEL 11	LEVEL 12	LEVEL 13	LEVEL 14	LEVEL 15	LEVEL 16	LEVEL 17	LEVEL 18	LEVEL 19	LEVEL 20
80	87	94	101	108	115	122	129	136	143

FREEZE DURATION (SECONDS)

LEVEL 1	LEVEL 2	LEVEL 3	LEVEL 4	LEVEL 5	LEVEL 6	LEVEL 7	LEVEL 8	LEVEL 9	LEVEL 10
3	3.2	3.4	3.6	3.8	4	4.2	4.4	4.6	4.8

LEVEL 11	LEVEL 12	LEVEL 13	LEVEL 14	LEVEL 15	LEVEL 16	LEVEL 17	LEVEL 18	LEVEL 19	LEVEL 20
5	6.2	5.4	5.6	5.8	6	6.2	6.4	6.6	6.8

SHIVER ARMOR (LEVEL 12; MANA COST = 11; COLD LENGTH = 4 SECONDS)

This is an armor that will not only cause damage to the enemy when they hit you, bu will also hit them with a cold blast that slows them for four seconds. The 'offensive nature of Shiver Armor masks the fact that it also increases your defense rating whe active, making it a 'three-in-one' tool that can hit, protect, and slow your enemies all a once. Shiver Armor is effective at level 1, so you don't necessarily have to put a lot c skill points into it for it to be effective. Obviously, this is a spell that's best used whe your Sorceress is involved in melee combat situations.

DEFENSE BONUS (%)

LEVEL 1	LEVEL 2	LEVEL 3	LEVEL 4	LEVEL 5	LEVEL 6	LEVEL 7	LEVEL 8	LEVEL 9	LEVEL 10
45	51	57	63	69	75	81	87	93	99
LEVEL 11	LEVEL 12	LEVEL 13	LEVEL 14	LEVEL 15	LEVEL 16	LEVEL 17	LEVEL 18	LEVEL 19	LEVEL 20
105	111	117	123	129	135	141	147	153	159

DAMAGE

LEVEL 1	LEVEL 2	LEVEL 3	LEVEL 4	LEVEL 5	LEVEL 6	LEVEL 7	LEVEL 8	LEVEL 9	LEVEL 10
6-8	8-10	10-12	12-14	14-16	16-18	18-20	20-22	22-24	24-26
LEVEL 11	LEVEL 12	LEVEL 13	LEVEL 14	LEVEL 15	LEVEL 16	LEVEL 17	LEVEL 18	LEVEL 19	LEVEL 20
26-28	28-30	30-32	32-34	34-36	36-38	38-40	40-42	42-44	44-46

DURATION (SECONDS)

LEVEL 1	LEVEL 2	LEVEL 3	LEVEL 4	LEVEL 5	LEVEL 6	LEVEL 7	LEVEL 8	LEVEL 9	LEVEL 10
120	132	144	156	168	180	192	204	216	228
LEVEL 11	LEVEL 12	LEVEL 13	LEVEL 14	LEVEL 15	LEVEL 16	LEVEL 17	LEVEL 18	LEVEL 19	LEVEL 20
240	252	264	276	288	300	312	324	336	348

GLACIAL SPIKE (LEVEL 18)

Glacial Spike is one of the most powerful cold spells in the game because it freezes a group of monsters rather than just one. Its damage is so substantial that enemies often simply smash into a hundred shards of ices and melt away after they take a single hit. Glacial Spike is a must-have skill that becomes considerably more powerful with just a few skill points. Use it against any group of enemies and watch them all freeze or shatter with just a few shots. Unfortunately, the radius of effect (2.6 yards) for Glacial Spike does not change when more skill points are added, but this is offset by the increased attack value and length of cold effect that the enemy must endure with each successive skill level.

Glacial Spike severely punish es any group of enemies it hit. Those that aren't destroyed will be slowed by the cold.

DAMAGE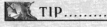

LEVEL 1	LEVEL 2	LEVEL 3	LEVEL 4	LEVEL 5	LEVEL 6	LEVEL 7	LEVEL 8	LEVEL 9	LEVEL 10
16-24	23-31	30-38	37-45	44-52	51-59	58-66	65-73	72-80	79-87
LEVEL 11	LEVEL 12	LEVEL 13	LEVEL 14	LEVEL 15	LEVEL 16	LEVEL 17	LEVEL 18	LEVEL 19	LEVEL 20
86-94	93-101	100-108	107-115	114-122	121-129	128-136	135-143	142-150	149-157

FREEZE DURATION (SECONDS)

LEVEL 1	LEVEL 2	LEVEL 3	LEVEL 4	LEVEL 5	LEVEL 6	LEVEL 7	LEVEL 8	LEVEL 9	LEVEL 10
2	2.1	2.2	2.3	2.4	2.6	2.7	2.8	2.9	3
LEVEL 11	LEVEL 12	LEVEL 13	LEVEL 14	LEVEL 15	LEVEL 16	LEVEL 17	LEVEL 18	LEVEL 19	LEVEL 20
3.2	3.3	3.4	3.5	3.6	3.8	3.9	4	4.1	4.2

MANA COST

LEVEL 1	LEVEL 2	LEVEL 3	LEVEL 4	LEVEL 5	LEVEL 6	LEVEL 7	LEVEL 8	LEVEL 9	LEVEL 10
10	10.5	11	11.5	12	12	13	13	14	14
LEVEL 11	LEVEL 12	LEVEL 13	LEVEL 14	LEVEL 15	LEVEL 16	LEVEL 17	LEVEL 18	LEVEL 19	LEVEL 20
15	15	16	16	17	17	18	18	19	19

BLIZZARD (LEVEL 24)

Blizzard is the most visually impressive of the cold skills, but along with the great eye-candy it also packs a massive punch.

Blizzard creates a massive hailstorm that damages all enemies caught beneath its fury with a cascade of icy mayhem. More skill points in this skill means a longer duration of effect and more damage done from each ice shard that falls from the sky. Needless to say, this is a show-stopper when you're facing a large group of tightly packed enemies. Blizzard also works well indoors, and is probably best used when you come across a room full of enemies trapped within an enclosed area. The Mana Cost of this spell ranges between 23 and 42 (see Appendix).

TIP

Blizzard is a great spell to invoke multiple times in a specific area, giving your enemies nowhere to run from the icy wrath you have summoned from above. This technique of blanketing the enemy with this spell can be continued indefinitely as long as you have enough mana.

DAMAGE (PER SECOND)

LEVEL 1	LEVEL 2	LEVEL 3	LEVEL 4	LEVEL 5	LEVEL 6	LEVEL 7	LEVEL 8	LEVEL 9	LEVEL 10
16-24	20-28	24-32	28-36	32-40	36-44	40-48	44-52	48-56	52-60
LEVEL 11	LEVEL 12	LEVEL 13	LEVEL 14	LEVEL 15	LEVEL 16	LEVEL 17	LEVEL 18	LEVEL 19	LEVEL 20
56-64	60-68	64-72	68-76	72-80	76-84	80-88	84-92	88-96	92-100

DURATION (SECONDS)

LEVEL 1	LEVEL 2	LEVEL 3	LEVEL 4	LEVEL 5	LEVEL 6	LEVEL 7	LEVEL 8	LEVEL 9	LEVEL 10
4	5	6	7	8	9	10	11	12	13
LEVEL 11	LEVEL 12	LEVEL 13	LEVEL 14	LEVEL 15	LEVEL 16	LEVEL 17	LEVEL 18	LEVEL 19	LEVEL 20
14	15	16	17	18	19	20	21	22	23

CHILLING ARMOR (LEVEL 24; MANA COST = 17)

Chilling Armor is another multipurpose spell that both attacks and defends. It offers yo
an armor bonus while also launching an Ice Bolt at any enemies that hit you, thus dam
aging and slowing your attacker. This spell is most useful when you're alone facing thre
or four enemies at once.

DEFENSE BONUS (%)

LEVEL 1	LEVEL 2	LEVEL 3	LEVEL 4	LEVEL 5	LEVEL 6	LEVEL 7	LEVEL 8	LEVEL 9	LEVEL 10
45	50	55	60	65	70	75	80	85	90

LEVEL 11	LEVEL 12	LEVEL 13	LEVEL 14	LEVEL 15	LEVEL 16	LEVEL 17	LEVEL 18	LEVEL 19	LEVEL 20
95	100	105	110	115	120	125	130	135	140

DAMAGE

LEVEL 1	LEVEL 2	LEVEL 3	LEVEL 4	LEVEL 5	LEVEL 6	LEVEL 7	LEVEL 8	LEVEL 9	LEVEL 10
4-6	5-7	6-8	7-9	8-10	9-11	10-12	11-13	12-14	13-15

LEVEL 11	LEVEL 12	LEVEL 13	LEVEL 14	LEVEL 15	LEVEL 16	LEVEL 17	LEVEL 18	LEVEL 19	LEVEL 20
14-16	15-17	16-18	17-19	18-20	19-21	20-22	21-23	22-24	23-25

DURATION (SECS.)

LEVEL 1	LEVEL 2	LEVEL 3	LEVEL 4	LEVEL 5	LEVEL 6	LEVEL 7	LEVEL 8	LEVEL 9	LEVEL 10
144	150	156	162	168	174	180	186	192	198

LEVEL 11	LEVEL 12	LEVEL 13	LEVEL 14	LEVEL 15	LEVEL 16	LEVEL 17	LEVEL 18	LEVEL 19	LEVEL 20
204	210	216	222	228	234	240	246	252	258

FROZEN ORB (LEVEL 30; MANA COST = 25)

Frozen Orb is a very powerful spell that serves multiple purposes. When cast, it send
out a large orb of ice that flies out in a straight line while spinning out Ice Bolts in a
directions. This is a great weapon for a narrow hallway where there's a lineup of ene
mies, but it is also of great use in places such as a Carver camp because the bolts fl
everywhere. It is an impressive display when you can eliminate the Shaman in a Carve
Camp with the Frozen Orb (preventing him from resurrecting his minions) while the Ic
Bolts literally carve up the Carvers.

MANA COST

LEVEL 1	LEVEL 2	LEVEL 3	LEVEL 4	LEVEL 5	LEVEL 6	LEVEL 7	LEVEL 8	LEVEL 9	LEVEL 10
25	27	29	31	33	35	37	39	41	43

LEVEL 11	LEVEL 12	LEVEL 13	LEVEL 14	LEVEL 15	LEVEL 16	LEVEL 17	LEVEL 18	LEVEL 19	LEVEL 20
45	47	49	51	53	55	57	59	61	65

CHAPTER 2: THE CHARACTERS

DAMAGE

LEVEL 1	LEVEL 2	LEVEL 3	LEVEL 4	LEVEL 5	LEVEL 6	LEVEL 7	LEVEL 8	LEVEL 9	LEVEL 10
32-35	38-41	44-47	50-53	56-59	62-65	68-71	74-77	80-83	86-89

LEVEL 11	LEVEL 12	LEVEL 13	LEVEL 14	LEVEL 15	LEVEL 16	LEVEL 17	LEVEL 18	LEVEL 19	LEVEL 20
92-95	98-101	104-107	110-113	116-119	122-125	128-131	134-137	140-143	146-149

COLD DURATION (SECONDS)

LEVEL 1	LEVEL 2	LEVEL 3	LEVEL 4	LEVEL 5	LEVEL 6	LEVEL 7	LEVEL 8	LEVEL 9	LEVEL 10
8	9	10	11	12	13	14	15	16	17

LEVEL 11	LEVEL 12	LEVEL 13	LEVEL 14	LEVEL 15	LEVEL 16	LEVEL 17	LEVEL 18	LEVEL 19	LEVEL 20
18	19	20	21	22	23	24	25	26	27

COLD MASTERY (LEVEL 30)

While Cold Mastery doesn't reduce the mana cost of your Cold spells, it does lower your enemy's resistance to cold-based damage by a percentage. Just two extra skill points nearly doubles the effectiveness of any of your damaging cold spells, so it's well worth the investment.

ENEMY RESISTANCE (%)

LEVEL 1	LEVEL 2	LEVEL 3	LEVEL 4	LEVEL 5	LEVEL 6	LEVEL 7	LEVEL 8	LEVEL 9	LEVEL 10
23	34	42	49	55	59	63	65	59	71

LEVEL 11	LEVEL 12	LEVEL 13	LEVEL 14	LEVEL 15	LEVEL 16	LEVEL 17	LEVEL 18	LEVEL 19	LEVEL 20
73	75	77	79	80	82	82	83	84	85

The Barbarian

The Barbarian is usually a member of any of several tribes living on the fringe of civilization. These tribes refuse the influence of those they see as soft and weak, and the Barbarian is no different. Ceaseless clan warfare and the constant struggle to survive in the hostile wilderness are reflected in the Barbarian's sturdy and powerful frame.

Perhaps lacking the sophistication of the other characters, the Barbarian has an acute awareness of his surroundings. Because of his shamanistic belief in the animal powers with which he identifies, the Barbarian is sometimes associated with stories of lycanthropy. In fact, he believes he can call upon totemic animal spirits to infuse him with supernormal strengths and abilities but these abilities only work to improve his already superb battle tactics.

BARBARIAN SKILLS

The Barbarian is a pure fighter, and most of his skills augment these core abilities. His three skill sets are Combat Skills, Combat Masteries, and Warcries. As with the other characters, the skills that are developed in each area will ultimately affect the abilities of the Barbarian as he progresses through *Diablo II*.

Out of the Masteries, the higher level weapons that the Barbarian is likely to find are swords. Therefore, if you're looking to create an uber-barbarian, it is usually prudent to put points into sword mastery.

COMBAT

This skill tree is the main attack skill tree of the Barbarian, and includes the critical skills of Bash and Leap Attack. Although the Barbarian's Masteries are very important, he'd be hard pressed to succeed without having at least a few of the skills in the Combat skill tree.

BASH (LEVEL 1; MANA COST = 2)

This skill delivers a powerful smashing blow that knocks the target back, stuns it, and inflicts a substantial amount of damage. Bash not only adds additional damage, it also increases the damage and attack modifiers, thus giving you a powerful hit that knocks back the enemy and stuns it for a brief time. Bash is a skill that is great to use against monsters that are exceptionally tough, because it will get them out of your way while providing a brief period of time for you to attack again, run, or switch skills.

Bash is a Level 1 skill, but you can use it for effect throughout the entire game.

ADDITIONAL DAMAGE

LEVEL 1	LEVEL 2	LEVEL 3	LEVEL 4	LEVEL 5	LEVEL 6	LEVEL 7	LEVEL 8	LEVEL 9	LEVEL 10
1	2	3	4	5	6	7	8	9	10

LEVEL 11	LEVEL 12	LEVEL 13	LEVEL 14	LEVEL 15	LEVEL 16	LEVEL 17	LEVEL 18	LEVEL 19	LEVEL 20
11	12	13	14	15	16	17	18	19	20

DAMAGE MODIFIER (+%)

LEVEL 1	LEVEL 2	LEVEL 3	LEVEL 4	LEVEL 5	LEVEL 6	LEVEL 7	LEVEL 8	LEVEL 9	LEVEL 10
50	55	60	65	70	75	80	85	90	95

LEVEL 11	LEVEL 12	LEVEL 13	LEVEL 14	LEVEL 15	LEVEL 16	LEVEL 17	LEVEL 18	LEVEL 19	LEVEL 20
100	105	110	115	120	125	130	135	140	145

ATTACK MODIFIER (+%)

LEVEL 1	LEVEL 2	LEVEL 3	LEVEL 4	LEVEL 5	LEVEL 6	LEVEL 7	LEVEL 8	LEVEL 9	LEVEL 10
20	25	30	35	40	45	50	55	60	65

LEVEL 11	LEVEL 12	LEVEL 13	LEVEL 14	LEVEL 15	LEVEL 16	LEVEL 17	LEVEL 18	LEVEL 19	LEVEL 20
70	75	80	85	90	95	100	105	110	115

LEAP (LEVEL 6; MANA COST = 2)

Perhaps the Barbarian's most versatile and important skill, Leap enables him to jump over obstacles. Leap not only moves you around the map nicely, but it enables you to do things that other players cannot do. For example, you can leap over rivers or cut corners over areas that the other party members or monsters must walk around. With the Leap skill, you can access places you otherwise couldn't such as in the Arcane Sanctuary, or use it to escape a scary situation from which you normally couldn't run.

Of course, to get the kind of distance that will *really* make a difference, you must put six or seven skill points into this skill. As an added bonus, when you land after performing a Leap there's a small amount of 'knock-back' that occurs against enemies. Although this doesn't damage the enemies, it gives you a cushion of space when you land.

NOTE......

In multiplayer action, you can often use Leap to reach an item before a party member. This is just one of the advantages of being a Barbarian.

RADIUS (YARDS)

LEVEL 1	LEVEL 2	LEVEL 3	LEVEL 4	LEVEL 5	LEVEL 6	LEVEL 7	LEVEL 8	LEVEL 9	LEVEL 10
4.6	7.3	8.6	10	11.3	12	12.6	13.3	14	14

LEVEL 11	LEVEL 12	LEVEL 13	LEVEL 14	LEVEL 15	LEVEL 16	LEVEL 17	LEVEL 18	LEVEL 19	LEVEL 20
14.6	14.6	15.3	16	16	16	16.6	16.6	16.6	16.6

DOUBLE SWING (LEVEL 6; MANA COST = 2)

This skill provides a quick double attack that enables you to use weapons held in both hands in the space of a single attack. For example, if you have an axe in one and a sword in the other, Double Swing quickly swings both weapons and causes damage with both. However, this isn't the only benefit of this skill. It also provides a bonus to your attack rating that makes each attack a little better.

Oftentimes, it's a good idea to make Double Swing your standard attack for your le
mouse button. Therefore, each time you attack, you're performing a Double Swing an
getting the attack rating modifier. This will enable you to cause more damage faster, plu
it's a great technique to use throughout the game.

The drawback to using Double Swing is that it costs two mana each time it is used. Thi
skill is best used when you have a mana recharge item or if have additional man
potions to keep up your mana reserve.

ATTACK MODIFIER (+%)

LEVEL 1	LEVEL 2	LEVEL 3	LEVEL 4	LEVEL 5	LEVEL 6	LEVEL 7	LEVEL 8	LEVEL 9	LEVEL 10
15	20	25	30	35	40	45	50	55	60
LEVEL 11	LEVEL 12	LEVEL 13	LEVEL 14	LEVEL 15	LEVEL 16	LEVEL 17	LEVEL 18	LEVEL 19	LEVEL 20
65	70	75	80	85	90	95	100	105	110

STUN (LEVEL 12; MANA COST = 2)

This skill not only stuns the enemy that you're attacking, it also increases the attac
rating for that attack. Similar to skills like Bash and Smite, Stun is great for keeping a
enemy stunned and unable to retaliate against your attacks.

If you consistently use Stun against an enemy, your foe won't be able to respond to you
attacks because it will be perpetually stunned until its death. When you put a few ski
points into Stun, the duration of the stun increases so that you can have more time ir
between attacks. This provides more time to choose how to finish off the enemy, attac
another enemy, or run if you need to.

ATTACK MODIFIER (+%)

LEVEL 1	LEVEL 2	LEVEL 3	LEVEL 4	LEVEL 5	LEVEL 6	LEVEL 7	LEVEL 8	LEVEL 9	LEVEL 10
15	20	25	30	35	40	45	50	55	60
LEVEL 11	LEVEL 12	LEVEL 13	LEVEL 14	LEVEL 15	LEVEL 16	LEVEL 17	LEVEL 18	LEVEL 19	LEVEL 20
65	70	75	80	85	90	95	100	105	110

DURATION (SECONDS)

LEVEL 1	LEVEL 2	LEVEL 3	LEVEL 4	LEVEL 5	LEVEL 6	LEVEL 7	LEVEL 8	LEVEL 9	LEVEL 10
1.2	1.4	1.6	1.8	2.0	2.2	2.4	2.6	2.8	3.0
LEVEL 11	LEVEL 12	LEVEL 13	LEVEL 14	LEVEL 15	LEVEL 16	LEVEL 17	LEVEL 18	LEVEL 19	LEVEL 20
3.2	3.4	3.6	3.8	4.0	4.2	4.4	4.6	4.8	5.0

DOUBLE THROW (LEVEL 12; MANA COST = 2)

Like Double Swing, Double Throw simply allows you to quickly throw two weapon
(one from each hand). In addition, it increases the attack rating of each throw
weapon. The importance of the attack rating increase cannot be overstated. Afte
adding just a few skill points to Double Throw, the attack improves by 50 percent!

ATTACK MODIFIER (+%)

LEVEL 1	LEVEL 2	LEVEL 3	LEVEL 4	LEVEL 5	LEVEL 6	LEVEL 7	LEVEL 8	LEVEL 9	LEVEL 10
20	30	40	50	60	70	80	90	100	110

LEVEL 11	LEVEL 12	LEVEL 13	LEVEL 14	LEVEL 15	LEVEL 16	LEVEL 17	LEVEL 18	LEVEL 19	LEVEL 20
120	130	140	150	160	170	180	190	200	210

NOTE......

The only downside to Double Throw is that you must have weapons that you can throw. When fighting lots of enemies, you need plenty of throwing weapons at your disposal. If not, you'll run out of weapons and be left without a weapon with which to fight.

LEAP ATTACK (LEVEL 18; MANA COST = 9)

This is a skill that allows you to leap onto a target and then immediately attack. The Leap Attack is a very powerful attack because you cannot be hit *while* you're in the act of leaping. After adding just a few skill points, you can leap about 10 yards and increase the damage inflicted by nearly 200 percent. Many Blizzard employees use Leap Attack to jump in and out of melee fighting so as to avoid taking hits while still causing substantial damage.

This may be the Barbarian's best skill—use it for attacks or getting around!

Leap Attack is also useful because you can leap further at level 1 than with the standard Leap skill at the same level, and can use it to leap from place to place, regardless of the presence of enemies. For example, there are enemies in the Arcane Sanctuary on nearby platforms that attack you. In this case, you can simply Leap Attack over and take out the enemies rather than looking for the proper teleporter usually required to transport you to the action.

ATTACK RADIUS (YARDS)

LEVEL 1	LEVEL 2	LEVEL 3	LEVEL 4	LEVEL 5	LEVEL 6	LEVEL 7	LEVEL 8	LEVEL 9	LEVEL 10
4.6	7.3	8.6	10	11.3	12.	12.6	13.3	14	14

LEVEL 11	LEVEL 12	LEVEL 13	LEVEL 14	LEVEL 15	LEVEL 16	LEVEL 17	LEVEL 18	LEVEL 19	LEVEL 20
14.6	14.6	15.3	16	16	16	16.6	16.6	16.6	16.6

ATTACK DAMAGE MODIFIER (+%)

LEVEL 1	LEVEL 2	LEVEL 3	LEVEL 4	LEVEL 5	LEVEL 6	LEVEL 7	LEVEL 8	LEVEL 9	LEVEL 10
100	130	160	190	220	250	280	310	340	370

LEVEL 11	LEVEL 12	LEVEL 13	LEVEL 14	LEVEL 15	LEVEL 16	LEVEL 17	LEVEL 18	LEVEL 19	LEVEL 20
400	430	460	490	520	550	580	610	640	670

CONCENTRATE (LEVEL 18; MANA COST = 2)

With this skill, your attack can be uninterrupted, which for the Barbarian can be critical. When surrounded by enemies, having your attack interrupted by being hit is a common occurrence. However, when using Concentrate, your attack will finish regardless of any damage you take.

Concentrate is also a handy skill because it improves your attack and defense rating while you're attacking the enemy. It's nice to have at least one point in this skill just in case you get surrounded by a pack of creatures.

DEFENSE MODIFIER (+%)

LEVEL 1	LEVEL 2	LEVEL 3	LEVEL 4	LEVEL 5	LEVEL 6	LEVEL 7	LEVEL 8	LEVEL 9	LEVEL 10
20	30	40	50	60	70	80	90	100	110

LEVEL 11	LEVEL 12	LEVEL 13	LEVEL 14	LEVEL 15	LEVEL 16	LEVEL 17	LEVEL 18	LEVEL 19	LEVEL 20
120	130	140	150	160	170	180	190	200	210

ATTACK MODIFIER (+%)

LEVEL 1	LEVEL 2	LEVEL 3	LEVEL 4	LEVEL 5	LEVEL 6	LEVEL 7	LEVEL 8	LEVEL 9	LEVEL 10
25	30	35	40	45	50	55	60	65	70

LEVEL 11	LEVEL 12	LEVEL 13	LEVEL 14	LEVEL 15	LEVEL 16	LEVEL 17	LEVEL 18	LEVEL 19	LEVEL 20
75	80	85	90	95	100	105	110	115	120

FRENZY (LEVEL 24; MANA COST = 2)

When this skill is invoked, a successful hit increases the attack speed and velocity fo each successive hit. After placing a few points into this skill, the duration of action long enough that you can deliver many consecutive, faster, and more powerful hi because Frenzy also increases your attack rating.

This skill is considerably more powerful after adding six or seven skill points into it, b even then it's most effective against enemies that require several hits to kill. For exampl if you use Frenzy on an enemy that requires only one or two hits to kill, then the cumu lative effects of Frenzy will be lost. Therefore, Frenzy is best used against tougher enemie that require many hits to take down and is not as useful against run-of-the-mill fodder.

DURATION (SECONDS)

LEVEL 1	LEVEL 2	LEVEL 3	LEVEL 4	LEVEL 5	LEVEL 6	LEVEL 7	LEVEL 8	LEVEL 9	LEVEL 10
2	3	4	5	6	7	8	9	10	11

LEVEL 11	LEVEL 12	LEVEL 13	LEVEL 14	LEVEL 15	LEVEL 16	LEVEL 17	LEVEL 18	LEVEL 19	LEVEL 20
12	13	14	15	16	17	18	19	20	21

ATTACK MODIFIER (+%)

LEVEL 1	LEVEL 2	LEVEL 3	LEVEL 4	LEVEL 5	LEVEL 6	LEVEL 7	LEVEL 8	LEVEL 9	LEVEL 10
10	20	30	40	50	60	70	80	90	100

LEVEL 11	LEVEL 12	LEVEL 13	LEVEL 14	LEVEL 15	LEVEL 16	LEVEL 17	LEVEL 18	LEVEL 19	LEVEL 20
110	120	130	140	150	160	170	180	190	200

WHIRLWIND (LEVEL 30)

As the folks at Blizzard like to say, "Think Tasmanian Devil." With this skill, your Barbarian's weapons actually go into a 'whirlwind' and hack away at anything in the path. It's important to note that in the first few levels it actually penalizes you by decreasing the damage it causes. However, after you get past Level 4, Whirlwind not only increases the damage you inflict (substantially), but it also increases the attack rating as well.

Whirlwind is a skill that's been likened to watching the Tasmanian Devil of cartoon fame.

great tactic for Whirlwind is to click on an area behind a group of enemies and have our Barbarian clear a path as he chops them into little pieces.

MANA COST

LEVEL 1	LEVEL 2	LEVEL 3	LEVEL 4	LEVEL 5	LEVEL 6	LEVEL 7	LEVEL 8	LEVEL 9	LEVEL 10
25	27	29	31	33	35	37	39	41	43
LEVEL 11	LEVEL 12	LEVEL 13	LEVEL 14	LEVEL 15	LEVEL 16	LEVEL 17	LEVEL 18	LEVEL 19	LEVEL 20
45	47	49	51	53	55	57	59	61	63

DAMAGE MODIFIER (%)

LEVEL 1	LEVEL 2	LEVEL 3	LEVEL 4	LEVEL 5	LEVEL 6	LEVEL 7	LEVEL 8	LEVEL 9	LEVEL 10
-50	-35	-20	-5	+10	+25	+40	+55	+70	+85
LEVEL 11	LEVEL 12	LEVEL 13	LEVEL 14	LEVEL 15	LEVEL 16	LEVEL 17	LEVEL 18	LEVEL 19	LEVEL 20
+100	+115	+130	+145	+160	+175	+190	+205	+220	+235

ATTACK MODIFIER (+%)

LEVEL 1	LEVEL 2	LEVEL 3	LEVEL 4	LEVEL 5	LEVEL 6	LEVEL 7	LEVEL 8	LEVEL 9	LEVEL 10
25	30	35	40	45	50	55	60	65	70
LEVEL 11	LEVEL 12	LEVEL 13	LEVEL 14	LEVEL 15	LEVEL 16	LEVEL 17	LEVEL 18	LEVEL 19	LEVEL 20
75	80	85	90	95	100	105	110	115	120

BERSERK (LEVEL 30; MANA COST = 5)

his is a powerful skill that makes your Barbarian go berserk. You attack with a greater ttack rating and a greater magical damage rating. You must remember that when you ut points into this skill and receive the huge attack bonuses, its duration actually goes *own* rather than up. This is because the effect of the skill is so great that any duration onger than 1.5 seconds at higher levels would make the skill too powerful.

ATTACK MODIFIER (+%)

LEVEL 1	LEVEL 2	LEVEL 3	LEVEL 4	LEVEL 5	LEVEL 6	LEVEL 7	LEVEL 8	LEVEL 9	LEVEL 10
56	72	88	104	120	136	152	168	184	200
LEVEL 11	LEVEL 12	LEVEL 13	LEVEL 14	LEVEL 15	LEVEL 16	LEVEL 17	LEVEL 18	LEVEL 19	LEVEL 20
216	232	248	264	280	296	312	328	344	360

MAGIC DAMAGE (+%)

LEVEL 1	LEVEL 2	LEVEL 3	LEVEL 4	LEVEL 5	LEVEL 6	LEVEL 7	LEVEL 8	LEVEL 9	LEVEL 10
56	66	76	86	96	106	116	126	136	146
LEVEL 11	LEVEL 12	LEVEL 13	LEVEL 14	LEVEL 15	LEVEL 16	LEVEL 17	LEVEL 18	LEVEL 19	LEVEL 20
156	166	176	186	196	206	216	226	236	246

DURATION (SECONDS)

LEVEL 1	LEVEL 2	LEVEL 3	LEVEL 4	LEVEL 5	LEVEL 6	LEVEL 7	LEVEL 8	LEVEL 9	LEVEL 10
2.7	2.4	2.2	2.1	2.0	1.9	1.8	1.7	1.6	1.6
LEVEL 11	LEVEL 12	LEVEL 13	LEVEL 14	LEVEL 15	LEVEL 16	LEVEL 17	LEVEL 18	LEVEL 19	LEVEL 20
1.6	1.5	1.5	1.4	1.4	1.4	1.4	1.3	1.3	1.3

COMBAT MASTERIES

A Barbarian who's mastered the six arts (mace, axe, sword, pole arm, throwing, an spear) is be a force to be reckoned with. Unfortunately, putting many points into all the Masteries is not feasible, so the best thing to do is choose a Mastery and run wit it. Oftentimes, gamers will wait and hold onto skill points until they pick up a weapo that they like, and then put the skill points into the area that matches that weapon

MASTERIES (ALL AVAILABLE AT LEVEL 1)

TIP..........

Derek Simmons, Senior QA Analyst at Blizzard, suggests that you save skill points that you have earmarked for Masteries until you find a weapon that you'll want to keep and use throughout the game. Usually around Act II, you will have found a few desirable weapons, and one is probably a favorite. When you've decided on the class of weapon you are going to keep, you can put your points into that Mastery so that you can best use the great weapon you've found!

This set of skills adds to the damage inflicted by the class of weapons that you've pu the skill points into. The masteries include Sword, Axe, Mace, Pole Arm, Throwing, an Spear. When points are added to these skills, the damage inflicted by the improve weapon class increases dramatically. For example, if you want to use swords throug out the game, then Sword Mastery is the skill to put your skill points into.

The player that puts points into the Masteries will always be more successful than th player that puts their points into other Barbarian skills exclusively. The reason wh Masteries are so powerful is that they dramatically improve the performance of group of weapons. Therefore, no matter which weapon in that class you're using, you'll alway have the benefit of the Mastery.

If a Barbarian invests heavily in Axe Mastery, the benefits of the Mastery will always b there, no matter which axe he uses as he passes through the game. No casting required to utilize Masteries. You only need the kind of weapon that will benefit fro the Mastery into which you've put your points.

SWORD MASTERY DAMAGE MODIFIER (+%)

LEVEL 1	LEVEL 2	LEVEL 3	LEVEL 4	LEVEL 5	LEVEL 6	LEVEL 7	LEVEL 8	LEVEL 9	LEVEL 10
28	33	38	43	48	53	58	63	68	73
LEVEL 11	LEVEL 12	LEVEL 13	LEVEL 14	LEVEL 15	LEVEL 16	LEVEL 17	LEVEL 18	LEVEL 19	LEVEL 20
78	83	88	93	98	103	108	113	118	123

SWORD MASTERY ATTACK MODIFIER (+%)

LEVEL 1	LEVEL 2	LEVEL 3	LEVEL 4	LEVEL 5	LEVEL 6	LEVEL 7	LEVEL 8	LEVEL 9	LEVEL 10
28	36	44	52	60	68	76	84	92	100
LEVEL 11	LEVEL 12	LEVEL 13	LEVEL 14	LEVEL 15	LEVEL 16	LEVEL 17	LEVEL 18	LEVEL 19	LEVEL 20
108	116	124	132	140	148	156	164	172	180

AXE MASTERY DAMAGE MODIFIER (+%)

LEVEL 1	LEVEL 2	LEVEL 3	LEVEL 4	LEVEL 5	LEVEL 6	LEVEL 7	LEVEL 8	LEVEL 9	LEVEL 10
28	33	38	43	48	53	58	63	68	73
LEVEL 11	LEVEL 12	LEVEL 13	LEVEL 14	LEVEL 15	LEVEL 16	LEVEL 17	LEVEL 18	LEVEL 19	LEVEL 20
78	83	88	93	98	103	108	113	118	123

AXE MASTERY ATTACK MODIFIER (+%)

LEVEL 1	LEVEL 2	LEVEL 3	LEVEL 4	LEVEL 5	LEVEL 6	LEVEL 7	LEVEL 8	LEVEL 9	LEVEL 10
28	36	44	52	60	68	76	84	92	100
LEVEL 11	LEVEL 12	LEVEL 13	LEVEL 14	LEVEL 15	LEVEL 16	LEVEL 17	LEVEL 18	LEVEL 19	LEVEL 20
108	116	124	132	140	148	156	164	172	180

MACE MASTERY DAMAGE MODIFIER (+%)

LEVEL 1	LEVEL 2	LEVEL 3	LEVEL 4	LEVEL 5	LEVEL 6	LEVEL 7	LEVEL 8	LEVEL 9	LEVEL 10
28	36	44	52	60	68	76	84	92	100
LEVEL 11	LEVEL 12	LEVEL 13	LEVEL 14	LEVEL 15	LEVEL 16	LEVEL 17	LEVEL 18	LEVEL 19	LEVEL 20
108	116	124	132	140	148	156	164	172	180

MACE MASTERY ATTACK MODIFIER (+%)

LEVEL 1	LEVEL 2	LEVEL 3	LEVEL 4	LEVEL 5	LEVEL 6	LEVEL 7	LEVEL 8	LEVEL 9	LEVEL 10
28	36	44	52	60	68	76	84	92	100
LEVEL 11	LEVEL 12	LEVEL 13	LEVEL 14	LEVEL 15	LEVEL 16	LEVEL 17	LEVEL 18	LEVEL 19	LEVEL 20
108	116	124	132	140	148	156	164	172	180

SPEAR MASTERY DAMAGE MODIFIER (+%)

LEVEL 1	LEVEL 2	LEVEL 3	LEVEL 4	LEVEL 5	LEVEL 6	LEVEL 7	LEVEL 8	LEVEL 9	LEVEL 10
30	35	40	45	50	55	60	65	70	75
LEVEL 11	LEVEL 12	LEVEL 13	LEVEL 14	LEVEL 15	LEVEL 16	LEVEL 17	LEVEL 18	LEVEL 19	LEVEL 20
80	85	90	95	100	105	110	115	120	125

SPEAR MASTERY ATTACK MODIFIER (+%)

LEVEL 1	LEVEL 2	LEVEL 3	LEVEL 4	LEVEL 5	LEVEL 6	LEVEL 7	LEVEL 8	LEVEL 9	LEVEL 10
30	38	46	54	62	70	78	86	94	102
LEVEL 11	LEVEL 12	LEVEL 13	LEVEL 14	LEVEL 15	LEVEL 16	LEVEL 17	LEVEL 18	LEVEL 19	LEVEL 20
110	118	126	134	142	150	158	166	174	182

THROWING MASTERY DAMAGE MOD. (+%)

LEVEL 1	LEVEL 2	LEVEL 3	LEVEL 4	LEVEL 5	LEVEL 6	LEVEL 7	LEVEL 8	LEVEL 9	LEVEL 10
30	35	40	45	50	55	60	65	70	75
LEVEL 11	LEVEL 12	LEVEL 13	LEVEL 14	LEVEL 15	LEVEL 16	LEVEL 17	LEVEL 18	LEVEL 19	LEVEL 20
80	85	90	95	100	105	110	115	120	125

THROWING MASTERY ATTACK MOD. (+%)

LEVEL 1	LEVEL 2	LEVEL 3	LEVEL 4	LEVEL 5	LEVEL 6	LEVEL 7	LEVEL 8	LEVEL 9	LEVEL 10
30	38	46	54	62	70	78	86	94	102
LEVEL 11	LEVEL 12	LEVEL 13	LEVEL 14	LEVEL 15	LEVEL 16	LEVEL 17	LEVEL 18	LEVEL 19	LEVEL 20
110	118	126	134	142	150	158	166	174	182

POLEARM MASTERY DAMAGE MOD. (+%)

LEVEL 1	LEVEL 2	LEVEL 3	LEVEL 4	LEVEL 5	LEVEL 6	LEVEL 7	LEVEL 8	LEVEL 9	LEVEL 10
30	35	40	45	50	55	60	65	70	75
LEVEL 11	LEVEL 12	LEVEL 13	LEVEL 14	LEVEL 15	LEVEL 16	LEVEL 17	LEVEL 18	LEVEL 19	LEVEL 20
80	85	90	95	100	105	110	115	120	125

POLEARM MASTERY ATTACK MODIFIER (+%)									
LEVEL 1	LEVEL 2	LEVEL 3	LEVEL 4	LEVEL 5	LEVEL 6	LEVEL 7	LEVEL 8	LEVEL 9	LEVEL 10
30	38	46	54	62	70	78	86	94	102
LEVEL 11	LEVEL 12	LEVEL 13	LEVEL 14	LEVEL 15	LEVEL 16	LEVEL 17	LEVEL 18	LEVEL 19	LEVEL 20
110	118	126	134	142	150	158	166	174	182

INCREASED STAMINA (LEVEL 12)

While this skill simply improves your stamina, just a few skill points gives you a stamina bonus of 60 percent! The catch is whether or not you're the kind of player that need
to have increased stamina. For example, if you rarely run, then there isn't much need
put skill points into this skill. Likewise, if you occasionally run but often find yourse
with Stamina Potions that you don't use, then it's probably not a good idea to waste
point in Increased Stamina.

However, if you constantly run to move, attack, or get away from the enemy, then ha
ing a higher level of Stamina will be important to you. Obviously, you'll want to inve
a skill point or two into Increased Stamina to lower your dependence on resting or co
lecting and drinking Stamina Potions.

BONUS (%)									
LEVEL 1	LEVEL 2	LEVEL 3	LEVEL 4	LEVEL 5	LEVEL 6	LEVEL 7	LEVEL 8	LEVEL 9	LEVEL 10
30	45	60	75	90	105	120	135	150	165
LEVEL 11	LEVEL 12	LEVEL 13	LEVEL 14	LEVEL 15	LEVEL 16	LEVEL 17	LEVEL 18	LEVEL 19	LEVEL 20
180	195	210	225	240	255	270	285	300	315

IRON SKIN (LEVEL 18)

Iron Skin is a skill that improves your overall defense rating. With a few points adde
to it, this skill becomes very powerful because the Barbarian often has a high defen:
rating since his strength allows him to wear massive armor.

Iron Skin modifies the defense rating by a percentage. So, if you put in eight skill point
your Barbarian's defense rating will double, which is an impressive boost to a ve
important statistic. For example, if your Barbarian has a defense rating of 200, ar
you've put eight skill points into Iron Skin, then your Barbarian will have a defense ra
ing of 400.

DEFENSE RATING BOOST (%)									
LEVEL 1	LEVEL 2	LEVEL 3	LEVEL 4	LEVEL 5	LEVEL 6	LEVEL 7	LEVEL 8	LEVEL 9	LEVEL 10
30	40	50	60	70	80	90	100	110	120
LEVEL 11	LEVEL 12	LEVEL 13	LEVEL 14	LEVEL 15	LEVEL 16	LEVEL 17	LEVEL 18	LEVEL 19	LEVEL 20
130	140	150	160	170	180	190	200	210	220

INCREASED SPEED (LEVEL 24)

his skill increases the speed at which the Barbarian walks
nd runs. Having the ability to walk and run faster has
ajor implications in *Diablo II*. If you can walk faster, then
ou don't have to rely on Run to escape from certain ene-
nies, thus sparing your Stamina. Likewise, if you can run
aster, you can escape from fast enemies that you would
ot have been able to previously elude. Even in the first
ouple of levels, it's well worth adding a point or two into
nis skill.

Having increased speed can make running away from, or catching up to, enemies much easier.

WALK/RUN SPEED BONUS (%)

LEVEL 1	LEVEL 2	LEVEL 3	LEVEL 4	LEVEL 5	LEVEL 6	LEVEL 7	LEVEL 8	LEVEL 9	LEVEL 10
13	18	22	25	28	30	32	33	35	36

LEVEL 11	LEVEL 12	LEVEL 13	LEVEL 14	LEVEL 15	LEVEL 16	LEVEL 17	LEVEL 18	LEVEL 19	LEVEL 20
37	38	39	40	40	41	41	42	42	43

NATURAL RESISTANCE (LEVEL 30)

n the higher levels of *Diablo II*, one of the main dangers to your character comes from
nagical attacks (fire, cold, poison, and electrical). Natural Resistance is a skill that
ncreases your resistance to these attacks, thus making your Barbarian considerably
ess vulnerable at higher levels.

he benefit you receive from putting skill points into this skill may seem small; howev-
r, even a 12 percent protection from a magical attack can mean the difference between
fe and death.

ALL RESISTANCES (+%)

LEVEL 1	LEVEL 2	LEVEL 3	LEVEL 4	LEVEL 5	LEVEL 6	LEVEL 7	LEVEL 8	LEVEL 9	LEVEL 10
12	21	28	35	40	44	47	49	52	54

LEVEL 11	LEVEL 12	LEVEL 13	LEVEL 14	LEVEL 15	LEVEL 16	LEVEL 17	LEVEL 18	LEVEL 19	LEVEL 20
56	58	60	61	62	64	64	65	66	67

VARCRIES

he skills in this area are great tools for the Barbarian at any time. However, many of
nem, like Taunt and Battle Command, really shine when used in a multiplayer team
ituation.

Battle Command, for example, gives each party member who's close to you an extr[a] skill point in every skill they have for a brief period of time. The first skill in this set [is] Howl, which forces the enemies to run away from your position. This skill is hand[y] whether you're in the Blood Moor of Act I or the deepest recesses of Hell.

HOWL (LEVEL 1; MANA COST = 4)

Howl is a very handy skill that will send your enemies running!

TIP..........

You can use Howl to make a group of enemies more manageable. For example, if a pack of monsters runs at you, you can invoke Howl and send the first row of enemies away, leaving only those that weren't affected by Howl to fight you. This can reduce the number of enemies you must face at once, thus making your task easier.

This skill frightens monsters into retreating from your position. Howl works within a specific radius around your character which you can see when Howl is used. Upon using this skill, enemies will run for a set distance or a set amount of time, depending on how many skill points have been put into Howl. This skill works just as well in Act IV as it does in Act I, so it's valuable to use at any time during the game.

ENEMY RUNS (YARDS)

LEVEL 1	LEVEL 2	LEVEL 3	LEVEL 4	LEVEL 5	LEVEL 6	LEVEL 7	LEVEL 8	LEVEL 9	LEVEL 10
16	19.3	22.6	26	29.3	32.6	36	39.3	42.6	46

LEVEL 11	LEVEL 12	LEVEL 13	LEVEL 14	LEVEL 15	LEVEL 16	LEVEL 17	LEVEL 18	LEVEL 19	LEVEL 20
49.3	52.6	56	59.3	62.6	66	69.3	72.6	76	79.3

ENEMY RUNS (SECONDS)

LEVEL 1	LEVEL 2	LEVEL 3	LEVEL 4	LEVEL 5	LEVEL 6	LEVEL 7	LEVEL 8	LEVEL 9	LEVEL 10
3	4	5	6	7	8	9	10	11	12

LEVEL 11	LEVEL 12	LEVEL 13	LEVEL 14	LEVEL 15	LEVEL 16	LEVEL 17	LEVEL 18	LEVEL 19	LEVEL 20
13	14	15	16	17	18	19	20	21	22

FIND POTION (LEVEL 1; MANA COST = 2)

With this skill, there's a chance that you may find a potion on a dead body. The potio[n] you find is generated randomly, but the most common potions are Health Potions [or] Mana Potions.

As a rule, this skill doesn't need more than one or two skill points added to it. Even wit[h] a 15 percent chance of getting a Health Potion, this usually creates enough potions th[at] your Barbarian won't have to worry about buying potions in town. This is a great skill f[or] multiplayer action as well, because you can search the bodies of the dead and turn u[p] Health Potions for your party members that may be in need of healing.

CHANCE TO FIND (%)

LEVEL 1	LEVEL 2	LEVEL 3	LEVEL 4	LEVEL 5	LEVEL 6	LEVEL 7	LEVEL 8	LEVEL 9	LEVEL 10
15	27	36	44	50	55	59	62	66	68

LEVEL 11	LEVEL 12	LEVEL 13	LEVEL 14	LEVEL 15	LEVEL 16	LEVEL 17	LEVEL 18	LEVEL 19	LEVEL 20
71	73	75	77	78	80	81	82	83	84

⚔ TAUNT (LEVEL 6; MANA COST = 3)

This skill taunts a monster to approach and fight. Although this may not seem like a skill you'd use often (because enemies come to you anyway), there are uses for this skill that will help your Barbarian in single and multiplayer mode.

In single-player combat, you can use Taunt to bring ranged-weapon enemies directly to you rather than having to run them down yourself. Also, you can bring enemies out of a room where they may be lurking (for example, when you want to pull minions away from their controller, such as the Countess in the Tower). Lastly, you can use Taunt in multiplayer mode to pull an enemy off a party member that's taking a beating, thus sparing them from death in certain situations.

TARGET'S DAMAGE (-%)

LEVEL 1	LEVEL 2	LEVEL 3	LEVEL 4	LEVEL 5	LEVEL 6	LEVEL 7	LEVEL 8	LEVEL 9	LEVEL 10
5	7	9	11	13	15	17	19	21	23
LEVEL 11	LEVEL 12	LEVEL 13	LEVEL 14	LEVEL 15	LEVEL 16	LEVEL 17	LEVEL 18	LEVEL 19	LEVEL 20
25	27	29	31	33	35	37	39	41	43

TARGET'S ACCURACY RATING (-%)

LEVEL 1	LEVEL 2	LEVEL 3	LEVEL 4	LEVEL 5	LEVEL 6	LEVEL 7	LEVEL 8	LEVEL 9	LEVEL 10
5	7	9	11	13	15	17	19	21	23
LEVEL 11	LEVEL 12	LEVEL 13	LEVEL 14	LEVEL 15	LEVEL 16	LEVEL 17	LEVEL 18	LEVEL 19	LEVEL 20
25	27	29	31	33	35	37	39	41	43

> **NOTE......**
>
> It should be noted that Taunt also decreases the attack and defense rating of the enemy, so it has value beyond simply drawing enemies toward you.

⚔ SHOUT (LEVEL 6; MANA COST = 6)

Shout is a skill that dramatically increases the defense rating of your Barbarian and any allies. Even a level 1 Shout skill adds 100 to your defense bonus for 16 seconds. When playing multiplayer, this skill will attach to any ally that's close enough to you, so they will also enjoy the greatly enhanced defense rating. This skill is excellent to use just before you move into a heavy melee battle.

DEFENSE BONUS (%)

LEVEL 1	LEVEL 2	LEVEL 3	LEVEL 4	LEVEL 5	LEVEL 6	LEVEL 7	LEVEL 8	LEVEL 9	LEVEL 10
100	110	120	130	140	150	160	170	180	190
LEVEL 11	LEVEL 12	LEVEL 13	LEVEL 14	LEVEL 15	LEVEL 16	LEVEL 17	LEVEL 18	LEVEL 19	LEVEL 20
200	210	220	230	240	250	260	270	280	290

DURATION (SECONDS)

LEVEL 1	LEVEL 2	LEVEL 3	LEVEL 4	LEVEL 5	LEVEL 6	LEVEL 7	LEVEL 8	LEVEL 9	LEVEL 10
16	18	20	22	24	26	28	30	32	34
LEVEL 11	LEVEL 12	LEVEL 13	LEVEL 14	LEVEL 15	LEVEL 16	LEVEL 17	LEVEL 18	LEVEL 19	LEVEL 20
36	38	40	42	44	46	48	50	52	54

🅰 FIND ITEM (LEVEL 12; MANA COST = 7)

Like Find Potion, this skill increases the chance to find an item. The item you find randomly generated, but it could range from gold to weapons and everything in between.

Using Find Item is a great way to gain wealth for the Barbarian. Simply use Find Item to scour every corpse you come across, and then sell the results of your searches in town.

CHANCE TO FIND (%)									
LEVEL 1	LEVEL 2	LEVEL 3	LEVEL 4	LEVEL 5	LEVEL 6	LEVEL 7	LEVEL 8	LEVEL 9	LEVEL 10
19	21	26	31	35	38	40	42	44	45
LEVEL 11	LEVEL 12	LEVEL 13	LEVEL 14	LEVEL 15	LEVEL 16	LEVEL 17	LEVEL 18	LEVEL 19	LEVEL 20
47	48	50	51	51	53	53	54	54	55

🪓 BATTLECRY (LEVEL 18; MANA COST = 4)

Battlecry reduces the defense rating of enemies within the radius of effect of this skill. The result is a dramatic reduction in the enemy's ability to cause damage and defend itself; and an enemy that can't defend itself or fight back well is exactly what you want in melee combat.

This skill is best used when fighting in tight quarters or against several enemies that are in close proximity. The duration of this skill is the most important part of Battlecry especially when you're facing tough monsters that may take more than a minute to kill. To increase the duration of this skill, just add more skill points.

DURATION (SECONDS)									
LEVEL 1	LEVEL 2	LEVEL 3	LEVEL 4	LEVEL 5	LEVEL 6	LEVEL 7	LEVEL 8	LEVEL 9	LEVEL 10
12	14.4	16.8	19.2	21.6	24	26.4	28.8	31.2	33.6
LEVEL 11	LEVEL 12	LEVEL 13	LEVEL 14	LEVEL 15	LEVEL 16	LEVEL 17	LEVEL 18	LEVEL 19	LEVEL 20
36	38.4	40.8	43.2	45.6	48	50.4	52.8	55.2	57.6

DEFENSE MODIFIER (-%)									
LEVEL 1	LEVEL 2	LEVEL 3	LEVEL 4	LEVEL 5	LEVEL 6	LEVEL 7	LEVEL 8	LEVEL 9	LEVEL 10
50	52	54	56	58	60	62	64	66	68
LEVEL 11	LEVEL 12	LEVEL 13	LEVEL 14	LEVEL 15	LEVEL 16	LEVEL 17	LEVEL 18	LEVEL 19	LEVEL 20
70	72	74	76	78	80	82	84	86	88

DAMAGE MODIFIER (-%)									
LEVEL 1	LEVEL 2	LEVEL 3	LEVEL 4	LEVEL 5	LEVEL 6	LEVEL 7	LEVEL 8	LEVEL 9	LEVEL 10
25	26	27	28	29	30	31	32	33	34
LEVEL 11	LEVEL 12	LEVEL 13	LEVEL 14	LEVEL 15	LEVEL 16	LEVEL 17	LEVEL 18	LEVEL 19	LEVEL 20
35	36	37	38	39	40	41	42	43	44

BATTLE ORDERS (LEVEL 24; MANA COST = 7)

This skill is especially powerful in multiplayer situations because it gives you *and* your party boosts in Life, Stamina, and mana for a relatively small mana cost. The downside to Battle Orders is that it costs one-third of your hit points to invoke! You should use Battle Orders only when it can benefit your party in multiplayer, or when you have a life-stealing piece of equipment that will compensate for the lost you as you attack.

Since the Barbarian can use Find Potion to scrounge up healing potions, you may want to use the extra potions you find to counteract the life lost when you use this skill. On the upside, the benefits this skill bestows on you and your party are very worthwhile, and the more points you put into this skill, the longer the effects will last.

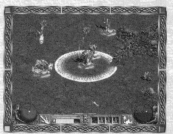

Battle Orders boosts several categories of stats for you and your nearby party members.

DURATION (SECONDS)

LEVEL 1	LEVEL 2	LEVEL 3	LEVEL 4	LEVEL 5	LEVEL 6	LEVEL 7	LEVEL 8	LEVEL 9	LEVEL 10
30	36	42	48	54	60	66	72	78	84

LEVEL 11	LEVEL 12	LEVEL 13	LEVEL 14	LEVEL 15	LEVEL 16	LEVEL 17	LEVEL 18	LEVEL 19	LEVEL 20
90	96	102	108	114	120	126	132	138	144

MAX. STAMINA/HIT POINTS/MANA (+%)

LEVEL 1	LEVEL 2	LEVEL 3	LEVEL 4	LEVEL 5	LEVEL 6	LEVEL 7	LEVEL 8	LEVEL 9	LEVEL 10
40	44	47	50	52	54	55	56	58	58

LEVEL 11	LEVEL 12	LEVEL 13	LEVEL 14	LEVEL 15	LEVEL 16	LEVEL 17	LEVEL 18	LEVEL 19	LEVEL 20
59	60	61	61	62	63	63	63	64	64

GRIM WARD (LEVEL 24; MANA COST = 4; DURATION = 40 SEC.)

This skill turns a fallen enemy into a gruesome totem that frightens away enemies and prevents them from coming near the area where the ward stands. When you use Grim Ward, the enemies will not pass the area near the ward until it disappears, thus giving you extra time to regroup or create a town portal. It is especially effective when you need to run from enemies and there are bodies in your path.

RADIUS

LEVEL 1	LEVEL 2	LEVEL 3	LEVEL 4	LEVEL 5	LEVEL 6	LEVEL 7	LEVEL 8	LEVEL 9	LEVEL 10
2	2.6	3.3	4	4.6	5.3	6	6.6	7.3	8

LEVEL 11	LEVEL 12	LEVEL 13	LEVEL 14	LEVEL 15	LEVEL 16	LEVEL 17	LEVEL 18	LEVEL 19	LEVEL 20
8.6	9.3	10	10.6	11.3	12	12.6	13.3	14	14.6

WARCRY (LEVEL 30)

This is a powerful and useful skill that damages and stuns nearby monsters. Th[e] amount of damage and the length of the stun effect is limited by the number of ski[ll] points in the skill. However, even at level 1, Warcry packs a substantial punch.

The stun effect from Warcry should provide ample time to prepare another attack whi[le] the enemy recovers from the effect. It costs between 17 and 36 mana points to ca[st] Warcry, but in the right situations it's a skill that's worth having. Use Warcry to slo[w] down the pace of a frenzied battle by stunning or killing all the enemies near you.

MANA COST

LEVEL 1	LEVEL 2	LEVEL 3	LEVEL 4	LEVEL 5	LEVEL 6	LEVEL 7	LEVEL 8	LEVEL 9	LEVEL 10
17	18	19	20	21	22	23	24	25	26
LEVEL 11	LEVEL 12	LEVEL 13	LEVEL 14	LEVEL 15	LEVEL 16	LEVEL 17	LEVEL 18	LEVEL 19	LEVEL 20
27	28	29	30	31	32	33	34	35	36

DAMAGE

LEVEL 1	LEVEL 2	LEVEL 3	LEVEL 4	LEVEL 5	LEVEL 6	LEVEL 7	LEVEL 8	LEVEL 9	LEVEL 10
15-20	20-25	25-30	30-35	35-40	40-45	45-50	50-55	55-60	60-65
LEVEL 11	LEVEL 12	LEVEL 13	LEVEL 14	LEVEL 15	LEVEL 16	LEVEL 17	LEVEL 18	LEVEL 19	LEVEL 20
65-70	70-75	75-80	80-85	85-90	90-95	95-100	100-105	105-110	110-115

STUN DURATION (SECONDS)

LEVEL 1	LEVEL 2	LEVEL 3	LEVEL 4	LEVEL 5	LEVEL 6	LEVEL 7	LEVEL 8	LEVEL 9	LEVEL 10
1	1.2	1.4	1.6	1.8	2	2.2	2.4	2.6	2.8
LEVEL 11	LEVEL 12	LEVEL 13	LEVEL 14	LEVEL 15	LEVEL 16	LEVEL 17	LEVEL 18	LEVEL 19	LEVEL 20
3	3.2	3.4	3.6	3.8	4	4.2	4.4	4.6	4.8

BATTLE COMMAND (LEVEL 30)

This is a very powerfu[l] and, important skill for use with a party in multiplayer game[s.] Battle Command increases *all* of your skills (and those of nearby allies) by one lev[el.] This means that each party member that was within the radius of your Battle Comma[nd] when it was cast has an additional level of each skill they have, regardless of the ty[pe] of character they are.

In a tough battle against formidable opponents, this skill can turn the tide in yo[ur] party's favor. As you add skill points to Battle Command, you receive only one benef[it] time. The more points you add, the longer the duration of this skill's effect. Having t[he] ability to fight for 30 seconds with a higher skill level for a party of six players amour[ts] to a huge advantage.

DURATION (SECONDS)

LEVEL 1	LEVEL 2	LEVEL 3	LEVEL 4	LEVEL 5	LEVEL 6	LEVEL 7	LEVEL 8	LEVEL 9	LEVEL 10
12	16	20	24	28	32	36	40	44	48
LEVEL 11	LEVEL 12	LEVEL 13	LEVEL 14	LEVEL 15	LEVEL 16	LEVEL 17	LEVEL 18	LEVEL 19	LEVEL 20
52	56	60	64	68	72	76	80	84	88

DIABLO II
COLOR GALLERY

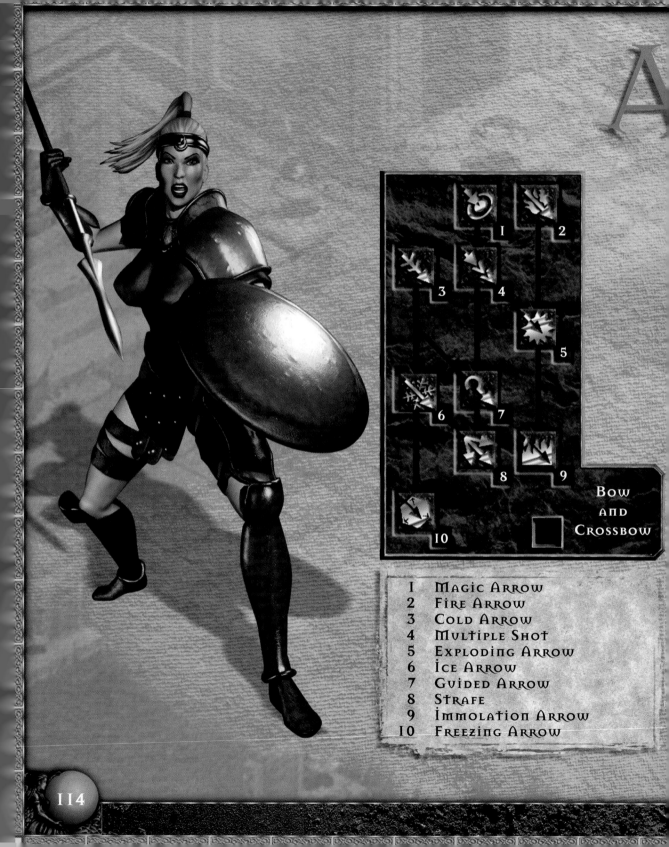

Bow
and
Crossbow

1	Magic Arrow
2	Fire Arrow
3	Cold Arrow
4	Multiple Shot
5	Exploding Arrow
6	Ice Arrow
7	Guided Arrow
8	Strafe
9	Immolation Arrow
10	Freezing Arrow

nAZON

Passive
and
Magic

Javelin
and
Spear

1	Inner Sight
2	Critical Strike
3	Dodge
4	Slow Missiles
5	Avoid
6	Penetrate
7	Decoy
8	Evade
9	Valkyrie
10	Pierce

1	Jab
2	Power Strike
3	Poison Javelin
4	Impale
5	Lightning Bolt
6	Charged Strike
7	Plague Javelin
8	Fend
9	Lightning Strike
10	Lightning Fury

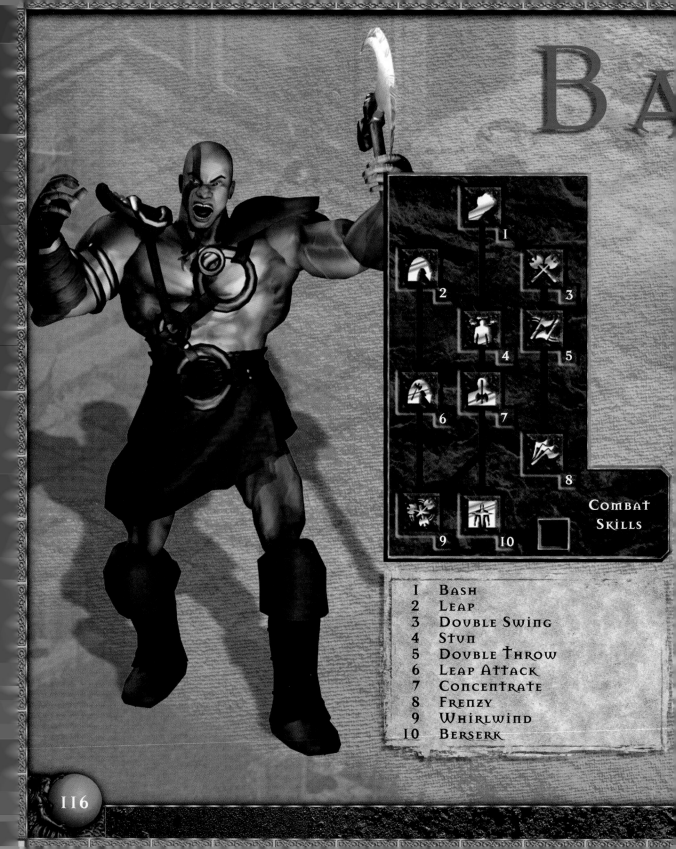

BA

COMBAT SKILLS

1   BASH
2   LEAP
3   DOUBLE SWING
4   STUN
5   DOUBLE THROW
6   LEAP ATTACK
7   CONCENTRATE
8   FRENZY
9   WHIRLWIND
10 BERSERK

Combat Masteries

Warcries

1 Sword Mastery	1 Howl
2 Axe Mastery	2 Find Potion
3 Mace Mastery	3 Taunt
4 Pole Arm Mastery	4 Shout
5 Throwing Mastery	5 Find Item
6 Spear Mastery	6 Battlecry
7 Increased Stamina	7 Battle Orders
8 Iron Skin	8 Grim Ward
9 Increased Speed	9 Warcry
10 Natural Resistance	10 Battle Command

CURSES

1 AMPLIFY DAMAGE
2 DIM VISION
3 WEAKEN
4 IRON MAIDEN
5 TERROR
6 CONFUSE
7 LIFE TAP
8 ATTRACT
9 DECREPIFY
10 LOWER RESIST

Poison
and
Bone

Summoning
and
Control

I	Teeth
2	Bone Armor
3	Poison Dagger
4	Corpse Explosion
5	Bone Wall
6	Poison Explosion
7	Bone Spear
8	Bone Prison
9	Poison Nova
10	Bone Spirit

I	Skeleton Mastery
2	Raise Skeleton
3	Clay Golem
4	Golem Mastery
5	Raise Skeletal Mage
6	Blood Golem
7	Summon Resist
8	Iron Golem
9	Fire Golem
10	Revive

PA

COMBAT

1   Sacrifice
2   Smite
3   Holy Bolt
4   Zeal
5   Charge
6   Vengeance
7   Blessed Hammer
8   Conversion
9   Holy Shield
10 Fist of the Heavens

Offensive
Auras

Defensive
Auras

1 Might	1 Prayer
2 Holy Fire	2 Resist Fire
3 Thorns	3 Defiance
4 Blessed Aim	4 Resist Cold
5 Concentration	5 Cleansing
6 Holy Freeze	6 Resist Lightning
7 Holy Shock	7 Vigor
8 Sanctuary	8 Meditation
9 Fanaticism	9 Redemption
10 Conviction	10 Salvation

FIRE

1	FIRE BOLT
2	WARMTH
3	INFERNO
4	BLAZE
5	FIRE BALL
6	FIRE WALL
7	ENCHANT
8	METEOR
9	FIRE MASTERY
10	HYDRA

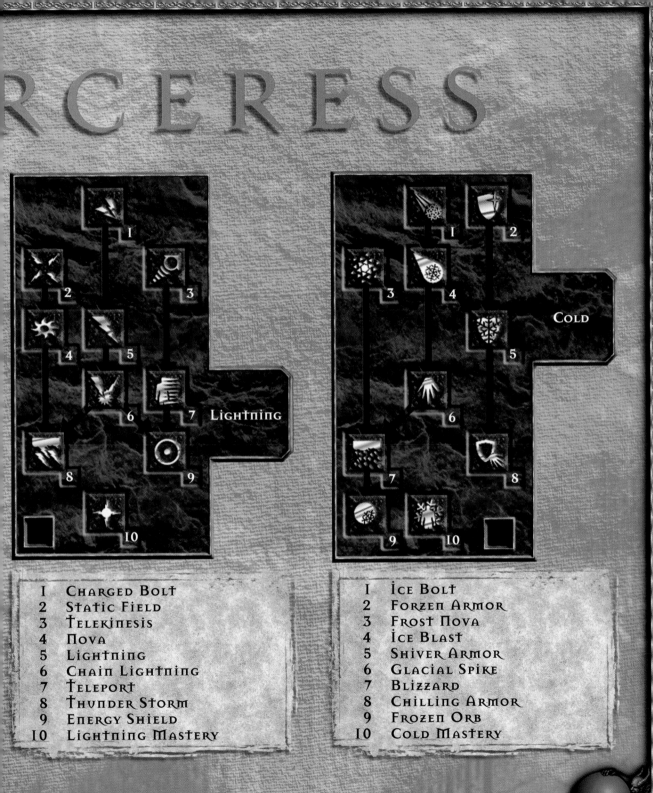

Lightning

COLD

I	CHARGED BOLT
2	STATIC FIELD
3	TELEKINESIS
4	NOVA
5	LIGHTNING
6	CHAIN LIGHTNING
7	TELEPORT
8	THUNDER STORM
9	ENERGY SHIELD
10	LIGHTNING MASTERY

I	ICE BOLT
2	FORZEN ARMOR
3	FROST NOVA
4	ICE BLAST
5	SHIVER ARMOR
6	GLACIAL SPIKE
7	BLIZZARD
8	CHILLING ARMOR
9	FROZEN ORB
10	COLD MASTERY

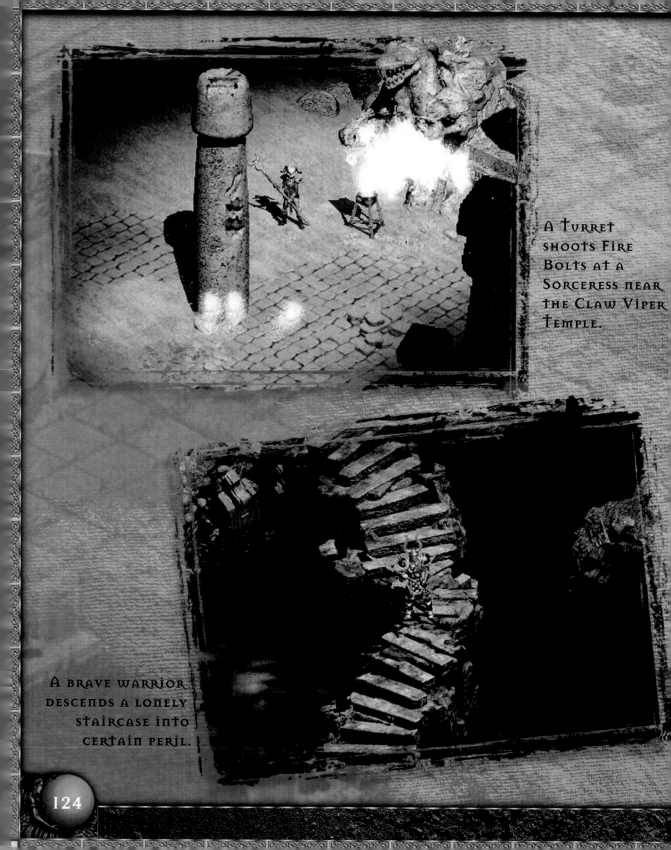

A Turret shoots Fire Bolts at a Sorceress near the Claw Viper Temple.

A brave warrior descends a lonely staircase into certain peril.

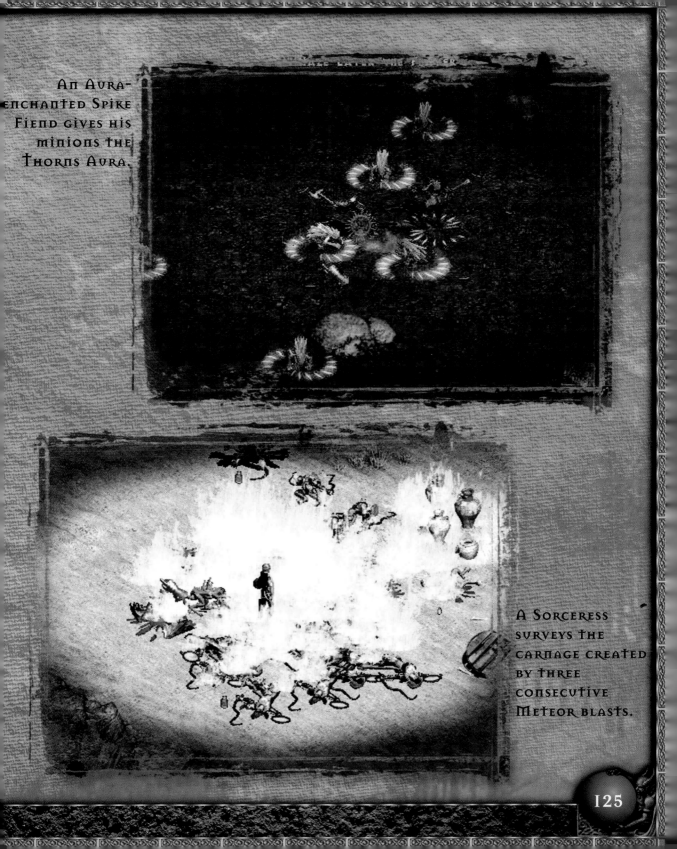

An Aura-enchanted Spike Fiend gives his minions the Thorns Aura.

A Sorceress surveys the carnage created by three consecutive Meteor blasts.

One of the seals (that helps to bring Diablo) is opened in the final area.

Two awesome spells (Meteor and Blizzard) rain down from the sky at the same time!

Beat the crowd —
get all the latest Diablo II tips and secrets
at www.bradygames.com!

Horadric Cube Recipes

Rejuvenation Potion

3 Health Potions
+ 3 Mana Potions
= 1 Rejuvenation Potion

There may be other ways to create or use potions, but this recipe is the only one found in the Library of Lut Gholein.

Amulets & Rings

3 Rings = 1 Amulet
3 Amulets = 1 Ring

Rings and amulets are strange creations that share many magical qualities. It makes sense that they are so closely linked within the mysteries of the Cube.

Gem of the Next Higher Grade

3 Gems of the Same Type and Grade = 1 Gem of the Next Higher Grade

Gems are excellent foci for magic and the most powerful of these are highly coveted treasures. Perfect Gems are extremely valuable and are sure to be used in creating remarkable items of all types.

Coral Ring

1 Ring
+ 2 Topazes
= 1 Coral Ring

Much of the powers found in rings come from the Gems and precious metals used in their crafting. Combining even the simplest of rings with other magical elements is a logical path for the adventurous to follow.

Javelin

1 Spear
+ 1 Quiver of Arrows
= 1 Javelin

There may be ways to craft other weapons, both mundane and magical, but those recipes can only be found through experimentation.

Chapter 3
THE QUESTS

THE PATH TO VICTORY

The quest walkthroughs supplied here are meant as skeletal guides to help you to find your way and complete each of the quests. Because the distances that you must travel in **Diablo II**, the random nature of many of the maps, and the randomness of monsters, items, and shrines, it would be very cumbersome and ineffective to provide a detailed walkthrough. Instead, this section is designed to give you the high points and keep you going in the right direction. Also, whenever there is a monster that's in the same place every time the game is played (Unique Monsters), we mention them so that you know what to expect when you get there.

The other aspect of **Diablo II** that affects this chapter is the variance within each character's skill classes. The number of possible strengths and weaknesses for an individual character may have is enormous, making it impossible to give specific advice about fighting individual battles. Rather than discussing that strategy here, the detailed information about how to use each skill is covered in the Chapter 2: The Characters. We recommend that you review the tactics for each skill you chose to develop for your character class before using them in your quests.

Act I: The Sightless Eye

ROGUE ENCAMPMENT

The non-player characters or NPCs in the Rogue Encampment play important roles in your efforts to complete Act I. Here is a list that points out each character's role in terms of buying, selling, identifying, and repairing items. Knowing just who to go to can save time when you're in a rush to buy a particular item or heal your aching wounds. Keep in mind that any NPC who sells items will buy any type of saleable item from you.

WARRIV

Warriv: A caravan master who is involved in the first two acts and helps to advance Diablo II's story. He stands near Your Private Stash in the Rogue Encampment.

CHARSI

Charsi: A blacksmith who repairs, buys, and sells Weapons, Armor, and Arrows/Bolts. Charsi seems to have an affinity for Barbarians.

AKARA

Akara: Not only is Akara important for some of the quests, she also fully replenishes your health and mana when you talk to her. This spiritual guide of the Rogues buys and sells Scrolls, Tomes, Potions, Wands, Staffs, and Scepters.

KASHYA

Kasha: The leader of the Rogues is willing to hire some of her warriors out to aid you in your quests.

CAIN

Deckard Cain: Your guide from the original Diablo, he is available to assist you after you complete the Cairn Stones quest. Apart from sagely advice and information, Cain will identify items free of charge for the rest of the game.

GHEED

Gheed: A slick salesman who deals in Armor, Weapons, Magic Items, and Keys. You can also Gamble on his unidentified magical wares and possibly gain Rare, Unique, or even Set Piece items.

MERCENARIES

Mercenary names and attributes are randomly assigned at the beginning of the game, so it's not possible for this book to list which of the mercenaries will match up with a particular set of stats. Therefore, we supply the important information about the range of abilities a group of mercenaries will have so that you can decide whether it's worth shelling out the gold for their services or not. The mercenaries in the Rogue Encampment can be hired from Kasha, and will have attributes that are within the following ranges:

Level: 3-10

Gold (cost): 150-490

Damage: 1-3 or 2-4

Life: 30-60

Defense: 15-45

Special Attack:
None/Cold Arrow/Fire Arrow

QUEST: DEN OF EVIL

As you would expect from the first quest of the game, this one begins near the Rogu[e] Encampment in the Blood Moor and is meant to help you cut your teeth and get a fee[l] for your character. Before you begin this quest, move around the Blood Moor and figh[t] until you gain a level. This will earn you a skill point and some more attribute points t[o] improve your character. Akara will now give this speech to begin your first quest:

AKARA

"There is a place of great evil in the wilderness. Rashya's rogue scouts have informed me that a cave nearby is filled with shadowy creatures and horrors from beyond the grave.

I fear that these creatures are massing for an attack against our encampment. If you are sincere about helping us, find the dark labyrinth and destroy the foul beasts. May the Great Eye watch over you."

Move through the Blood Moor and keep an eye out for a cavern entrance. When you discover the entrance, you can descend into the Den of Evil.

Descend into the Den of Evil— look for a cave entrance some where in the Blood Moor.

The Den of Evil is a one-level cavern that must be cleared of all monsters.

The Den of Evil consists of only one level, and the completion of the quest requires you to clear it of all monsters. The Quest log (which can be accessed by pressing the letter 'Q') will inform you of your progress. Toward the end o[f] the quest, it will tell you just how many enemies remai[n] for you to destroy.

As you work your way through the Den of Evil, you will meet one Unique monster by the name of Corpse Fire whose special attack (Spectral Hit) does massive damage. When the all of the enemies have been defeated, you will have completed the quest. At this point, you can visit Akara who will give you a rare extra Skill Point to put into one of your character's skills.

When the quest is complete, the sun will shine into the Den of Evil.

You will meet one Unique mon ster in the Den of Evil.

Quest: Sisters' Burial Grounds

This quest is triggered by either talking to Kasha after completing the Den of Evil quest or by stumbling across the Cemetery. When it's over, Kasha will then offer you the option to hire Rogue mercenaries from her.

KASHYA

"My Rogue scouts have reported an abomination in the Monastery graveyard! Apparently, Andarial is not content on taking only our living. Blood Raven, one of our finest captains in the battle against Diablo at Tristram, was also one of the first to be corrupted by Andariel. Now you'll find her in the Monastery graveyard raising our dead as zombies! We cannot abide this defilement! If you are truly our ally you will help us destroy her."

The battle to kill Blood Raven occurs in the Burial Grounds, located off the Cold Plains. Fight your way through the Cold Plains, gaining experience and money along the way—an extra level of experience never hurts when facing an adversary like Blood Raven.

You must cross the Cold Plains to reach the Burial Grounds.

When you enter the Burial Grounds you'll encounter a multitude of undead monsters. Kill off all of the enemies you see and work your way toward the Cemetery in the central area.

Blood Raven will put up a good fight!

There will be plenty of undead to deal with as you approach the Cemetery.

Eventually you'll see Blood Raven. She's fast and raises new zombies straight out of the ground to fight for her cause! Blood Raven fights with a bow and likes to run away if she takes any hits. Because she's so fast, you'll need to run to catch up to her. It's also important to remember that Blood Raven does fire damage with fire arrows, so she's one tough customer.

If you're a character class that can fight hand-to-hand battles, it's best to pin Blood Raven in a corner to fight her; otherwise, she'll repeatedly run away, and then fire arrows at you when she stops. Her 'run and shoot' approach can result in you taking a lot of damage without hitting her much.

TIP

Don't follow Blood Raven in a straight line because she'll turn and shoot quickly, and most certainly hit you if you're right behind her.

When Blood Raven is dead, descend into the Crypt and Mausoleum—there's some great loot and cool items in these areas. Both the Crypt and Mausoleum are designed to raise your character's level and give them wealth, so it could hurt you not to explore these areas.

TIP.........

When using an Amazon against Blood Raven, attack by throwing javelins. This is a wise tactic because it provides your best chance to do a lot of damage from a distance. As a Necromancer, Amplify Damage is a key spell to use on her. When you're a Barbarian, Bash can knock Blood Raven off her rhythm.

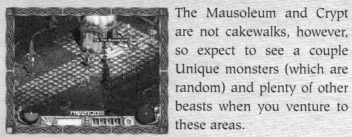

The Crypt and Mausoleum are both worth exploring to boost your experience and wealth.

The Mausoleum and Crypt are not cakewalks, however, so expect to see a couple Unique monsters (which are random) and plenty of other beasts when you venture to these areas.

When Blood Raven dies, she'll often drop a magic item or two!

QUEST: THE CAIRN STONES

Your character should be between level 6 and 8 to approach The Cairn Stones ques. This quest is enabled either by completing the Blood Raven quest or discovering th Tree of Inifuss. Once the quest is enabled, you must talk to Akara, at which time she' tell you to get the scroll from the Tree of Inifuss (unless you've already been there).

AKARA

"It is clear that we are facing an Evil difficult to comprehend, let alone combat. There is only one Horadrim Sage, schooled in the most arcane history and lore, who could help us... his name is Deckard Cain. You must travel to Tristram. I pray that he still lives."

The Tree of Inifuss is in the Dark Wood. To get there, you must enter the Stony Fiel and find the Underground Passageway.

You will face plenty of enemies In the Underground Passageway, so be ready to fight. When you exit, you'll be in the Dark Wood. Here, you must explore and attempt to find the Tree of Inifuss. Once again, your task is seriously challenged by a host of monsters.

The Underground Passagewa is found in the Stony Field or the side of a cliff.

When you reach the Tree of Inifuss, you must fight a Unique Gargantuan Beast that is extremely strong and fast, as well as his minions. Once they are disposed of, you can click on the tree to get the Bark Scroll, then use a Town Portal or Waypoint to get back to the Rogue Encampment or Akara's help in deciphering your new-found artifact. Once the Scroll has been deciphered, you'll be able to visit the Cairn Stones and open the Portal to Tristram.

A Unique Gargantuan Beast, Treehead Woodfist, guards the Tree of Inifuss.

The Cairn Stones are in the Stony Field. They're guarded by Rakanishu, a Unique monster that's Lightning Enchanted and returns damage to you every time you hit him.

A fight against Rakanishu and his minions awaits you at the Cairn Stones. Once he's dead, touch the stones in the order written on the scroll by right-clicking its image in your inventory to open a red portal that transports you to Tristram.

Tristram is swarming with enemies. Release Deckard Cain from his prison in the middle of Tristram to open a Portal back to the Rogue Encampment.

When the stones are touched in the correct order, a portal to Tristram opens.

Releasing Cain will satisfy this quest, but there's more to do in Tristram than releasing Cain.

After Cain is released you can fight Griswold—a Unique monster who's cursed. Griswold puts up a tough fight, but he's relatively slow—a ranged attack should take him out fairly easily.

In the far (left) side of Tristram you'll see Wirt. Pick up his leg, which can at the very least be used as a weapon and may have other uses (hint, hint!). When you take Wirt's leg, his corpse will spew out all that gold he bilked you out of in the first game like a slot machine giving up a jackpot!

Take Wirt's leg and collect all of the money he dishes out.

> **TIP**..........
>
> You can run to Tristram, hit the cage Cain is in, then run out quickly and get out; but if you do this, you will miss a lot of monsters and you won't get Wirt's Leg. While this may or may not be of any significance, it's not within the scope of this book to milk it any further, even if the results might be moving.

Griswold is cursed and will fight you to the death.

Return to the Rogue Encampment and Deckard Cain will thank you. From this point forward he'll identify items for free.

QUEST: THE FORGOTTEN TOWER

Finding the Moldy Tome in the Stony Field activates this quest. Your character shoul[d] be between levels 6-9 character to undertake this quest. When you read the Tome you'[ll] learn this:

TOME

"...And so it came to pass that the Countess, who once bathed in the rejuvenating blood of a hundred virgins, was burned alive. And her castle in which so many cruel deeds took place fell rapidly to ruin. Rising over the buried dungeons in that god-for-saken wilderness, a solitary tower, like some monument to Evil, is all that remains.

The Countess's fortune was believed to be divided among the clergy, although some say that more remains unfound, still buried alongside the rotting skulls that bear mute witness to the inhumanity of the human creature."

The Forgotten Tower is in the Black Marsh, which can be reached by traveling through the Dark Wood. Needless to say, there will be all kinds of monsters getting in your way as you move through these areas, so keep a Town Portal scroll on hand at all times, and remember to activate any waypoints you come across on your travels.

You must find this book in the Stony Field to activate the Forgotten Tower quest.

As you travel through the Dark Wood and the Black Marsh, you'll face a lot of opposition, so be prepared to fight.

When you reach the Forgotten Tower you'll soon realize that the tower has been razed and the real adventure lies underground. Ente[r] and be prepared to hack through five levels before yo[u] reach the Countess (the boss for this quest). Each level [of] the Forgotten Tower has at least one Unique monster [or] Champion group that you must face. These monsters ar[e] generated randomly so we can't tell you for sure wha[t] you'll face, but it's safe to say that these five Tower level[s] will keep you busy.

There are a few things you need to know about the Countess before you meet her. First, she's Fire Enchanted, so she's capable of dealing fire damage. Specifically, the Countess likes to conjure up Fire Walls in your way, so be prepared to do some fancy footwork to avoid the flames.

You may face a group of Champions or a Unique monster on every level of the Forgotten Tower.

The Countess is a formidable foe.

Formidable minions also guard the Countess, and it's important to take them out first or you'll never be able to successfully fight her. The Barbarian's Taunt skill is excellent for this situation because the Countess won't leave the room she's in, llowing you to use Taunt to pull her minions out one at a me and kill them individually. After her servants are out f the way, move in and fight the Countess one-on-one.

Once the Countess has been defeated, you'll discover all the riches to be had!

TIP
The Fire Walls used by the Countess are to be reckoned with. If you have an item that reduces the effect of an enemy's magic or some fire resistance, you can endure the flames without taking much damage.

QUEST: TOOLS OF THE TRADE

his quest is enabled after completing the Forgotten Tower quest and having a conversation with Charsi. Upon completion Charsi will imbue one of your items with magical roperties, making this a significant accomplishment in your on-going adventure. To egin this quest you should be around level 10 before you talk to Charsi.

"When I fled the Monastery, I left behind my Horadric Malus, an enchanted smithing hammer. If you can retrieve it for me, I will use its magic to strengthen your equipment."

CHARSI

ou must now visit the Outer Cloister (be sure to hit the Vaypoint marker there). Follow this path to get there: nove from the Dark Wood to the Black Marsh to the amoe Highlands to the Monastery. This is a long and rduous journey that will require you to be victorious in nany battles.

You'll have many battles to fight as you move toward the Outer Cloister.

TIP
In Multiplayer, every player that is in the party of the character that returns the Malus to Charsi gets the reward, so make sure you are grouped before completing the quest!!

The Barracks will provide lots of monsters for you to fight before you actually meet up with The Smith.

Eventually, you'll work your way into the Barracks. As you fight through, you'll notice a small image on your map that looks like a hammer—this is where the Malus (and The Smith) are located.

The Smith is a Unique monster that's extra strong. There's a Devilkin and his minions in with The Smith, as well, so take them out before you go toe to toe with this beast.

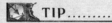

TIP..........

There are two important things to know about Charsi imbuing items. First, she does this only **once** in the game, so choose your item carefully. Secondly, if you imbue things like gloves or belts (items not normally chosen to be imbued), you can often acqrire good attributes such as increased statistics or health regeneration.

The Smith is a powerful enemy, but you should be able to handle him if you take his minions out first. Keeping your distance and using ranged attacks is always a good idea.

When you've finished off The Smith, grab the Malus and return it to Charsi; she'll imbue something for you. Charsi can imbue any non-magical, non-thrown, non-socketed, non-jewelry item, making it a rare item in the process by granting it 3-5 magical attributes. Many

You get only once chance to imbue an item, so choose carefully.

players hold off on imbuing an item until they find a particular weapon or piece of armor that's especially good. They then journey back to Charsi to get their rare item.

QUEST: SISTERS TO THE SLAUGHTER

This is the last quest of Act I, and is given to you by Deckard Cain. When you face this quest, your character should be between level 12 and 16. After you've completed the five other quests of Act I, talk to Cain in the Rogue Encampment and he'll give you the quest while passing along some words of wisdom.

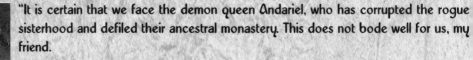

CAIN

"It is certain that we face the demon queen Andariel, who has corrupted the rogue sisterhood and defiled their ancestral monastery. This does not bode well for us, my friend.

Ancient Horadric texts record that Anderial and the other lesser evils once overthrew the three prime evils—Diablo, Mephisto, and Baal—banishing them from Hell to our world.

Here, they caused mankind untold anguish and suffering before they were finally bound within the Soulstones.

Andariel's presence here could mean that the forces of Hell are once again aligned behind Diablo and his brothers. If this is true, then I fear for us all. You must kill her before the Monastery becomes a permanent outpost of Hell and the way east lost forever."

To reach your destination, you must travel to the Barracks, down three levels of the Jail, onward to the Inner Cloister, then to the Cathedral, and finally into the Catacombs. Your battles in the Jail will be difficult. Often you'll take damage from enemies behind bars—you cannot immediately reach them, but they can still use ranged weapons against you.

The Jail can be a difficult place to fight.

After passing through the three Jail levels, you'll find yourself in the Inner Cloister where you'll face a Unique Spike Fiend by the name of Flame Spike the Crawler. Eliminate the creature and then proceed to the Cathedral.

Fight your way through the Cathedral to the Catacombs entrance, then descend and get ready for a rough ride. There are plenty of randomly generated Unique and Champion monsters to face in the Catacombs, so be sure to hit the Waypoint marker on level 2—you'll probably need to use it.

Expect to fight a Unique Spike Fiend named Flame Spike the Crawler in the Inner Cloister.

The Catacombs are full of Unique and Champion monsters.

There's a small room in the Catacombs level 4. Clear it and the surrounding area, then open the double doors to face Andariel. Andariel is tough, scary, and a vicious opponent. In addition to her other attacks, she throws out a lot of poison, so anything you have that can give you poison resistance will help considerably. Some items have Poison resistance, and the Paladin's Cleansing Aura is excellent—will help everyone in your party in Multiplayer.

Andariel is a ferocious creature, but you can defeat her!

TIP..........

Take a Mercenary or Golem (if you're a Necromancer) down with you to use as a decoy when you face Andariel, then use a bow or some other ranged weapon to hit Andariel while she attacks your sidekick.

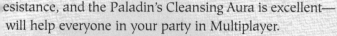

Act II: The Secret of the Vizjerei

Lut Gholein

As in the Rogue Encampment, the NPCs in Lut Gohlein play important roles in you efforts to complete Act II. This list gives a brief description of each character's role i this act.

WARRIV

FARA

ATMA

DROGNAN

ELZIX

MESHIF

LYSANDER

CAIN

GEGLASH

GRIEZ

JERHYN

Warriv: After providing your transportation from the Rogue Encampment, he now setting up trade routes in Lut Gholein.

Lysander: This addled alchemist buys and sells Potions, Keys, and various othe items.

Fara: A former Paladin, she automatically replenishes your health and man when you deal with her. Fara also repairs and sells Armor and Weapons, bot mundane and Magical.

Deckard Cain: Coming with you from the Rogue encampment, he continues t identify your needs as well as any items you may find.

Atma: The owner of the public house, she is looking for a hero to avenge her mu dered husband and son. Atma gives you the Radament's Lair quest.

Geglash: The town drunk who offers a few laughs and some cryptic informatio on the current state of affairs.

Drognan: This aged sorcerer buys and sells Staffs, Scepters, Wands, Scroll: Tomes, and Health Potions.

Griez: In charge of guarding the city, he also hires out his well-traine Mercenaries.

Elzix: His days as a renowned bandit behind him, he buys and sells Weapons an Armor. He is also willing to let you Gamble on his unidentified magical items.

Jerhyn: The troubled young leader of Lut Gholein.

Kaelan: A Guard of the Palace.

Meshif: The captain of a ship that will be your eventual transport to the next Ac

Mercenaries

As in the Rogue Encampment, mercenary names and attributes are randomly assigne in Lut Gohlein. Therefore, we supply the important information about the range of abi ities a group of mercenaries will have so that you can decide whether it's worthwhile t hire them or not. The mercenaries in Lut Gohlein can be hired from Griez, and will hav attributes that are within the following ranges:

Level: 9-17

Gold (cost): 300-700

Damage: 2-6 or 3-8

Life: 120-180

Defense: 25-60

Special Attack: None/Jab Attack/Poison Resistance (ability)

140

QUEST: RADAMENT'S LAIR

Since Atma has a personal stake in Radament being destroyed, she is the one who assigns you this quest. Your character should be between level 16 and 18 by the time you reach this quest. She provides you the following valuable information:

ATMA

"In the sewers below our city, there lurks a horrid creature that hungers for human flesh. The creature has killed many, including my son and my husband. If you destroy it, I will reward you. Please be careful though, that beast has taken enough from us already. The sewer entrance is through the trap door just up the street."

Once you enter the Sewers, you must pass through several levels before you reach the area where Radament is located. Be sure to hit the Waypoint marker on Level 2 of the Sewers in case you die. This will make your journey back much quicker. There are plenty of new enemies in the Sewers; you'll typically face Burning Archers and Burning Dead, so ready an item that gives you fire resistance.

The trap door to the sewers below Lut Gohlien is easy to find.

The Sewers teem with new and ferocious enemies.

When you reach Radament, you'll have a tough fight indeed. Radament can poison you, and he's also magic resistant, which can make life hard for the Sorceress. He's also surrounded by his minions, which he can resurrect after you've killed them. Using cold based or freezing attacks is an excellent way to deal with Radament because if you can shatter one of his servants, it's gone forever and cannot be resurrected. Likewise, when the Necromancer uses Raise Skeleton on a fallen minion, it means that it can no longer work in Radament's favor.

Radament can resurrect his minions after you kill them.

When Radament dies, you can get the Horadric Scroll and take it to Cain.

When Radament is dead, pick up the Book of Skill that he drops and read it to get an extra skill point! Then, search for the Horadric Scroll in a nearby chest. Take this Scroll to Cain and you'll receive an important new quest.

QUEST: THE HORADRIC STAFF

Once you have delivered the Horadric Scroll to Cain, he will send you on a quest for the Horadric Staff. He also reveals some important details when describing your quest

CAIN

"Ahh... The lost Horadric Scroll! What a fortunate turn of events...

As the last living Horadrim, I **alone** have knowledge of its meaning. Now, to read the Horadric runes it bears... Hmmm...

The Horadric Mages, after binding Baal within Tal Rasha, magically sealed off his Burial Chamber from the mortal realm. Those same Mages also crafted fearsome Horadric Staves and imbued them with the special power to open the Chamber's hidden door.

After nearly losing one to the thievery of a rogue sorcerer, they divided all the Horadric Staves into two parts—wooden shaft and metal headpiece—hiding them separately to safeguard them.

The Horadrim foresaw our current plight and designed the hiding places to reveal themselves to worthy heroes like you.

Collect both parts of a Horadric Staff and unite them using a Horadric Cube. Then, you may enter Tal Rasha's Burial Chamber."

> ### 🗡 TIP..........
> The Horadric Cube is a special item that you'll want to keep throughout the game. The cube can be used to 'transmute' objects and create new ones. Check out Chaper 1: The Basics to learn more about the Horadric Cube, including a few recipes for making interesting things.

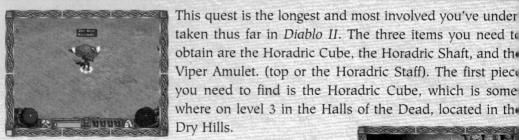
You must venture through the Dry Hills to reach the Halls of the Dead.

This quest is the longest and most involved you've under taken thus far in *Diablo II*. The three items you need to obtain are the Horadric Cube, the Horadric Shaft, and the Viper Amulet. (top or the Horadric Staff). The first piece you need to find is the Horadric Cube, which is some where on level 3 in the Halls of the Dead, located in the Dry Hills.

When you get to level 3 of the Halls of the Dead you'll find a Unique Sabre Cat guarding the Horadric Cube, along with a bevy of other monsters that would like nothing better than to destroy you. Once these enemies have been dealt with, pick up the Horadric Cube and put it in your inventory.

Monsters that do not like uninvited guests guard the Horadric Cube.

he next item you'll need is the Horadric Shaft, which ou'll find on level 3 in the Sand Maggot Lair, located in ne Far Oasis. The Shaft is guarded by a Unique monster alled Cold Worm the Devourer.

Next, you'll need to enter the Sand Maggot Lair in the Far Oasis.

Cold Worm the Devourer will put up a fight for the Horadric Shaft.

Cold Worm the Devourer will be only part of the enemy equation in your quest to obtain the Horadric Shaft, so be prepared to fight long and hard, and carry potions and Town Portal Scrolls with you.

The final item you must acquire to complete this uest is the Viper Amulet. You'll find it on level 2 of the 'law Viper Temple in the Valley of the Snakes, which is ast the Lost City, and then beyond the Far Oasis.

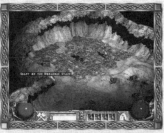

You must find your way through the Valley of the Snakes to the Claw Viper Temple.

You'll have to face Fang Skin before acquiring the Viper Amulet.

You'll meet a host of enemies in the Claw Viper Temple, and when you come to the Viper Amulet you must fight a Unique monster named Fang Skin. This beast is extremely fast and presents a challenging battle. Take along Plenty of Thawing potions and some Cold resistance would be a good idea, too. Once the last piece of the quest is in your inventory, head back to Lut Gohlein and visit Deckard Cain to have him identify both parts of the Staff. Then, follow his directions carefully to restore it to usefulness..

QUEST: TAINTED SUN

f you finish the Horadric Staff quest, then the Tainted Sun uest is already complete. If you haven't accomplished this et, then Tainted Sun is a stand-alone quest. You are tasked vith your new quest when you enter the Lost City. The sun oes out and you must find the Viper Template and destroy he evil altar (thus releasing the Viper Amulet) to undo the vil that has blackened the day.

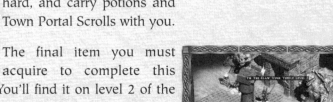

This quest overlaps with the Horadric Staff quest. If you are attempting The Tainted Sun quest first, then go to the Lost City to trigger it.

QUEST: THE ARCANE SANCTUARY

Drognan in Lut Gohlein gives you the quest to seek out the Arcane Sanctuary. After you kill Radament, Jheryn will give you the Seven Tombs quest. Drognan will activate the Arcane Sanctuary quest, which will allow you to enter the palace. You'll proceed through the Harem to the Palace Cellar, where you'll find the Arcane Sanctuary. When accepting this quest from Drognan, he gives you some advice.

DROGAN

"I've been researching the old records, trying to find the location of Tal Rasha's Tomb. Though I haven't found the Tomb itself, I may have a good lead for you.

The great Vizjerei Summoner, Horazon, built his Arcane Sanctuary somewhere around here. He was a powerful spellcaster and kept demons as slaves within the Sanctuary. He kept a close eye on great events, too—such as the imprisonment of Baal within Tal Rasha's Tomb.

If you could find Horazon's Sanctuary, I'm sure that it would hold some clue as to the Tomb's location. Though I doubt Horazon is still alive, you must proceed with caution. There's no telling what could be waiting inside.

When I spoke of this with Lord Jerhyn, he asked that I send you to him. Perhaps he knows of a secret entrance or the like."

In Lut Gohlein, go to the Palace and request entrance. Once inside, descend to Harem level 1, then further to level 2. Of course, the Harem is not easy; you'll have enemies to fight the whole way, so be prepared.

The Harem is not a walk in the park—there will be many battles to be fought.

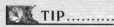

TIP

When moving in the Arcane Sanctuary, the Barbarian and the Sorceress have definite advantages over the other character classes. The Barbarian's Leap is very effective for bypassing teleporters to get from one ledge to another, while the Teleport Skill of the Sorceress achieves the same ends.

Take out Fire Eye to clear the way to the Arcane Sanctuary.

After the Harem you'll descend through three levels of Palace Cellar, eventually finding the entrance to the Arcane Sanctuary. Fire Eye, a Unique Sand Raider, guards this passage. Destroy this monster to finish the quest, then enter the Arcane Sanctuary.

Enter the Arcane Sanctuary and start working your way through it. Be absolutely sure to hit the Waypoint in the middle of the Sanctuary because it's entirely possible that you'll die in this area and will need to get back quickly.

Be sure to hit this Waypoint in the Arcane Sanctuary.

QUEST: THE SUMMONER

This quest is activated when you meet the Summoner in the Arcane Sanctuary. During his encounter, he'll taunt you with a tortured laugh.

"Muhuhahaha!"

SUMMONER

The Summoner is impersonating Horazon. When you find him, you must destroy him. Resistance to cold is important when fighting the Summoner because he uses Ice Blast. The Paladin's Resist Cold aura is very useful in this situation, and will not only help the Paladin, but also any party members (in Multiplayer), as well. As a rule, it's best to use ranged weapons against the Summoner rather than getting into hand-to-hand combat because he packs a substantial punch.

The Summoner is tough, but he must be taken out if you are to proceed.

QUEST: THE SEVEN TOMBS

Jerhyn gives this quest. He tells you that you need to search for Diablo himself, and that the search will take you to Tal Rasha's Tomb. Here, you must find the chamber with the Circle of Seven Symbols, place the Horadric Staff into receptacle in its center, and kill Duriel. Thus begins the quest for the Seven Tombs. Jerhyn has some advice to give during this exchange.

JERHYN

"I have heard of your many deeds of skill and bravery. I feel I can trust you with something I have been hesitant to speak of...

Drognan and I have concluded that the Dark Wanderer who passed through here recently was Diablo, himself! Drognan believes that Diablo is searching the desert for the secret tomb where the great Horadrim, Tal Rasha, keeps Baal imprisoned.

You must find Diablo and put an end to the terrible evil that has fallen upon our city! Drognan is wise and is sure to have some helpful advice for you as to how Tal Rasha's tomb may be found.

It may take you quite some time to find The Tomb. May you be **ready** when you do."

Take the portal to the Canyon of the Magi. When you arrive, touch the Waypoint marker in case you need to go back. You must now find the Tomb of Tal Rasha (by matching the symbols).

Match the Symbols to locate the Tomb of Tal Rasha.

Once inside the chamber, place the staff in the Horadric Orifice; this will blow a hole in the wall and open a doorway to the tomb of Tal Rasha. You must then kill Duriel.

Placing the staff in the Orifice will open a passage to the Tomb of Tal Rasha.

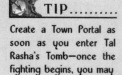

TIP..........

Create a Town Portal as soon as you enter Tal Rasha's Tomb—once the fighting begins, you may not have time to do this and get out alive!

When fighting Duriel, it helps to have something that reduces freeze/cold duration, because Duriel will use this magic on you. It is important to note, however, that his chilling field is a Demonic power and not an Elemental magic, so resistances to cold are ineffective in staving of this attack. Keep Duriel at a distance and you'll fair much better than if you engage him in close combat. Duriel closes fast and has a powerful melee attack that will do both stun and knock back. He also has a huge amount of hi points, so you'll have to pound away to take him out.

Duriel is a powerful foe with plenty of hit points, so prepare for a long battle.

The one exception for the ranged-weapon advice is the Barbarian. His powerful abilities in Melee attack make it best for him to go toe-to-toe and use Double Swing with two weapons against Duriel. Once Duriel's dead, click on Tyrael the Angel to free him. Tyrael delivers a speech and a portal to Jerhyn opens (near palace steps). Back in Lut Gohlein, go to Meshif and head east.

Click on the Angel Tyrael to release him and hear about what happened to Baal.

Act III: The Infernal Gate

KURAST DOCKTOWN

s in the Rogue Encampment and Lut Gohlein, the NPCs in Kurast Docktown play mportant roles in your efforts to complete Act III. This list gives a brief description of ach character's role in this act.

Meshif: His ship stands ready to take a full cargo and you back to Lut Gohlein, should you wish to return.

Deckard Cain: He continues to offer guidance and his skills as a master of identification as you continue your journeys here.

Ormus: An enigmatic figure, he automatically replenishes your health and mana when you talk with him. He also buys and sells Masks, Scepters, Wands, Staffs, Scrolls, and Tomes.

Alkor: Living in a small hut, this secluded fellow buys and sells Potions while inviting the wayward adventurer to Gamble on his unknown magical treasures.

Hralti: An enchanter by trade, he buys, sells, and repairs Armor and Weapons of many kinds.

Asheara: Leader of the Iron Wolves, she will gladly sell you the services of her magic-wielding Mercenaries.

Natalya: A shadowy woman who offers advice cloaked in mysteries.

MESHIF

CAIN

ORMUS

ALKOR

HRALTI

ASHEARA

NATALYA

MERCENARIES

s in the other two towns, mercenary names and attributes are randomly assigned, so gain only the important information about the range of abilities a group of mercenar- s has is included. The mercenaries in Kurast Docktown can be hired from Asheara, nd will have attributes that are within the following ranges:

Level: 15-26	**Life:** 240-400
Gold (cost): 600-1285	**Defense:** 80-150
Damage: 3-8 or 4-10	**Special Attack:** None/Cold Spells/ Fire Spells/Lightning Spells/Fast Cast

QUEST: THE GOLDEN BIRD

The first Unique monster you meet in the wilds outside of the Kurast Docktown will be the monster you must kill to begin this quest.

This quest starts when you meet the first Unique monster after leaving Kurast Docktown.

The quest is begun when you kill the first Unique monster you meet. It doesn't matter where; it's simply the first one you find. Destroy it and you receive the Jade Figurine as your treasure. This item must be given to Meshif. In exchange, he will present you with the Golden Bird. You can now go to Alkor. He will take the Golden bird. Finally, leave Alkor and return for your reward. Do this and you'll get a potion of life that adds a permanent +20 to your life!

QUEST: BLADE OF THE OLD RELIGION

Find the Pygmy village in the Flayer Jungle. Hratli will then give you the quest to fin[d] an enchanted dagger called the Gidbinn. You must kill a Unique Pygmy in the villag[e] and return the blade to Ormus. Hralti gives you the quest and shares some advice.

HRALTI — "As I told you before, I placed an enchantment upon the dockside in order to keep the demons at bay. But lately, the enchantment seems to be weakening. If memory serves me correctly, there is a holy Skatsimi blade that could revitalize the enchantment. The blade is called Gidbinn. Find it, and our sanctuary here will remain safe."

Venture into the Flayer Jungle and move around until you find the Pygmy Village. This area can be confusing to find your way around. Just remember that you're entering a new area when you see two pillars.

Navigating the Flayer Jungl[e] isn't easy, especially when there are enemies to face.

You must kill the Pygmy to get the Gidbinn.

You'll find the Gidbinn in the Pygmy Village. You must kill the Pygmy with the Gidbinn in his hand. To take the Pygmy out, remember that he will always charge you, so you don't have to worry abou[t] chasing him down—even if he runs away briefly.

Use a Town Portal to go back to Kurast Docktown and ta[lk] to Ormus. He will give you a rare magical ring that [is] random in nature, but always useful. As an additional reward, Asheara will make th[e] hiring of her Iron Wolf mercenaries free!

QUEST: KHALIM'S WILL

Deckard Cain gives this huge, over-arching quest to you. He adds some words of wis[-] dom and a stern reminder as to your true purpose in Kurast for good measure.

CAIN — "Never forget that your ultimate purpose here in Kurast is to destroy Mephisto. The ancient Horadrim imprisoned the Lord of Hatred inside the Guardian Tower that is located within the Temple City of Travincal.

Know this, friend—the only way to gain entry to Mephisto's prison is to destroy the artifact known as the Compelling Orb. Mephisto used this device to control the Zakarum Priests and their followers. The Orb can only be destroyed with an ancient flail imbued with the spirit of the one incorruptible priest."

Soon after his imprisonment, Mephisto worked his evil corruption on the Zakarum priesthood. All were turned to his dark ways, save one—Rhalim, the Que-Hegan of the High Council.

Mephisto directed the other Council priests to slay and dismember Rhalim and then scatter his remains across the Kingdom. The Priest Sankekur succeeded Rhalim as Que-Hegan, eventually becoming the embodiment of Mephisto here on the mortal plane.

The corrupted High Council fashioned an Orb to control the rest of the Zakarum faithful and used their powers to hide the lair of their master from mortals.

Your task is to collect the scattered relics of Rhalim—his Heart, his Brain, and his Eye. Then, using the Horadric Cube, transmute Rhalim's Flail with his relics. Once this is accomplished, you must destroy the Compelling Orb with Rhalim's Will to open the way into the corrupt sanctum of Mephisto."

In this quest you must find three body parts and a Flail. You will find the first body part, the Eye, in the Spider Cavern, which is located in the Spider Forest. Be sure not to confuse the Spider Cavern with the Arachnid Lair.

You must journey to the Spider Cavern, which will require you to move through the Spider Forest and fight the creatures that stand in your way.

A Unique monster called Sszark the Burning, a Fire Spinner, guards the first body part. When you've defeated Sszark (fire resistance is helpful when fighting him), you'll be able to open a chest that contains the Eye and some other valuables; take them.

After you defeat Sszark the Burning, you can get the Eye of Khalim

The next piece to collect is the Brain of Khalim. It's located on the third level of the Flayer Dungeon and is guarded by Witch Doctor Endugu (a Flayer Shaman). Once you defeat him, the Brain is yours for the taking.

TIP..........

The Flayer Dungeon is located near the Pygmy Village.

You must destroy Endugu in the Flayer Dungeon to get at the Brain of Khalim.

The third piece of the body, the Heart, is in level 2 of the Sewers. There are two entrances in Upper Kurast and two in the Bazaar. Once in the Sewer, you'll find a lever that opens level 2. Within this small area is a chest containing the Heart.

The Heart of Khalim is on level 2 of the Sewers.

You must get the Flail by fighting the High Council in Travincal.

The last thing you need to find is the Flail. It is held in Travincal by one of the members of the High Council, whom you have to kill. You must put the body parts and the Flail into the Horadric Cube, and then transmute them into a very powerful Flail called Khalim's Will.

Put the body parts and th Flail into the Horadric Cub and then transmute them in Khalim's Will.

When fighting the High Council, hire an Iron Wolf Mercenary, if you don't already have one

Quest: Lam Esen's Tome

This quest asks you to find the Book in a particular area of the city, then return it t Alkor, who impatiently gives you directions.

ALKOR

"It pains me to waste time with you, so I'll get right to the point. There is a very special book, which you must find for me. It was written long ago by a sage known as Lam Esen, who studied Skatsimi magic and the effects of the Prime Evils on the mortal world. The Black Book was lost when the Children of Zakarum took over this land. Now, you must reclaim it without delay! Its knowledge may aid us in this dark time ahead."

In Upper Kurast, the Bazaar, and the Causeway there are staircases, which when clicked on descend into temples below the surface. One of these is a ruined temple, and this is where you need to go.

Descend into a ruined temple from one of these locations.

You must fight the Battlemaid Sarina to get Lam Esen's Tome.

In the ruined temple you find Lam Esen's Tome, which is guarded by the Unique monster Battlemaid Sarina, a Flesh Hunter. Defeat her to get the book, then give it to Alkor to earn five attribute points.

QUEST: THE BLACKENED TEMPLE

This quest is given by Ormus. You must find the Temple City of Travincal, kill the evil High Council there, and smash the Compelling Orb with Khalim's Will. Ormus congratulates you, then presents you with this new challenge.

ORMUS

"You have done well, my friend. Your courage and valor are an inspiration to us all. But now the time has come to face those responsible for the evil that has stifled our land. You must destroy the High Council of Zakarum! Long ago, these elders were charged with the stewardship of Mephisto, the Lord of Hatred, who was imprisoned within the Guardian Tower. Through the generations, these pious men slowly fell more and more under the sway of Mephisto's malevolent power and the Council became an evil mockery of its former glory.

It is Mephisto's Hatred that has corrupted Zakarum and turned its devout followers into paranoid fanatics. That is why you must travel to the Temple City of Tavincal and slay the Council. Once they are gone, Mephisto's hold over this land and its people will be broken!"

The council members are in the Temple City of Travincal.

The three council members are Unique monsters with minions, which will make them more than a handful to battle. Once you take them out, you'll end up inside the Travincal area and find a Compelling Orb. Smash this Orb to open the doorway to the Durance of Hate.

Locate the Compelling Orb and smash it with Khalim's Will.

> **NOTE......**
>
> This quest is related to the Rhalim's Will quest.

QUEST: THE GUARDIAN

This quest is given by Ormus after you smash the Compelling Orb in the previous quest. You must find the Tower and entrance, then race through to confront Mephisto and kill him. Ormus explains the critical nature of your quest.

ORMUS

"Diablo and Baal have surely found the Temple City by now. They seek to free their brother, Mephisto, who was imprisoned by the Horadrim in the Temple's Guardian Tower. You must reach him before his brothers do and prevent them from releasing Hatred upon the world."

While in the Durance of Hate, you should hit the Waypoint on level 2 for an easy way to return here should you die or need to flee. If you don't, you'll regret it later.

The Durance of Hate is guarded well.

Mephisto is well guarded by Blood Lords and Council Members.

When you reach Mephisto, you'll see that he has many Blood Lords and Council Members defending him. Meteors, Firewalls, and other destructive forces will be flying at you as you try to take him down. Obviously, fire resistance is is helpful when you're dealing with his minions, but Lightning resistance vital when dueling with Mephisto.

Mephisto also inflicts poison, launches charged bolts, and fires lightning bolts. In short, he's your worst nightmare. In order to be successful you must first kill all of Mephisto's minions, then go after him. Upon his defeat, Mephisto drops his Soulstone and a rare or unique item!

Take out Mephisto's minions first or you'll never bring him down.

152

Act IV: The Harrowing

PANDEMONIUM FORTRESS

The Pandemonium Fortress is the last of the encampments that you will find in Diablo II, and there are just four NPCs to interact with. There are also no mercenaries for you to hire here, which adds to the pressure you're no doubt feeling as the game reaches its climax.

Deckard Cain: Following you to the very edge of Hell, his dedication to your quest, as well as his continued help in identifying items, is well appreciated.

Tyrael: The Archangel who fought Diablo and Baal and the crafter of the runeblade Azurewrath. What else needs to be said?

Jamella: This Warrior of Light who outfits those making assaults upon Hell will buy and sell Weapons, Armor, Scrolls, and Potions. She will also allow you to test your hand against the fates by Gambling on the unknown items in her stock.

Halbu: Brother in arms to Jamella, he buys, sells, and repairs Weapons and Armor.

CAIN

TYRAEL

JAMELLA

HALBU

QUEST: THE FALLEN ANGEL

Tyrael charges you with seeking out and destroying the Unique monster that harbors the spirit of the fallen Angel Izual. Tyrael describes the perilous situation.

TYRAEL

"There is a dark, tortured soul who was trapped within this forsaken realm long ago. He was called Izual by mortal men, and in ages past he was my most trusted Lieutenant. Yet against my wishes he led an ill-fated assault upon the fiery Hellforge itself.

Despite his valor and strength, Izual was captured by the Prime Evils and twisted by their perverse power. They forced him to betray his own kind and give up Heaven's most guarded secrets. He became a corrupt shadow of his former self; a fallen angel trusted neither by Heaven nor Hell.

For his transgressions, Izual's spirit was bound within the form of a terrible creature, which was summoned from the Abyss. His maddened spirit has resided within that tortured husk for many ages now.

It seems to me that he has suffered long enough. I implore you, hero, find Izual and release him from his cruel imprisonment. Put an end to his guilt and suffering."

Search the Plains of Despair until you come across the wandering Izual.

In this quest you must kill Izual in the Plains of Despai[r]. Izual is randomly wandering the area, so you must fir[st] search for him.

Izual has a Frost Nova attack and a sword, so cold resistance will help. It's also a good idea to fight him from afar so that you don't feel the wrath of his sword. When Izual has been destroyed you get two skill points to allocate as you see fit.

As you would expect this lat[e] in the game, you'll have you[r] hands full during your battl[e] against Izual.

QUEST: THE HELLFORGE

Cain tells you, "The time has come for you to destroy Mephisto's Soulstone!" and sends you to the Hellforge to do the job. If you didn't take the Soulstone earlier, he'll give it to you anyway (saying he picked it up for you).

Descend this staircase to get to the Hellforge.

To reach the Hellforge, cross the Plains of Despair. When you arrive in the City of the Dammed, descend the large staircase. Make sure to activate the nearby Waypoint!

To reach the Hellforge, you must cross the Plains of Despair and enter the City of the Dammed.

At the bottom of the staircase, go into the River of Flam[e]. About halfway through, you'll enter the Hellforge. This [is] where you will meet Hephasto, the Smith's big brother. Yo[u] must not only kill him, but all the other monsters, as well– this is no small task.

When Hephasto dies, you pick up the Hellforge Hammer. This will be used to destroy the Soulstone on the Hellforge. Equip the Hellforge Hammer, then click on the forge. The Soulstone will leave your inventory and arrive on the Hellforge. Smash the stone and you'll get a large number of high-quality Gems (just in time to throw them into your socketed items/ weapons). Take a Town Portal back to the Pandemonium Fortress and prepare for the final quest.

In the Hellforge you'll face off against Hephasto.

The Soulstone will be destroyed on the Hellforge, and you will get some high-quality Gems for your efforts[.]

Quest: Terror's End

Tyrael gives you the final quest where you must find and kill Diablo. Tyrael has some important things to say before you begin this enormous task.

TYRAEL "The time has come to hunt down and destroy Diablo himself. But beware, the Lord of Terror is not to be underestimated. He single-handedly destroyed the town of Tristram and corrupted the last noble hero who tried to stop him. This time, you must defeat him for good. Only by destroying the Soulstone, which he carries, will his spirit be banished forever. Good luck. Though this be our darkest hour, it may yet be your greatest moment!"

At the end of the River of the Flame there's a Waypoint. You need to activate it because you'll most certainly be coming back.

You must open five seals in Diablo's lair to trigger his appearance. Move around the Chaos Sanctum and hit the five seals to open them. Unfortunately, three of these seals will randomly spawn a Unique monster:

The Waypoint is important because this is the toughest part of the game, and it's likely that you'll be working your way back.

- The Grand Vizier of Chaos (Burning Soul)
- Lord De Seis (Oblivion Knight)
- The Infector of Souls (Venom Lord)

This is one of the seals you must open to make Diablo appear.

When you've broken all five seals, Diablo shows up and you must defeat him to complete the game. He has numerous attacks, ranging from his awesome Flame Circle that acts as a Fire Nova, to a special Bone Cage spell that will imprison you, to the snaking Fire Serpent to his Lightning Inferno that is a devastating stream of red death. On top of this he has and a powerful melee attack and a charge that deals massive damage. He's the toughest enemy in the game, as he should be.

Killing Diablo

If there is more than one character in his lair (including minions or mercenaries) and you try to run from Diablo, he will try and imprison you in the Bone Cage. You are then at the mercy of any of his potent spells and death is a mere heartbeat away. Therefore, in a multiplayer situation, you're better off standing and fighting.

The following are strategies for destroying the final boss as each of the character classes.

TIP.........

Don't be afraid to go out and try to build up your levels more before you face Diablo, and be sure to take LOTS of Mana and Health potions when you do take him on. There's no magic way to destroy the Lord of Terror, so you'll have to use your wiles and chip away at him. Use Town Portal often; in fact, open one up ahead of time so that you can be ready to run. Finally, build up your fire and lightning resistances as these are his main forms of magical attack.

BARBARIAN

Go toe-to-toe with Diablo, but run when he is about to launch the Lightning Inferno (Diablo makes a certain gesture when this is about t[o] happen), then go back and fight. Also use your Leap attack because you can't be h[it] when you're actively Leaping. Make sure you are stocked with healing or, better ye[t,] Rejuvenation potions.

NECROMANCER

Use a Golem to distract, then curse Diablo with Amplify Damage. The lesse[r] Necromancer minions are largely wasted on Diablo, so only use a Golem to distract hi[m] and then attack him with anything you've got. If you are using Poison or Bone spell[s,] be sure you bring along plenty of mana or Rejuvenation potions.

SORCERESS

Use the Meteor skill plus Static Field to knock down his hit points quickly. Remembe[r] the Static Field skill takes the enemy's hit points down by 1/3 every time you use it. I[n] Diablo's case, that's a LOT of hit points. Be sure to keep a good supply of mana or rej[u]venation potions at your fingertips.

PALADIN

The Paladin should use Thorns for the same reason the Sorceress uses Static Fiel[d.] Every time Diablo hits the Paladin, the damage will be returned (many times over [if] Thorns has skill points in it). Make sure to keep a full belt of health and rejuvenatio[n] potions as well.

AMAZON

The Amazon needs to put some points into the Decoy skill to keep Diablo distracted. [If] she's using a bow, then fire the Immolation Arrow with a Long War Bow or Heav[y] Crossbow. Her battle strategy can be summed up quite simply—hit and run! Points int[o] the passive skills such as Dodge, Evade, and Critical Strike are also crucial to secu[re] victory. Having Health, Mana, Rejuvenation, and even stamina potions are all goo[d] ideas.

Chapter 4
THE LISTS

THE BESTIARY

This section of the book covers all of the enemy monsters you'll face in *Diablo* including the Standard monsters, the Unique monsters, and the Champion mosters. Every creature is examined thoroughly so that you can get a solid handle just what to expect as you move through the game. For your convenience, much of the information is presented in table form, allowing you to glean just what you need quickly and then move on to playing the game.

The Standard Monsters

These are the standard monsters of *Diablo II*. There is a multitude of enemies in the game—you could play through an entire game and not see all of the monsters listed here—but you can rest assured that you'll see *most* of them on your travels. This section tells you a little about each monster, shows you what the class of creature looks like, and includes some important statistics about each one. The 'Variant' column merely the name of the creature within the category. The Resistance tells you if the monster is resistant to any elemental or magical attacks or if it has increased resistance to physical damage. This information is very important when deciding how to attack an enemy. Any Special Attacks (such as Burning Arrows) have also been listed, as well the range of Hit Points that you can expect from each beast. Lastly, the Act(s) where the creature is found is identified—this location information is not set in stone, however due to *Diablo II*'s random nature (sometimes, for example, you can find an Act I enemy in Act III, or visa versa).

SKELETON

VARIANTS	RESISTANCE	SPECIAL ATTACKS	HIT POINT RANGE	FOUND IN
Skeleton	Poison	None	6-9	Act I/II
Returned	Poison	None	9-21	Act I/II
Bone Warrior	Cold/Poison	None	9-30	Act I/II
Burning Dead	Fire/Poison/Physical	Flaming Hits	11-30	Act II
Horror	Magic/Lightning/Poison	Shocking Hits	30-45	Act II/III

The enemies in the Skeleton class are the most common of the undead monsters you'll face in Acts I and II. Of course, any weapon you have that has extra power against the undead will be of great value to you when you're fighting these creatures. Therefore, skills like the Paladin's Holy Bolt or Sanctuary Aura are very useful when confronting these creatures.

ZOMBIE

VARIANTS	RESISTANCE	SPECIAL ATTACKS	HIT POINT RANGE	FOUND IN
Zombie	Poison	None	5-9	Act I
Hungry Dead	Poison	None	7-13	Act I
Ghoul	Poison	None	28-51	Act I
Drowned Carcass	Fire/Poison/Damage	None	47-85	Act III
Plague Bearer	Magic/Poison	Poison	39-69	Act II

The enemies in the Zombie class are also undead monsters and, like the Skeletons, you'll be seeing a lot of them. Again, any weapon with extra abilities against the undead will be of great value to you when you're fighting them. The Sanctuary Aura or Holy Bolt of the Paladin is also very effective.

TAINTED

VARIANTS	RESISTANCE	SPECIAL ATTACKS	HIT POINT RANGE	FOUND IN
Afflicted	Lightning	Shoots Lightning Globe	28-40	Act I
Tainted	Lightning	Shoots Lightning Globe	26-37	Act I
Misshapen	Lightning	Shoots Lightning Globe	13-19	Act I
Disfigured	Lightning	Shoots Lightning Globe	20-28	Act II
Damned	Lightning	Shoots Lightning Globe	60-84	Act IV

As the above table suggests, having resistance to Lightning is important when fighting any of these monsters. In a multiplayer game, the Paladin can greatly aid his party by using the Resist Lightning Aura.

BLOOD HAWK

VARIANTS	RESISTANCE	SPECIAL ATTACKS	HIT POINT RANGE	FOUND IN
Foul Crow	None	None	2-5	Act I
Blood Hawk	None	None	3-6	Act I
Black Raptor	Poison	None	7-15	Act II
Cloud Stalker	Fire/Lightning	None	8-18	Act III

These annoying creatures are spawned from nests that are dotted around the wilderness areas. Blood Hawks perform quick attacks, then fly away. Fortunately, these feathered foes are not particularly dangerous, as they don't do a great deal of damage unless they attack you in numbers. As a rule, it's best to go after the nests rather than slug it out with the individual creatures.

FALLEN

VARIANTS	RESISTANCE	SPECIAL ATTACKS	HIT POINT RANGE	FOUND IN
Fallen	None	None	1-3	Act I
Carver	None	None	3-7	Act I
Devilkin	None	None	3-9	Act I
Dark One	None	None	5-12	Act I
Warped One	All	None	10-25	Act III

Fallen Ones are small creatures that are very common throughout Act I. They will always attack in numbers, but run away if they take a hit. Their tendency to retreat can make them difficult to kill, but the fact that Fallen Shamans can resurrect them makes them even more troublesome. If you can't get to the Shamans, the best way to deal with these creatures is to shatter them with cold spells so that they cannot be resurrected.

WENDIGO

VARIANTS	RESISTANCE	SPECIAL ATTACKS	HIT POINT RANGE	FOUND IN
Gargantuan Beast	None	None	9-15	Act I
Brute	None	None	18-29	Act I
Yeti	Cold	None	29-47	Act I
Crusher	Magic	None	57-92	Act II
Wailing Beast	Magic/Fire	None	54-87	Act III

These creatures are large and frightening when you first run into them—and they can do a heck of a lot of damage if you get surrounded by a group of them! Your first encounter with Gargantuan Beasts will occur in the Den of Evil (the first quest), so be ready to face them down!

SAND RAIDER

VARIANTS	RESISTANCE	SPECIAL ATTACKS	HIT POINT RANGE	FOUND IN
Sand Raider	None	Flaming Sword Hits	38-59	Act II
Marauder	None	Cold Charge	48-76	Act II
Invader	None	Flaming Sword Hits	51-80	Act II
Infidel	None	Cold Charge	61-96	Act III
Assailant	None	Flaming Sword Hits	72-113	Act III

Sand Raiders are fearsome creatures that wield four swords at the same time! Needless to say, with the fire damage they do it's best to keep your distance from these enemies, but if you must fight them in melee it can help to have some resistance to fire. The Paladin's Resist Fire Aura is an excellent defense in these battles.

WRAITH

VARIANTS	RESISTANCE	SPECIAL ATTACKS	HIT POINT RANGE	FOUND IN
Ghost	Magic/Poison/Physical	Drains Mana	14-28	Act I
Wraith	Magic/Poison/Physical	Drains Mana	19-38	Act I
Specter	Poison/Physical	Drains Mana	34-69	Act II
Apparition	Poison/Physical	Drains Mana	36-72	Act II
Dark Shape	Poison/Physical	Drains Mana	41-82	Act III

Wraiths are tough monsters, especially for the Sorceress, because they drain mana with every attack. It is best to *use* your spells or skills that require mana when fighting these horrors or they will drain away your reserves and leave you without enough mana to finish them off. Keep Wraiths at a distance if possible, or slow them with cold.

CORRUPT ROGUE

VARIANTS	RESISTANCE	SPECIAL ATTACKS	HIT POINT RANGE	FOUND IN
Dark Hunter	None	None	4-7	Act I
Vile Hunter	None	None	8-13	Act I
Dark Stalker	None	None	12-20	Act I
Black Rogue	None	None	13-22	Act I
Flesh Hunter	Physical	None	26-43	Act III
Dark Spear Woman	None	None	6-9	Act I
Vile Lancer	None	None	11-16	Act I
Dark Lancer	None	None	16-24	Act I
Black Lancer	None	None	16-24	Act I
Flesh Lancer	None	None	34-52	Act III

Corrupt Rogues are melee fighters that like to mix it up in hand-to-hand combat. Slowing them with cold or using a skill like Iron Maiden (Necromancer) or Thorns (Paladin) that returns melee damage is effective against these monsters. Beware that the Black Rogue and Flesh Hunter are resistant to Poison, so skills like Poison Explosion (Necromancer) and Poison Javelin (Amazon) are not as effective against these creatures.

BABOON DEMON

VARIANTS	RESISTANCE	SPECIAL ATTACKS	HIT POINT RANGE	FOUND IN
Dune Beast	None	None	41-57	Act II
Jungle Hunter	None	None	45-63	Act III
Doom Ape	None	None	49-69	Act III
Temple Guard	None	None	53-75	Act III

Baboon Demons are huge, hulking monsters that are built exclusively for hand-to-hand combat. Keeping these enemies at range is your best bet. They lack resistances to any elemental damage, so use cold, fire, lightning, and poison against them.

GOATMEN

VARIANTS	RESISTANCE	SPECIAL ATTACKS	HIT POINT RANGE	FOUND IN
Moon Clan	None	None	12-17	Act I
Night Clan	None	None	17-21	Act I
Blood Clan	None	None	19-23	Act I
Death Clan	Magic/Fire	None	26-32	Act I
Hell Clan	Fire	None	46-57	Act II

The Goatmen are large, axe-wielding nasties. Although they are tough, they lack any magical or elemental resistances and are, therefore, susceptible to any weapon that adds this variety of damage. Poison works on them as well—a Rancid or Strangling Gas Potion is always great to have around if you can't create the poison yourself.

FALLEN SHAMAN

VARIANTS	RESISTANCE	SPECIAL ATTACKS	HIT POINT RANGE	FOUND IN
Fallen Shaman	Fire	Raises Fallen/Fire	4-7	Act I
Carver Shaman	Fire	Raises Carver/Fire	9-15	Act I
Devilkin Shaman	Fire	Raises Devilkin/Fire	13-22	Act I
Dark Shaman	Fire	Raises Dark Ones/Fire	16-26	Act I
Warped Shaman	Fire/magic	Raises Warped Ones/Fire	32-45	Act III

The Fallen Shaman are a group of monsters that you need to target first and foremost when you come across them. This is because they are capable of resurrecting other monsters of their kind once they've been killed. Often the best tactic is to wade through the Fallen (or Carvers, or whatever) and go straight to the Shaman so that they won't be able to raise up their minions again after you've killed them. When the Shaman is dead, the rest are easy to eliminate.

SPIKE FIEND

VARIANTS	RESISTANCE	SPECIAL ATTACKS	HIT POINT RANGE	FOUND IN
Quill Rat	None	None	1-4	Act I
Spike Fiend	None	None	3-11	Act I
Thorn Beast	None	None	4-16	Act I
Razor Spine	None	None	4-17	Act I
Jungle Urchin	None	None	8-33	Act III

Spike Fiends are challenging beasts because they discharge thorns over great distances, meaning they don't have to be nearby to hurt you. When they travel in packs they can do plenty of damage in a short time. The Amazon's Evade skill is excellent for avoiding the ranged attacks of these creatures. As with other monsters that lack elemental resistances, any weapon that has an elemental or magical attack is worth using on them.

Sand Maggot

VARIANTS	RESISTANCE	SPECIAL ATTACKS	HIT POINT RANGE	FOUND IN
Sand Maggot	None	Lays Eggs/Spits Poison	47-59	Act II
Rock Worm	None	Lays Eggs/Spits Poison	50-62	Act II
Devourer	None	Lays Eggs/Spits Poison	56-69	Act II
Giant Lamprey	None	Lays Eggs/Spits Poison	61-75	Act III
Blood Maggot	None	Lays Eggs/Spits Poison	78-96	Act IV

Sand Maggots are dangerous because they can not only burrow underground to protect themselves from attack, but can also lay eggs to propagate. Sand Maggots also have a Poison attack, so having a resistance to poison or some Antidote potions handy will be necessary when fighting these creatures. As a rule, Sand Maggots only inhabit caverns, but you never know when you might meet up with one.

Claw Viper

VARIANTS	RESISTANCE	SPECIAL ATTACKS	HIT POINT RANGE	FOUND IN
Tomb Viper	None	Freezing Charge Attack	16-26	Act II
Claw Viper	Cold	Freezing Charge Attack	21-34	Act II
Salamander	Cold	Freezing Charge Attack	25-41	Act II
Pit Viper	Cold/Poison	Freezing Charge Attack	27-45	Act II
Serpent Magus	Magic/Cold/Poison	Freezing Charge Attack	30-49	Act III

This creature's Freezing Charge Attack can slow you down considerably, so having some sort of cold resistance, like the Paladin's Resist Cold, is of great value in these battles. Claw Vipers are tough enemies to deal with, so don't take them lightly.

Sand Leaper

VARIANTS	RESISTANCE	SPECIAL ATTACKS	HIT POINT RANGE	FOUND IN
Sand Leaper	None	None	20-58	Act II
Cave Leaper	None	None	21-62	Act II
Tomb Creeper	Fire	None	23-69	Act II
Tree Lurker	Lightning/Fire	None	28-85	Act III
Cliff Lurker	Lightning/Fire/Physical	None	37-111	Act IV

Sand Leapers are difficult to score damage on because they cannot be hit when they're in the act of leaping, and that is quite often. Skills that can passively affect these creatures, such as the Paladin's Holy Fire, are great to use when near groups of Sand Leapers; cold is also effective because it will slow their scurrying and leaping enough for you to get in a clean hit.

PANTHER WOMAN

VARIANTS	RESISTANCE	SPECIAL ATTACKS	HIT POINT RANGE	FOUND IN
Huntress	None	None	17-29	Act II
Sabre Cat	None	None	18-31	Act II
Night Tiger	None	None	21-34	Act II
Hell Cat	None	None	23-38	Act II
Slinger	None	None	15-25	Act II
Spear Cat	None	None	17-29	Act II
Night Slinger	None	None	20-33	Act II
Hell Slinger	None	None	21-34	Act II

Panther Women are half-feline, half-human creatures that are swift and deadly. They travel in packs and will race after fleeing adventurers as they seek to deliver the killing blow. Some Panther Women launch barbed javelins, so it's always good to try and slow them down and focus your first attacks against them. Use ranged attacks against any of these beasts and, if you're an Amazon, put points into the Dodge and Evade skills.

SWARM

VARIANTS	RESISTANCE	SPECIAL ATTACKS	HIT POINT RANGE	FOUND IN
Itchies	Physical	Drains Stamina	7-15	Act II
Black Locust	Physical	Drains Stamina	8-16	Act II
Plague Bugs	Physical	Drains Stamina	9-19	Act II
Hell Swarm	Lightning/Physical	Drains Stamina	10-21	Act III

A Swarm is, quite literally, thousands of hostile insects that move *en masse* to attack you. Surprisingly, for a bunch of insects, Swarms can carry a surprising array of items, which they drop when they die. They always attack in bunches, so try not to get surrounded by them.

SCARAB DEMON

VARIANTS	RESISTANCE	SPECIAL ATTACKS	HIT POINT RANGE	FOUND IN
Dung Soldier	None	Defend with Sparks	20-33	Act II
Death Beetle	None	Defend with Sparks	23-38	Act II
Scarab	None	Defend with Sparks	24-40	Act II
Steel Scarab	None	Defend with Sparks	27-44	Act II
Bone Scarab	None	Defend with Sparks	32-53	Act III

Scarab Demons are tough little creatures that emit electrical sparks when they sustain damage. Therefore, every time you land a hit, you can expect to take a shock of lightning in return. Any resistance to lightning that you can acquire will make the Scarab Demon's special attack manageable.

Mummy

VARIANTS	RESISTANCE	SPECIAL ATTACKS	HIT POINT RANGE	FOUND IN
Dried Corpse	Poison	Poison	19-44	Act II
Decayed	Poison	Poison	22-50	Act II
Embalmed	Poison	Poison	26-59	Act II
Preserved Dead	Poison	Poison	29-65	Act II/III
Cadaver	Poison	Poison	30-68	Act III

Mummies are part of the family of the undead, and will poison you when they die. They are also resistant to poison, so using this form of magic against them is ill advised. Your best bet is to use ranged attacks or, if you are a melee class, be careful where you tread and make sure you have antidotes at your disposal.

Greater Mummy

VARIANTS	RESISTANCE	SPECIAL ATTACKS	HIT POINT RANGE	FOUND IN
Hollow One	Poison	Poison Cloud/Unholy Bolt	62-75	Act II
Guardian	Poison	Poison Cloud/Unholy Bolt	69-85	Act II
Unraveller	Poison	Poison Cloud/Unholy Bolt	74-92	Act II
Horadrum Ancient	Poison	Poison Cloud/Unholy Bolt	82-120	Act II/III

Greater Mummies are very tough, and are usually protected by many minions. Like Fallen Shaman, Greater Mummies can raise slain enemies to fight again. As a rule, it's best to go after the Greater Mummies first so they cannot create more undead followers. If you can't get to them, destroy their minions with cold, or use a Necromancer to raise the dead into Skeletons before the Greater Mummy has a chance to the same.

Vulture Demon

VARIANTS	RESISTANCE	SPECIAL ATTACKS	HIT POINT RANGE	FOUND IN
Carrion Bird	None	None	20-32	Act II
Undead Scavenger	None	None	21-34	Act II
Hell Buzzard	None	None	26-43	Act III
Winged Nightmare	None	None	31-51	Act III

Vulture Demons are flying enemies that cannot be hit when they are airborne. You must be patient and wait until they land before you can deal them a killing blow. Just to be fair, these birds cannot damage you if they're in the air; they must land first before they can attack.

MOSQUITO DEMON

VARIANTS	RESISTANCE	SPECIAL ATTACKS	HIT POINT RANGE	FOUND IN
Sucker	None	Drains Mana & Stamina	8-41	Act III
Feeder	None	Drains Mana & Stamina	9-45	Act III

While Mosquito Demons are not particularly tough, they will suck you dry of all of your mana and stamina if you let them surround you. This can be a major problem if you need to cast spells to run away from trouble, so keep Mana and Stamina Potions on hand at all times.

WILLOWISP

VARIANTS	RESISTANCE	SPECIAL ATTACKS	HIT POINT RANGE	FOUND IN
Gloam	Lightning/Physical	Drains Mana	19-38	Act III
Swamp Ghost	Lightning/Physical	Drains Mana	21-41	Act III
Burning Soul	Lightning/Physical	Drains Mana	24-46	Act IV
Black Soul	Lightning/Physical	Drains Mana	25-50	Act IV

Willowisps are a vicious enemy that consumes the mana from your reserves, thus rendering any character that's relying on mana helpless. The only way to avoid this problem is to keep your distance from these pests, keep Mana Potions handy, or kill them before they have a chance to drain away your mana.

EVIL SPIDERS

VARIANTS	RESISTANCE	SPECIAL ATTACKS	HIT POINT RANGE	FOUND IN
Arach	None	Spins Web	37-46	Act I
Poison Spinner	None	Spins Web	66-84	Act III
Flame Spider	None	Spins Web	69-88	Act III
Spider Magus	None	Spins Web	75-95	Act III

When injured, these creatures are capable of spinning a web that, if you move through it, slows your movement as if you were hit by a cold spell. Fortunately, the duration of the Spider's web is very short.

Thorned Hulk

VARIANTS	RESISTANCE	SPECIAL ATTACKS	HIT POINT RANGE	FOUND IN
Thorned Hulk	None	Stun	67-109	Act III
Bramble Hulk	None	Stun	70-114	Act III
Thrasher	None	Stun	73-119	Act III
Spike Fist	None	Stun	85-138	Act IV

Thorned Hulks are big, tough brutes that inflict a lot of damage and have large number of hit points to back them up. Their basic attack is very similar to the Barbarian Frenzy skill. Don't get caught in the middle of a group of Thorned Hulks or you'll end up dead.

Vampires

VARIANTS	RESISTANCE	SPECIAL ATTACKS	HIT POINT RANGE	FOUND IN
Banished	Cold/Physical	Steals Life/Cold/Fire	40-55	Act I
Ghoul Lord	Cold/Physical	Steals Life/Cold/Fire	61-84	Act II
Night Lord	Cold/Physical	Steals Life/Cold/Fire	64-88	Act III
Dark Lord	Cold/Physical	Steals Life/Cold/Fire	70-96	Act III
Blood Lord	Cold/Physical	Steals Life/Cold/Fire	76-105	Act III

Much like Vampires of classic mythology, these creatures of the night steal life from your character when they come into contact with you. Vampires are also resistant to both Cold and Poison, making them dangerous to deal with. Keep your distance and attack with ranged weapons to destroy these fiends. It's also a good idea to keep some health potions on hand should they start to drain your life.

Bat Demon

VARIANTS	RESISTANCE	SPECIAL ATTACKS	HIT POINT RANGE	FOUND IN
Desert Wing	None	Shocking Hit	14-48	Act II
Fiend	None	Shocking Hit	18-16	Act III
Gloom Bat	None	Shocking Hit	19-66	Act III
Blood Diver	None	Shocking Hit	21-72	Act III
Dark Familiar	None	Shocking Hit	24-84	Act IV

Bat Demons are a class of creatures that fly, and are thus difficult to hit. They also deliver electrical damage when they hit you, and are fairly strong enemies.

FETISH

VARIANTS	RESISTANCE	SPECIAL ATTACKS	HIT POINT RANGE	FOUND IN
Rat Man	None	Blow Darts	14-24	Act I
Fetish	None	Blow Darts	28-47	Act III
Flayer	None	Blow Darts	30-49	Act III
Soul Killer	None	Blow Darts	31-51	Act III
Stygian Doll	None	Blow Darts	32-53	Act III

These monsters attack you with knives that are almost the size of their entire bodies! They also are capable of firing at you with blow darts from a distance. Fetishes tend to attack, then quickly run away. The Shaman of their tribes can resurrect them, so you must always be on the lookout for Fetishes that you've already killed since they might be summoned back into battle.

CORRUPT ARCHER

VARIANTS	RESISTANCE	SPECIAL ATTACKS	HIT POINT RANGE	FOUND IN
Dark Ranger	None	None	10-14	Act I
Vile Archer	None	None	12-17	Act I
Dark Archer	None	None	16-23	Act I
Black Archer	None	None	21-31	Act I
Flesh Archer	Physical	None	40-58	Act III

This is a group of enemies that you'll be seeing plenty of as you wind your way through *Diablo II*. All of these monsters specialize in ranged attacks, so you need to keep your distance from them. As with other enemies that launch ranged attacks, an Amazon skilled in Evade will gain an edge in these battles.

Skeleton Archer

VARIANTS	RESISTANCE	SPECIAL ATTACKS	HIT POINT RANGE	FOUND IN
Skeleton Archer	Poison	None	9-19	Act I
Corpse Archer	Poison	None	14-28	Act I
Bone Archer	Cold/Poison	None	14-28	Act I
Burning Dead Archer	Fire/Poison	Fire Arrows	21-42	Act II
Horror Archer	Lightning/Magic/Poison	Lightning Arrows	28-57	Act II

Skeleton Archers are undead that fire ranged weapons—and in the case of the Horror Archer and Burning Dead Archer, Lightning and Fire arrows respectively. All of these creatures have resistance to poison, so don't even attempt poison weapons or potions. Like all undead, skills such as Sanctuary and Holy Bolt are very effective against them.

Sand Maggot Young

VARIANTS	RESISTANCE	SPECIAL ATTACKS	HIT POINT RANGE	FOUND IN
Sand Maggot Young	None	None	7-22	Act II
Rock Worm Young	None	None	8-23	Act II
Devourer Young	None	None	8-26	Act II
Giant Lamprey Young	None	None	9-28	Act III
Blood Maggot Young	None	None	12-36	Act IV

This group of creatures is simply the young of the larger versions you see in the game. When eggs hatch, this is what you get.

Blunderbore

VARIANTS	RESISTANCE	SPECIAL ATTACKS	HIT POINT RANGE	FOUND IN
Blunderbore	None	Knockback Attack	41-73	Act II
Gorbelly	None	Knockback Attack	45-81	Act II
Mauler	None	Knockback Attack	45-81	Act II
Urdar	All	Knockback Attack	62-111	Act IV

Be wary of the knockback attack of these huge beasts. They attack with a skill that's similar to Smite or Bash, so keep your distance from them. You might want to let Hirelings or the Necromancer's Golems and/or Skeletons fight it out while you provide support from a distance.

ZEALOT

VARIANTS	RESISTANCE	SPECIAL ATTACKS	HIT POINT RANGE	FOUND IN
Zakarumite	None	None	52-69	Act III
Faithful	None	None	57-75	Act III
Zealot	None	None	62-82	Act III

These enemies are masters of the Pole-arm, and do massive damage when they land a hit. For the Amazon, a skill like Dodge would be ideal when facing these monsters.

FROG

VARIANTS	RESISTANCE	SPECIAL ATTACKS	HIT POINT RANGE	FOUND IN
Swamp Dweller	None	Spits Fire Bolts	57-75	Act III
Bog Creature	None	Spits Fire Bolts	60-79	Act III
Slime Prince	None	Spits Fire Bolts	62-82	Act III

During multiplayer games, be sure to have a Paladin with a Resist Fire aura activated when you face these monsters. In single-player action, if you're not a Paladin, strive to have at least one item (ring, amulet, or piece of armor) that offers some resistance to fire to dilute the damage dealt by their fire bolts.

CANTOR

VARIANTS	RESISTANCE	SPECIAL ATTACKS	HIT POINT RANGE	FOUND IN
Sexton	None	Lightning/Teleport/Blizzard	54-72	Act III
Cantor	None	Lightning/Teleport/Blizzard	60-79	Act III
Heirophant	None	Lightning/Teleport/Blizzard	65-86	Act III

If you let them get close enough, Cantors have either a Lightning Damage or Cold Damage melee attack in addition to the special attacks above. These creatures also can heal Zealots and other Cantors alike, so it is vital when you meet a band of these misguided denizens that you take the Cantors out first!

TENTACLE

VARIANTS	RESISTANCE	SPECIAL ATTACKS	HIT POINT RANGE	FOUND IN
Water Watcher	None	None	49-65	Act III
River Stalker	None	None	54-72	Act III
Stygian Watcher	None	None	60-79	Act III

Tentacles are a real challenge as they quickly slide out of the murky depths to land vicious, whip-like blows upon the backs of the unwary and then retreat back to their watery lair. Often it's best simply to avoid these creatures with all due haste.

TENTACLEHEAD

VARIANTS	RESISTANCE	SPECIAL ATTACKS	HIT POINT RANGE	FOUND IN
Water Watcher	None	Spits Poison	49-65	Act III
River Stalker	None	Spits Poison	54-72	Act III
Stygian Watcher	None	Spits Poison	60-79	Act III

The head of the Tentacle creature spits a highly toxic poison, making them an even more dangerous foe. Perhaps the best way to deal with them is to move past them quickly and carry antidote potions in case they happen to poison you during your escape.

SKELETON MAGE

VARIANTS	RESISTANCE	SPECIAL ATTACKS	HIT POINT RANGE	FOUND IN
Returned Mage	Poison	Posion	10-15	Act II
Bone Mage	Poison/Cold	Cold	12-16	Act II
Burning Dead Mage	Poison/Lightning	Lightning	14-20	Act II
Horror Mage	All	All	17-23	Act II

These Skeletal Mages are dangerous because they fire elemental attacks from afar, much as the Skeletal Mages of the Necromancer. The Horror Mage is especially deadly since there are four different types that cast Cold, Lightning, Fire, or Poison spells. Every Horror Mage is resistant to Poison as well as the specific type of magic that they wield. Facing a group of these monsters requires resistances to all of the elements.

FETISH SHAMAN

	VARIANTS	RESISTANCE	SPECIAL ATTACKS	HIT POINT RANGE	FOUND IN
	Fetish Shaman	None	Raises Fetishes/Inferno	30-49	Act III
	Flayer Shaman	None	Raises Flayers/Inferno	31-51	Act III
	Soul Killer Shaman	None	Raises Soul Killers/Inferno	32-53	Act III

The Fetish Shaman raise the Fetishes, Ratmen, and Flayers from the dead. Like the other Shaman, you must kill them first before you kill any of the minions or you'll just end up killing them many times over as the Shaman resurrects them again and again.

FINGER MAGE

	VARIANTS	RESISTANCE	SPECIAL ATTACKS	HIT POINT RANGE	FOUND IN
	Doom Caster	Fire/Lightning	Homing Missiles/Drains Mana	57-81	Act IV
	Strangler	Fire/Lightning	Homing Missiles/Drains Mana	60-84	Act IV
	Storm Caster	Fire/Lightning	Homing Missiles/Drains Mana	62-87	Act IV

Always carry extra mana potions when facing Finger Mages. These creatures of magic seek dominance over opposing users of the arcane arts by firing homing missiles that drain mana upon contact!

REGURGITATOR

	VARIANTS	RESISTANCE	SPECIAL ATTACKS	HIT POINT RANGE	FOUND IN
	Corpulent	None	Eats and spits corpses	57-81	Act IV
	Corpse Spitter	None	Eats and spits corpses	60-84	Act IV
	Maw Fiend	None	Eats and spits corpses	62-87	Act IV

Regurgitators actually eat corpses and then spew the semi-digested remains at their victims! Fortunately, you don't usually see these monsters until Act IV.

UNDEAD HORROR

VARIANTS	RESISTANCE	SPECIAL ATTACKS	HIT POINT RANGE	FOUND IN
Doom Knight	All	None	57-81	Act IV
Abyss Knight	All	All	60-84	Act IV
Oblivion Knight	All	Bone Spirirt/Curses	62-87	Act IV

This group is really the royalty of the undead realm. Doom knights are tough undead melee fighters that do a respectable amount of damage when hit. Abyss Knights are slightly more resilient and cast an array of elemental spells. Oblivion Knights can strike terror into the hearts of even the most stalwart adventurer as they cast curses and Bone Spirit to slay those who stand in their way. Use Holy Bolt if you're a Paladin; there's never a better time than during a battle with Undead Horror.

MEGADEMON

VARIANTS	RESISTANCE	SPECIAL ATTACKS	HIT POINT RANGE	FOUND IN
Balrog	Fire	Inferno	57-81	Act IV
Pit Lord	Fire	Inferno	60-84	Act IV
Venom Lord	Fire/Poison	Inferno	62-87	Act IV

Megademons are sword-wielding, fire-breathing beasts that absolutely look the part of a creature that belongs in Hell. They are fearsome and often travel in packs.

Champions

Champion Monsters are randomly distributed throughout Diablo II, and appear in small packs. Champions are much tougher versions of Standard monsters. When these powerful monsters die, they usually give up a little more loot than Standard monsters do. Because you never know when you'll meet a pack of Champions, be ready for them at any time.

Champions and Uniques are random and can be found anywhere in the game, so be ready for them.

Unique Monsters

Unique Monsters usually have two-word names, like 'Ooze Drool'. Occasionally this name is followed by an appellation, like 'the Hungry'. Uniques are randomly distributed throughout *Diablo II*, and they always appear with a small pack of Standard Monsters, labeled as 'minions'. Like Champions, they usually give up a little more loot than Standard monsters do.

SUPER UNIQUE MONSTERS

These are the preset 'boss' monsters that you'll face as you move through the quests of *Diablo II*. Each monster is listed below with their special abilities and the general locations where they appear in the game. Keep in mind that most of these monsters will appear with minions, making them extra difficult to defeat! For details about how to handle some of the trickier Super Unique Monsters, refer to The Quests chapter. Below is a table that shows you exactly what each of the attributes means so that you can judge what you're up against when facing each of the bosses.

ATTRIBUTE	EFFECT
EXTRA STRONG	Min Dam x3 Max Dam x3 To Hit Plus 25%
EXTRA FAST	Unique & Pack get Velocity Increase: Attack Rate x2 (unique only)
MAGICAL RESISTANCE	Resist All 75% (Fire, Cold, & Lightning)
CURSE	50% Hits, an Amp Dam Curse (MLVL / 4) on attacker
FIRE ENCHANTED	Fire Min Dam +(min dam) Fire Max Dam +(max dam) x2 To Hit Fire Resist 75%
COLD ENCHANTED	Cold Min +(min dam) Cold Max +(max dam) Cold Length +20 To Hit x2 Cold Resist 75%
LIGHTNING ENCHANTED	Light Min Dam +(min dam) Light Max Dam +(max dam) To Hit x2 Light Resist 75%
MANA BURN	Mana Min Dam +(min dam x4) Mana Max Dam +(max dam x4) To Hit x2 Magic Resist 75%
SPECTRAL HIT	Fire, Light, & Cold Resist 20% To Hit x2 (random fire, cold, light, magic, & poison do Element hit) +(min dam) +(max dam)
STONE SKIN	Dam Resist +80% AC x3
MULTI-SHOT	2 more missiles of the same type are shot
TELEPORT	(health <33%) or (ranged monster & someone is close) Teleport if (health <33%) add +25% of max. hit points to health
AURA ENCHANTED	Might (at monster level 4) Holy Fire (at monster level 2) Thorns (at monster level 4) Holy Freeze (at monster level 2) Holy Shock (at monster level 2) Conviction (at monster level 4) Fanaticism (at monster level 4)
THIEVING	Monster steals potions out of the Belt (Potions drop down to proper slot)
POISON STRIKE	Hit Poisons target
POISON CLOUD	Damages and poisons as Poison Javelin skill of the Amazon
FIRE ARROW	Damages as Fire Arrow skill of the Amazon

ANDARIEL
(SPECIAL)

Special Attributes: Poison Strike, Poison Cloud
Found in: Act I, Monastery

BISHIBOSH
(FALLEN SHAMAN)

Special Attributes: Magic Resistance, Fire Enchanted
Found in: Act I, The Cold Plains

BONEBREAK
(SKELETON)

Special Attributes: Extra Strong, Magic Resistant
Found in: Act I, The Crypt

BLOOD RAVEN
(CORRUPT ROGUE ARCHER)

Special Attributes: Fire Arrow
Found in: Act I, The Burial Grounds

COLDCROW
(DARK RANGER)

Special Attributes: Cold Enchanted
Found in: Act I, The Cave

RAKANISHU
(CARVER)

Special Attributes: Lightning Enchanted, Extra Fast
Found in: Act I, The Stony Field

TREEHEAD WOODFIST
(BRUTE)

Special Attributes: Extra Strong, Extra Fast
Found in: Act I, The Dark Woods

GRISWOLD
(CHARACTER FROM DIABLO)

Special Attributes: Cursed
Found in: Act I, Tristram

THE COUNTESS
(DARK STALKER)

Special Attributes: Fire Enchanted
Found in: Act I, Forgotten Tower

PITSPAWN FOULDOG
(TAINTED)

Special Attributes: Cursed, Cold Enchanted
Found in: Act I, Jail Level 2

FLAMESPIKE THE CRAWLER
(RAZOR SPINE)

Special Attributes: Fire Enchanted, Cursed
Found in: Act I, Inner Cloister

BONE ASH
(BURNING DEAD MAGE)

Special Attributes: Extra Strong, Cold Enchanted, Magic Resistant.
Found in: Act I, Cathedral

THE SMITH
(SPECIAL)

Special Attributes: Extra Strong
Found in: Act I, Barracks

CORPSEFIRE
(ZOMBIE)

Special Attributes: Spectral Hit
Found in: Act I, The Den of Evil

RADAMENT
(GREATER MUMMY)

Special Attributes: Extra Fast
Found in: Act II, The Sewers Level 3

BLOODWITCH THE WILD
(HUNTRESS)

Special Attributes: Extra Strong, Cursed
Found in: Act II, Halls of the Dead Level 3

FANGSKIN
(SALAMANDER)

Special Attributes: Light Enchanted, Extra Fast
Found in: Act II, Claw Viper Temple Level 2

BEETLEBURST
(SAND WARRIOR)

Special Attributes: Magic Resistant
Found in: Act II, Far Oasis

COLDWORM THE BURROWER
(SAND MAGGOT QUEEN)

Special Attributes: Cold Enchanted, Magic Resistant
Found in: Act II, Maggot Lair Level 3

FIRE EYE
(INVADER)

Special Attributes: Fire Enchanted, Extra Fast
Found in: Act II, Palace Cellar Level 3

DARK ELDER
(PLAGUE BEARER)

Special Attributes: Extra Fast, Magic Resistant
Found in: Act II, Lost City

THE SUMMONER
(SPECIAL)

Special Attributes: Extra Strong, Extra Fast
Found in: Act II, Arcane Sanctuary

ANCIENT KAA THE SOULLESS
(UNRAVELER)

Special Attributes: Magic Resistant, Extra Strong, Lightning Enchanted.
Found in: Act II, Tal Rasha's Tomb

CREEPING FEATURE
(DECAYED)

Special Attributes: Extra Strong, Cold Enchanted
Found in: Act II, Stony Tomb Level 2

WITCH DOCTOR ENDUGU
(SOUL KILLER SHAMAN)

Special Attributes: Magic Resistant, Fire Enchanted
Found in: Act III, Flayer Dungeon Level 3

STORMTREE
(THRASHER)

Special Attributes: Extra Fast, Lightning Enchanted
Found in: Act III, Lower Kurast

BATTLEMAID SARINA
(FLESH HUNTER)

Special Attributes: Extra Fast, Spectral Hit
Found in: Act III, Ruined Temple

ICEHAWK RIFTWING
(GLOOM BAT)

Special Attributes: Cold Enchanted, Teleportation
Found in: Act III, Sewers Level 1

SSZARK THE BURNING
(FLAME SPIDER)

Special Attributes: Extra Strong, Cursed
Found in: Act III, Spider Cavern

ISMAIL VILEHAND
(COUNCIL MEMBER)

Special Attributes: Extra Fast, Cursed
Found in: Act III, Travincal

GELEB FLAMEFINGER
(COUNCIL MEMBER)

Special Attributes: Extra Strong, Fire Enchanted
Found in: Act III, Travincal

TOORC ICEFIST
(COUNCIL MEMBER)

Special Attributes: Cold Enchanted, Stone Skin
Found in: Act III, Travincal

WYAND VOIDFINGER
(COUNCIL MEMBER)

Special Attributes: Mana Burn, Teleportation
Found in: Act III, Durance of Hate Level 3

MAFFER DRAGONHAND
(COUNCIL MEMBER)

Special Attributes: Extra Fast, Extra Strong, Teleportation
Found in: Act III, Durance of Hate Level 3

BREMM SPARKFIST
(COUNCIL MEMBER)

Special Attributes: Aura Enchanted, Lightning Enchanted
Found in: Act III, Durance of Hate Level 3

INFECTOR OF SOULS
(VENOM LORD)

Special Attributes: Extra Fast, Spectral Hit
Found in: Act IV, Chaos Sanctuary (seal)

HEPHASTO THE ARMORER
(OVERLORD)

Special Attributes: Aura Extra Strong, Cursed, Magic Resistant
Found in: Act IV, River of Flame

GRAND VIZIER OF CHAOS
(STORM CASTER)

Special Attributes: Extra Fast, Thieving, Aura Enchanted
Found in: Act IV, Chaos Sanctuary (seal)

LORD DE SEIS
(OBLIVION KNIGHT)

Special Attributes: Extra Fast, Aura, Thieving
Found in: Act IV, Chaos Sanctuary (seal)

WEAPONS & ARMOR

When you move the mouse over an item, the name of the item is color-coded. This is to inform you, even before an item is identified, what the class of the item is:

White = Standard   **Yellow** = Rare

Gray = Socketed   **Gold** = Unique

Blue = Magic   **Green** = Set Item

STANDARD WEAPONS

Choosing a weapon often depends on what kinds of weapons you pick up or purchase as you work through the *Diablo II* world. Ideally, you'll want to use magical weapons, but standard weapons will be the usual fare early in the game. Even the rarest of enchanted items are created from these basic types and, indeed, it must be a standard weapon that you ask Charsi to Imbue after you return the Hordric Malus to her near the end of Act I. The following list of basic weapons and armor will show you just what awaits you in *Diablo II*. You will undoubtedly come across each of these items at some point in the game, but what you use will depend on your preference. The kind of character you have will also play a role in this decision (a Barbarian with many skill points in Sword Mastery will naturally be attracted to swords), as well as the enemies you're facing within each Act.

NOTE......

The costs of these items can vary by a great deal depending on item type, number of special attributes (if any), and how much of the item's durability is remaining.

AXES

Hand Axe	Large Axe	Throwing Axe
Axe	Broad Axe	Balanced Axe
Double Axe	Battle Axe	
Military Pick	Great Axe	
War Axe	Giant Axe	

WANDS

Wand
Yew Wand
Bone Wand
Grim Wand

CLUBS

Club	War Hammer	War Scepter
Spiked Club	Maul	
Mace	Great Maul	
Morning Star	Scepter	
Flail	Grand Scepter	

SWORDS

Short Sword	Long Sword	Bastard Sword
Scimitar	War Sword	Flamberge
Saber	Two-Handed	Great Sword
Falchion	Sword	
Crystal Sword	Claymore	
Broad Sword	Giant Sword	

DAGGERS

Dagger	Throwing Knife
Dirk	Balanced Knife
Kris	
Blade	

JAVELINS/SPEARS

Javelin	Throwing Spear	Spetum
Pilum	Spear	Pike
Short Spear	Trident	
Glaive	Brandistock	

POLE-ARMS

Bardiche	Halberd
Voulge	War Scythe
Scythe	
Poleaxe	

STAVES

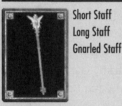

Short Staff	Battle Staff
Long Staff	War Staff
Gnarled Staff	

BOWS/CROSSBOWS

Short Bow	Long Battle Bow	Heavy Crossbow
Hunter's Bow	Short War Bow	Repeating
Long Bow	Long War Bow	Crossbow
Composite Bow	Light Crossbow	
Short Battle Bow	Crossbow	

POTIONS

Strangling Gas	Potion	Oil Potion
Potion	Exploding	
Fulminating	Potion	
Potion	Rancid Gas	
Choking Gas	Potion	

STANDARD ARMOR

HEAD PROTECTION

Cap	Great Helm
Skull Cap	Crown
Helm	Mask
Full Helm	Bone Helm

BODY ARMOR

Quilted Armor	Chain Mail	Ancient Armor
Leather Armor	Breast Plate	Light Plate
Hard Leather Armor	Splint Mail	
Studded Leather	Plate Mail	
Ring Mail	Field Plate	
Scale Mail	Gothic Plate	
	Full Plate Mail	

HIELDS

Buckler Tower Shield
Small Shield Gothic Shield
Large Shield Bone Shield
Kite Shield Spiked Shield

HAND PROTECTION

Gloves
Heavy Gloves
Chain Gloves
Light Gauntlets
Gauntlets

OOT PROTECTION

Leather Boots
Heavy Boots
Chain Boots
Light Plate Boots
Greaves

BELTS

Sash
Light Belt
Belt
Heavy Belt
Plate Belt

MAGIC WEAPONS & ARMOR

s in the original *Diablo*, there are plenty of magical items to be found as you work your ay through the game. And once again a series of prefixes and suffixes determines the ualities of the items. For example, you might pick up a Cobalt Sword of The Titan. This word would give you an added cold attack (21-30), as well as increased strength (21-0). In this way, literally hundreds-of-thousands of unique magical weapons and armor an be created in any given *Diablo II* game. Because of the vast complexity of this sys-em it's possible to never see the same magical em twice, even if you're a frequent player! Vhenever you find an item and identify it (either y talking to Cain or by using an Identify Scroll), ou will be able to see exactly what it does by sim-ly moving your mouse over the weapon in your nventory. For this reason you will not need to refer o these tables when playing; the purpose of these ables, however, is merely to show you what's pos-ible when different prefixes and suffixes combine!

NOTE......

You don't need to access these tables when you find an item in the game; indeed, you can simply move your mouse over the item to find out what it does.

Magic Items are always worth picking up, even if you intend to simply sell them.

SUFFIX	EFFECT	SUFFIX	EFFECT	SUFFIX	EFFECT
of Health	Damage reduced by 1	of Craftsmanship	Adds 1-2 to max damage	of the Bear	Causes knockback
of Protection	Damage reduced by 2	of Quality	Adds 2 to max damage	of Light	Light radius +1
of Absorption	Damage reduced by 3	of Maiming	Adds 3–4 to max damage	of Radiance	Light radius +3
of Life	Damage reduced by 4	of Slaying	Adds 5–7 to max damage	of the Sun	Light radius +5
of Warding	Magic damage reduced by 1	of Gore	Adds 8–10 to max damage	of Life	Adds 5 to Life
of the Sentinel	Magic damage reduced by 2	of Carnage	Adds 11–14 to max damage	of the Jackal	Adds 1–5 to Life
of Guarding	Magic damage reduced by 3	of Slaughter	Adds 15–20 to max damage	of the Fox	Adds 5–10 to Life
of Negation	Magic damage reduced by 4	of Worth	Adds 1 to min damage	of the Wolf	Adds 11–20 to Life
of Piercing	Ignores target defense	of Measure	Adds 2 to min damage	of the Tiger	Adds 21–30 to Life
of Bashing	Hit reduces monster defense by 25–40	of Excellence	Adds 3 to min damage	of the Mammoth	Adds 31–40 to Life
of Puncturing	Hit reduces monster defense by 10–20	of Performance	Adds 4-5 to min damage	of the Colossus	Adds 41–60 to Life
of Thorns	Attacker takes 1–3 damage	of Blight	Adds 2–7 poison damage over 3 seconds	of the Leech	Steals 4–7% of damage done and adds it to your Life
of Spikes	Attacker takes 2–6 damage	of Venom	Adds 4–14 poison damage over 3 seconds	of the Locust	Steals 8–10% of damage done and adds it to your Lif
of Readiness	Attack speed increased by 1 level	of Pestilence	Adds 12–28 poison damage over 4 seconds	of the Bat	Steals 4–8% of damage don and adds it to your Mana
of Alacrity	Attack speed increased by 2 levels	of Dexterity	Adds 1–3 to dexterity	of the Vampire	Steals 9–12% of damage done and adds it to your Mana
of Swiftness	Attack speed increased by 3 levels	of Skill	Adds 4–6 to dexterity		
of Quickness	Attack speed increased by 4 levels	of Accuracy	Adds 7–10 to dexterity	of Defiance	Poison length reduced by 75%
		of Precision	Adds 11–15 to dexterity	of Amelioration	Poison length reduced by 50%
		of Perfection	Adds 16–20 to dexterity		
of Blocking	+10% Chance of blocking	of Balance	Fast hit recovery	of Remedy	Poison length reduced by 25%
of Deflecting	+20% Chance of blocking	of Stability	Fastest hit recovery		
of the Apprentice	Fast cast rate	of Regeneration	Replenish life +3	of Simplicity	-40% to Requirements to us
of the Magus	Fastest cast rate	of Regrowth	Replenish life +5	of Ease	-20% to Requirements to us
of Frost	Adds 1–4 Cold damage	of Vileness	Prevents monster heal	of Strength	Adds 1–3 to Strength
of the Glacier	Adds 4–12 Cold damage	of Greed	40%-60% more gold when looting	of Might	Adds 4–6 to Strength
of Thawing	Half freeze duration			of the Ox	Adds 7–10 to Strength
of Flame	Adds 1 minimum to 2-6 maximum Fire damage	of Wealth	80%-120% more gold when looting	of the Giant	Adds 11–15 to Strength
of Fire	Adds 2 minimum to 6-11 maximum Fire damage	of Chance	10%–19% better chance of finding a magic item	of the Titan	Adds 16–20 to Strength
of Burning	Adds 10 minimum to 10-20 maximum Fire damage	of Fortune	20%–35% better chance of finding a magic item	of Pacing	Fast run/walk
				of Haste	Faster run/walk
of Shock	Adds 1–8 Lightning damage	of Energy	Adds 1–5 to Mana	of Speed	Fastest run/walk
of Lightning	Adds 1–16 Lightning damage	of the Mind	Adds 6–10 to Mana		
		of Brilliance	Adds 11–15 to Mana		
		of Sorcery	Adds 16–20 to Mana		
of Thunder	Adds 1–32 Lightning damage	of Wizardry	Adds 21–30 to Mana		

CHAPTER 4: THE LISTS

PREFIX	EFFECT	PREFIX	EFFECT	PREFIX	EFFECT
turdy	Defense is 120-130% of normal	Fine	+21–40 to Attack rating, Damage is 121–130% of normal	Crimson	+5–10% to Fire Resistance
trong	Defense is 131-140% of normal			Burgundy	+11–20% to Fire Resistance
lorious	Defense is 141-150% of normal	Warrior's	+41–60 to Attack rating, Damage is 131–140% of normal	Garnet	+21–30% to Fire Resistance
essed	Defense is 151-160% of normal			Ruby	+31–50% to Fire Resistance
aintly	Defense is 161-180% of normal	Soldier's	+61–80 to Attack rating, Damage is 141–150% of normal	Ocher	+5–10% to Lightning Resistance
oly	Defense is 181-200% of normal			Tangerine	+11–20% to Lightning Resistance
evious	Magic damage reduced by 1	Knight's	+81–100 to Attack rating, Damage is 151–165% of normal	Coral	+21–30% to Lightning Resistance
ortified	Magic damage reduced by 2			Amber	+31–50% to Lightning Resistance
agged	Damage is 110–120% of normal	Lord's	+101–120 to Attack rating, Damage is 166–180% of normal	Beryl	+5–10% to Poison Resistance
eadly	Damage is 121-130% of normal			Jade	+11–20% to Poison Resistance
icious	Damage is 131–140% of normal	King's	+121–150 to Attack rating, Damage is 181–200% of normal	Viridian	+21–30 to Poison Resistance
rutal	Damage is 141–150% of normal			Emerald	+31–50 to Poison Resistance
assive	Damage is 151–165% of normal	Howling	Hit causes monster to flee	Fletcher's	+1 to all Amazon skills
avage	Damage is 166–180% of normal	Fortuitous	+10-15% better chance of finding a magic item	Archer's	+2 to all Amazon skills
erciless	Damage is 181–200% of normal			Monk's	+1 to all Paladin skills
ulpine	10% damage taken goes to mana	Glimmering	Light radius +1	Priest's	+2 to all Paladin skills
reless	Stamina recovery +150%	Glowing	Light radius +2	Summoner's	+1 to all Necromancer skills
ugged	Base Stamina +3-5	Lizard's	+1–5 to Mana	Necromancer's	+2 to all Necromancer skills
ronze	+10–20 to Attack rating	Snake's	+5–10 to Mana	Angel's	+1 to all Sorceress skills
on	+21–40 to Attack rating	Serpent's	+11–20 to Mana	Arch-Angel's	+2 to all Sorceress skills
eel	+41–60 to Attack rating	Drake's	+21–30 to Mana	Slayer's	+1 to all Barbarian skills
lver	+61–80 to Attack rating	Dragon's	+31–40 to Mana	Berserker's	+2 to all Barbarian skills
old	+81–100 to Attack rating	Wyrm's	+41–60 to Mana	Triumphant	+1 Mana after each kill
latinum	+101–120 to Attack rating	Prismatic	+15–25 to All Resistances		
eteoric	+121–150 to Attack rating	Azure	+5–10% to Cold Resistance		
harp	+10–20 to Attack rating, Damage is 110–120% of normal	Lapis	+11–20% to Cold Resistance		
		Cobalt	+21–30% to Cold Resistance		
		Sapphire	+31–50% to Cold Resistance		

UNIQUE ITEMS

Unique weapons and armor are not random in their creation, but are specific items that randomly appear in the game. These Unique items have more modifiers than even the magic weapons, and usually have a different graphic, either in your inventory or on your character. Not all Unique items are spectacular in their abilities, but if a Unique item pops up, it's always worth picking up, even if you just plan on selling it. You can always tell Unique Items from other types since their names are displayed in Gold.

NAME	TYPE	EFFECT 1	EFFECT 2
ggin's Bonnet	Cap	Enhanced damage; +30 to attack rating	+15 to mana; +15 to life
rnhelm	Skull Cap	75% extra gold from monsters; 25-50% better chance of getting magic items (varies)	+1 to all skill levels
if of Glory	Helm	Attacker takes 4 lightning damage; Hit blinds target	Lightning resist 15%; +25 defense vs. missile
uskdeep	Full Helm	-2 to light radius; Damage reduced by 3	All resistances +5; +8 to max damage
wltusk	Great Helm	35% damage taken goes to mana; Enhanced defense	Magic damage reduced by 2; Attacker takes damage of 3
dead Crown	Crown	Half freeze duration; 4% life stolen per hit	Poison resist 50%; +8 defense
e Face of Horror	Mask	150% damage to undead; Hit causes monster to flee	All resistances +5; +20 to strength
eyform	Quilted Armor	5% life stolen per hit; Magic damage reduced by 3; Cold resist 20%	Fire resist 20%; +10 to dexterity

Name	Type	Effect 1	Effect 2
Blinkbat's Form	Leather Armor	Fast run/walk; Adds 3-6 fire damage	+16 defense vs. missile; +25 defense
The Centurion	Hard Leather Armor	Replenish life +3; Damage reduced by 2	+15 to mana; +15 to maximum stamina
		+30 defense	+15 to life
		+25 to attack rating	
Twitchthroe	Studded Leather	Increased chance of blocking; Slightly increased attack speed	+10 to strength; +15 defense
		+10 to dexterity	
Darkglow	Ring Mail	+3 to light radius	5% to maximum fire resist
		5% to maximum poison resist	All resistances +10
		5% to maximum cold resist	+25 defense vs. melee
		5% to maximum lightning resist	+20 to attack rating
Hawkmail	Scale Mail	Cannot be frozen; 15% to maximum cold resist	Cold resist 15%; +12 defense
Sparking Mail	Chain Mail	Attacker takes lightning damage of 1-10 (varies)	+40 defense
		Adds 1-10 lightning damage	
Venom Ward	Breast Plate	+2 to light radius; Adds 7-9 poison damage over 3 seconds	Poison resist 15%; Enhanced damage
		15% to maximum poison resist	
Iceblink	Splint Mail	Freezes target; +4 to light radius	Magic damage reduced by 1; Cold resist 30%
Boneflesh	Plate Mail	5% life stolen per hit; +35 defense	+35 to attack rating
Rockfleece	Field Plate	Requirements -10%; Damage reduced by 3	+25 defense; +5 to strength
		Poison resist 50%	
Rattlecage	Gothic Plate	25% chance of crushing blow; Hit causes monster to flee	+45 defense; +45 to attack rating
Goldskin	Full Plate Mail	+2 to light radius	+75 defense
		Attacker takes damage of 1-10 (varies)	All resistances +30
Silks of the Victor	Ancient Armor	+2 to light radius; +1 to all skill levels	5% mana stolen per hit
Heavenly Garb	Light Plate	Enhanced defense; Regenerate mana 25%	All resistances +10
Pelta Lunata	Buckler	+40 defense; +10 to mana	+10 to life; +2 to strength
Umbral Disk	Small Shield	Hit blinds target; -2 to light radius; +18 defense	+20 to life; +10 to dexterity
Stormguild	Large Shield	Magic damage reduced by 1	Adds 1-6 lightning damage
		Lightning resist 25%	+15 defense
Steelclash	Kite Shield	Increased chance of blocking; +3 to light radius	+1 to paladin skill levels; Damage reduced by 3
Bverrit Keep	Tower Shield	Magic damage reduced by 4; Fire resist 25%	+20 defense; +5 to strength
The Ward	Gothic Shield	Increased chance of blocking; Magic damage reduced by 2	+40 defense; +10 to strength
The Hand of Broc	Gloves	3% life stolen per hit; 3% mana stolen per hit	Poison resist 10%; +20 to mana
Bloodfist	Heavy Gloves	Fastest hit recovery; +40 to life	+5 to minimum damage
Chance Guards	Bracers	24% better chance og getting magic items	+2 to light radius
		200% extra gold from monsters; +25 to attack rating	+15 defense
Magefist	Light Gauntlets	+1 to fire skills; Faster cast rate	Regenerate mana 25%; Adds 1-5 fire damage
Frostburn	Gauntlets	Enhanced damage; Maximum mana 40%	Adds 1-6 cold damage; +30 defense
Hotspur	Leather Boots	15% to maximum fire resist; Fire resist 15%	Adds 3-6 fire damage; +15 to life
Gorefoot	Heavy Boots	Faster run/walk; 2% mana stolen per hit	Attacker takes damage of 2
Treads of Cthon	Chain Boots	50% stamina drain; Fastest run/walk	+50 defense vs. missile; +10 to life
Goblin Toe	Light Plate Boots	25% chance of crushing blow; -1 to light radius	Magic damage reduced by 1; +5 defense
		Damage reduced by 1	
Tearhaunch	Plate Boots	Faster run/walk	+5 to dexterity
		All resistances +10; +10 defense	+5 to strength
Lenymo	Sash	+1 to light radius; Regenerate mana 30%	All resistances +5; +15 to mana
Snakecord	Light Belt	Adds 4-6/7/8 poison damage over 3 seconds (varies)	Replenish life +5
		Poison resist 25%	+11 defense
Nightsmoke	Belt	50% damage taken goes to mana	All resistances +10
		Damage reduced by 2	+20 to mana
Goldwrap	Heavy Belt	Slightly increased attack speed	+2 to light radius
		30% better chance of getting magic items	+40 defense
Bladebuckle	Girdle	Damage reduced by 3; +20 defense	+5 to strength; Attacker takes damage of 8
		+10 to dexterity	
Wormskull	Bone Helm	+1 to necromancer skills; 5% life stolen per hit	Poison resist 25%; +10 to mana
Wall of the Eyeless	Bone Shield	+5 to mana after each kill; Faster cast rate	3% mana stolen per hit; Poison resist 20%
Swordback Hold	Spiked Shield	Attacker takes damage of 3/4/5 (varies)	50% chance of open wounds
		Increased chance of blocking	
The Gnasher	Hand Axe	20% chance of crushing blow	+30 to attack rating 50% chance of open wounds

CHAPTER 4: THE LISTS

NAME	TYPE	EFFECT 1	EFFECT 2
eathspade	Axe	+2 points of mana after each kill	Hit blinds target
		15% bonus to attack rating	+8 to minimum damage
adebone	Double Axe	+40 to attack rating against undead	+20 defense
		200% damage to undead	Increased attack speed
		Adds 4-7 fire damage	
ull Splitter	Military Pick	Hit blinds target; Regenerate mana 20%	Adds 1-12 lightning damage; +50 to attack rating
kescar	War Axe	Poison resist 50%	+50 to attack rating
		Adds 18-28 poison damage over 3 seconds	
e of Fechmar	Large Axe	Freezes target; +2 to light radius	Enhanced damage; Cold resist 30%
reshovel	Broad Axe	60% chance of open wounds	+25 to strength
		Greatly increased attack speed	
e Chieftain	Battle Axe	Enhanced damage; Poison resist 30%	Lightning resist 10%; Fire resist 10%
		Slightly increased attack speed	Cold resist 10%
ainhew	Great Axe	+4 to light radius; 10% mana stolen per hit	+25 to mana; +14 to minimum damage
mongous	Giant Axe	33% chance of crushing blow	Adds 8-15 damage
		Requirements 20%	+10 to strength
rch of Iro	Wand	+1 to necromancer skill levels; 6% life stolen per hit	Adds 5-9 fire damage
elstrom	Yew Wand	Half freeze duration	Adds 1-9 lightning damage
		Faster cast rate	+13 to mana
		Lightning resist 40%	
avenspine	Bone Wand	5% mana stolen per hit; Adds 4-8 cold damage	+10 to dexterity; +10 to strength
ne's Lament	Grim Wand	Hit causes monster to flee	Faster cast rate
		+2 to necromancer skill levels	+40 to mana
lloak	Club	Lightning resist 60%; Fire resist 20%	Adds 6-8 fire damage; Knockback
ell Striker	Scepter	25% chance of crushing blow	+35 to attack rating
		Poison resist 20%	+15 to mana
		Fire resist 20%	
sthandle	Grand Scepter	+1 to paladin skill levels; 8% life stolen per hit	Magic damage reduced by 1; Adds 3-7 damage
ormeye	War Scepter	Adds 1-6 lightning damage; Adds 3-5 cold damage	Replenish life +10
utnail	Spiked Club	Magic damage reduced by 2	Enhanced damage
		Attacker takes damage of 1-10 (varies)	+15 to life
ushflange	Mace	+2 to light radius; Fire resist 50%	+15 to strength; Knockback
oodrise	Morning Star	50% bonus to attack rating	Enhanced damage
		Slightly increased attack speed	+2 to light radius
e General's	Flail	Slows target by 50%	+25 defense
n Do Li Ga		5% mana stolen per hit	Adds 1-20 damage
nstone	War Hammer	Enhanced damage; Adds 1-10 lightning damage	+80 to attack rating; -5 to dexterity
nesnap	Maul	40% chance of crushing blow; Enhanced damage	Cold resist 30%; Fire resist 30%
eldriver	Great Maul	Heal stamina plus 25%; Greatly increased attack speed	Requirements -50%
xot's Keen	Short Sword	25% chance of crushing blow	+25 defense
		20% bonus to attack rating	+5 to minimum damage
		+2 to light radius	
ood Crescent	Scimitar	+4 to light radius; Enhanced damage	All resistances +15; +15 to life
ewer of Krintiz	Saber	Ignore target's defense	+10 to dexterity
		3% mana stolen per hit	+10 to strength
		Enhanced damage	
eamscythe	Falchion	+3 to light radius; Increased attack speed	+20 defense; +30 to mana
urewrath	Crystal Sword	Adds 3-6 cold damage	30% deadly strike
		10% better chance of getting magic item	
iswold's Edge	Broad Sword	Adds 8/9/10 to 12/13/14/15/16 fire damage	Knockback
		Slightly increased attack speed	+40 to attack rating
ellplague	Long Sword	5% life stolen per hit	5% mana stolen per hit
		Adds 28-56 poison damage over 6 seconds	
lwen's Point	War Sword	Poison length reduced by 50%	+1 to all skill levels
		Faster block rate	+60 to attack rating
		Faster hit recovery	
adowfang	Two-Handed Sword	-2 to light radius; 5% mana stolen per hit	Cold resist 20%; Adds 5-10 cold damage
ulflay	Claymore	4% life stolen per hit; 4-10% mana stolen per hit	Enhanced damage; All resistances +5

(continues)

NAME	TYPE	EFFECT 1	EFFECT 2
Kinemil's Awl	Giant Sword	Adds 6-12 fire damage; +45 to attack rating	+20 to mana
Blacktongue	Bastard Sword	Prevent monster heal	-10 to life
		Adds 14-18 poison damage over 3 seconds	Poison resist 50%
Ripsaw	Flamberge	50% chance of open wounds; 6% mana stolen per hit	+15 to maximum damage
The Patriarch	Great Sword	Magic damage reduced by 3;	Hit blinds target
		100% extra gold from monsters	Damage reduced by 3
Gull	Dagger	Adds 1-15 damage	-5 to mana
		50% better chance of getting magic item	
The Diggler	Dirk	Enhanced damage; +10 to dexterity	Cold resist 25%; Fire resist 25%
		Greatly increased attack speed	
The Jade Tan Do	Kris	+75 to attack rating; Adds 7-14 poison damage over 3 seconds	Cannot be frozen
Spectral Shard	Blade	Fastest cast rate; All resistances +10	+55 to attack rating; +50 to mana
The Dragon Chang	Spear	200% damage to undead; +10 to minimum damage	+2 to light radius; +35 to attack rating
Razortine	Trident	Slows target by 25%; 50% target defense	+8 to dexterity; +15 to strength
		Greatly increased attack speed	
Bloodthief	Brandistock	35% chance of open wounds; 8% life stolen per hit	+26 to life; +10 to strength
Lance of Yaggai	Spetum	Adds 1-40 lightning damage; Attacker takes damage of 8	All resistances +15
The Tannr Gorerod	Pike	+3 to light radius; 15% to maximum fire resist	Adds 12-18 fire damage; +60 to attack rating
		Fire resist 15%	+30 to life
Dimoak's Hew	Bardiche	Enhanced damage; Increased attack speed	-8 defense; +15 to dexterity
Steelgoad	Voulge	30% deadly strike; Hit causes monster to flee	All resistances +5; +30 to attack rating
Soul Harvest	Scythe	30% chance of open wounds	All resistances +20
		Adds 15-23 poison damage over 5 seconds	+45 to attack rating
The Battlebranch	Poleaxe	7% life stolen per hit; Enhanced damage	+40 to attack rating; +10 to dexterity
		Greatly increased attack speed	
Woestave	Halberd	Slows target by 50%	Poison resist 15%
		Adds 7-28 poison damage over 3 seconds	+2 to light radius
		15% to maximum poison resist	
The Grim Reaper	War Scythe	50% deadly strike; Prevent monster heal	5% mana stolen per hit; -20 to life
Bane Ash	Short Staff	Fire resist 50%; Adds 4-6 fire damage	+30 to mana; Increased attack speed
Serpent Lord	Long Staff	Adds 2-37 poison damage over 3 seconds	-1 to light radius
		+10 to mana	Poison resist 50%
Spire of Lazarus	Gnarled Staff	Magic damage reduced by 3; All resistances +30	+20 to mana; +9 to strength
		Adds 7-12 fire damage	Increased attack speed
The Salamander	Battle Staff	Adds 1-10 fire damage; +50 to attack rating	+2 to fire skills; Fire resist 20%
The Iron Jang Bong	War Staff	50% bonus to attack rating; Faster cast rate	Adds 1-25 lightning damage; +25 defense
		+1 to sorceress skill levels	
Pluckeye	Short Bow	+2 to light radius	+28 to attack rating
		3% mana stolen per hit	+10 to life
		Enhanced damage	
Witherstring	Hunter's Bow	Adds 1-3 damage; Greatly increased attack speed	Fires magic arrows; +50 to attack rating
Raven Claw	Long Bow	Fires explosive arrows; 50% bonus to attack rating	+3 to dexterity; +3 to strength
Rogue's Bow	Composite Bow	30% deadly strike; 200% damage to undead	All resistances +10; +60 to attack rating
Stormstrike	Short Battle Bow	Piercing attack; Lightning resist 25%	+28 to attack rating; +8 to strength
		Adds 1-10 lightning damage	
Wizendraw	Long Battle Bow	Fires magic arrows; Cold resist 26%	+30 to mana; Increased attack speed
		+36 to attack rating	
Hellclap	Short War Bow	Fire resist 40%	+20 to attack rating
		Adds 6-9 fire damage	+12 to dexterity
		Slightly increased attack speed	
Blastbark	Long War Bow	+1 to amazon skill levels; 3% mana stolen per hit	Enhanced damage; +5 to strength
Leadcrow	Light Crossbow	25% deadly strike; Enhanced damage	+40 to attack rating; +10 to life
		Poison resist 30%	+10 to dexterity
Ichorsting	Crossbow	Piercing attack; Adds 7-9 poison damage over 3 seconds	+50 to attack rating; +20 to dexterity
Hellcast	Heavy Crossbow	Fires explosive bolts; 15% to maximum fire resist	+70 to attack rating; Increased attack speed
		Fire resist 15%	
Doomslinger	Repeating Crossbow	Piercing attack; Greatly increased attack speed	+1 to amazon skill levels; +15 to life

CHAPTER 4: THE LISTS

NAME	TYPE	EFFECT 1	EFFECT 2
Hellforge Hammer	Hellforge Hammer	Fire resist 40%; Adds 5-20 fire damage	+35 defense
Horadric Staff	Horadric Staff	Fire resist 10%	Poison resist 35%
		+10 to mana	Cold resist 10%
		+10 to life	Lightning resist 10%
		Greatly increased attack speed	
Staff of Kings	Staff of Kings	Greater attack rate increase	All resistances +10
Khalim's Flail	Flail	Adds 1-20 lightning damage; Greatly increased attack speed	+40 to attack rating
Khalim's Will	Flail	6% mana stolen per hit; Greatly increased attack speed	Adds 1-40 lightning damage; +40 to attack rating
Nokozan Relic	Amulet	+3 to light radius; 10% to maximum fire resist	Fire resist 10%; Adds 3-6 fire damage
The Eye of Etlich	Amulet	3-7% life stolen per hit (varies)	+1 to 5 light radius (varies)
		Adds 1/2 to 3/4/5 cold damage (varies)	+1 to all skill levels
		+10 to 40 defense vs. missile (varies)	
The Mahim-Oak Curio	Amulet	+10 defense	+20 to life
		+40 to attack rating	+5 to dexterity
		+20 to mana	+5 to strength
Amulet of the Viper	Amulet	Poison resist 25%; +10 to mana	+10 to life
The Stone of Jordan	Ring	+1 to all skill levels	Adds 1-12 lightning damage
		Increase maximum mana 25%	+20 to mana
Nagelring	Ring	Attacker takes damage of 3	Magic damage reduced by 2
		15% better chance of getting magic items	+18 to attack rating
Manald Heal	Ring	4% mana stolen per hit; Replenish life +5	+20 to life

RARE WEAPONS & ARMOR

Rare weapons and armor are ultra-magical items that can have as many as four magical modifiers. These weapons are randomly generated in the game and vary widely in quality. You might get a powerful weapon that will help you to crush your enemies, or you may pick up a Rare item that is more or less worthless. Basically, Rare items (weapons and armor) allow a wider possible range of modifiers, which means that any one item has the potential to be exceptional! The following is a list of the Prefixes (which are general) and the Suffixes for each class of item that are used when generating the specific name of that item. While these names have no bearing on the specific abilities of the item, they do serve to make them special in their own way.

PREFIXES

Beast	Dread	Rune	Empyrian	Hailstone	Armageddon
Eagle	Doom	Plague	Bramble	Gale	Havoc
Raven	Grim	Stone	Pain	Dire	Bitter
Viper	Bone	Wraith	Loath	Soul	Entropy
Ghoul	Death	Spirit	Glyph	Brimstone	Chaos
Skull	Shadow	Demon	Imp	Corpse	Order
Blood	Storm	Cruel	Fiend	Carrion	Rift
					Corruption

BLADE SUFFIXES

bite	thirst	cleaver	wand
scratch	razor	sever	barb
scalpel	scythe	spike	needle
fang	edge	impaler	stinger
gutter	saw	skewer	song

AXE SUFFIXES

splitter	rend	beak	scythe
cleaver	mangler	gnash	edge
sever	slayer	bite	song
sunder	reaver	thirst	

BLUNT OBJECT SUFFIXES

star	crusher	mallet
blow	breaker	knell
smasher	grinder	
ram	crack	

SPEAR SUFFIXES

lance	scourge	dart	stinger
spike	wand	scratch	goad
impaler	wrack	fang	branch
skewer	barb	gutter	
prod	needle	thirst	

BOW SUFFIXES

bolt	nock	thirst
quarrel	horn	branch
fletch	stinger	song
flight	quill	

SCEPTERS & WAND SUFFIXES

star	breaker	song	weaver
blow	grinder	call	gnarl
smasher	crack	cry	
ram	mallet	spell	
crusher	knell	chant	

HELM SUFFIXES

visage	hood	visor
crest	mask	cowl
circlet	brow	horn
veil	casque	

STAFF SUFFIXES

goad	call	weaver
branch	cry	gnarl
spire	spell	
song	chant	

ARMOR SUIT SUFFIXES

hide	wrap	jack
pelt	suit	mantle
carapace	cloak	
coat	shroud	

SHIELD SUFFIXES

guard	ward	mark
badge	tower	emblem
rock	shield	
aegis	wing	

GLOVE SUFFIXES

hand	grip	finger
fist	grasp	knuckle
claw	hold	
clutches	touch	

BOOT SUFFIXES

shank	greaves	brogues
spur	blazer	track
tread	nails	slippers
stalker	trample	

BELT SUFFIXES

clasp	fringe	lash
buckle	winding	cord
harness	chain	
lock	strap	

RING SUFFIXES

knot	spiral	grip	knuckle
circle	coil	grasp	nails
loop	gyre	hold	
eye	band	touch	
turn	whorl	finger	

CHAPTER 4: THE LISTS

MULET SUFFIXES

talisman	collar	scarab
heart	beads	
noose	torc	
necklace	gorget	

Finding an entire item set is a time to celebrate; it's very rare!

SETS

Sets are groups of items that can function independently, but gain superior effectiveness when they are used in combination. The key is getting every single item in a set together, because sets are all or nothing—having five of six pieces won't cut it. The benefits, however, are substantial and make sets worth striving for. Set items are rare enough that it would be unlikely for you to put an entire set together in a single-player game, but in a multiplayer game (where there's plenty of other warriors fighting), you can trade with other players for pieces of the set that you need. If you find a set piece, put it into your Private Stash in case you find other pieces later, or come across another player that wants to trade something for it. The tables below include information on each individual item, as well as the bonus you'll get for having all of the items in a set equipped.

ANGELIC RAIMENT (4 ITEMS)

Item Name	Type	Individual Item Effect
Angelic Halo	Ring	Replenish life +6; +20 Life
Angelic Mantle	Ring Mail	Enhanced defense; Damage reduced by 3
Angelic Sickle	Sabre	350% damage to undead; +75 attack rating
Angelic Wings	Amulet	20% damage taken goes to mana; +3 light radius

Complete Set Attributes: Half freeze duration, All resistances +25, +40% chance of getting a magic item.

ARCANNA'S TRICKS (4 ITEMS)

Item Name	Type	Individual Item Effect
Arcanna's Deathwand	War Staff	25% deadly strike; +20 Life
Arcanna's Flesh	Light Plate	+2 light radius; Damage reduced by 3
Arcanna's Head	Skull Cap	Replenish life +4; Attacker takes damage of 2
Arcanna's Sign	Amulet	Regenerate mana 20 %; +15 % mana

Complete Set Attributes: Faster cast rate, 5% mana stolen per hit, +25 mana.

ARCTIC GEAR (4 ITEMS)

Item Name	Type	Individual Item Effect
Arctic Binding	Light Belt	Cold resist +40%; +30 defense
Arctic Furs	Quilted Armor	Enhanced defense; All resistances +10
Arctic Horn	Short War Bow	20% bonus to attack rating; Enhanced damage
Arctic Mitts	Light Gauntlets	+20 Life; Slightly increased attack speed

Complete Set Attributes: Cannot be Frozen, Adds 6-14 cold damage.

BERSERKER'S ARSENAL (3 ITEMS)

Item Name	Type	Individual Item Effect
Berserker's Hatchet	Double Axe	30% bonus to attack rating; 5% mana stolen per hit
Berserker's Hauberk	Splint Mail	+1 Barbarian skills; Magic damage reduced by 2
Berserker's Headgear	Helm	Fire resist +25%; +15 defense

Complete Set Attributes: Poison length reduced by 75%, Adds 4-9 poison damage over 3 seconds.

CATHAN'S TRAPS (5 ITEMS)

Item Name	Type	Individual Item Effect
Cathan's Mesh	Chain Mail	Requirements -50%; +15 defense
Cathan's Rule	Battle Staff	+1 fire skills; +10 max fire damage
Cathan's Seal	Ring	6% life stolen per hit; Damage reduced by 2
Cathan's Sigil	Amulet	Attacker takes 5 lightning damage; Fast hit recovery
Cathan's Visage	Mask	Cold resist +25%; +20 Mana

Complete Set Attributes: Fast cast rate, Magic damage reduced by 3, +20 mana, +6 attack rating, All resistances +25.

CIVERB'S VESTMENTS (3 ITEMS)

Item Name	Type	Individual Item Effect
Civerb's Cudgel	Grand Scepter	+75 attack rating; +17 to +23 max damage (varies)
Civerb's Icon	Amulet	Replenish life +4; Regenerate Mana +40%
Civerb's Ward	Large Shield	Increased block; +15 defense

Complete Set Attributes: 200% damage to undead, +15 Strength.

CLEGLAW'S BRACE (3 ITEMS)

Item Name	Type	Individual Item Effect
Cleglaw's Claw	Small Shield	Poison length reduced by 75%; +17 defense
Cleglaw's Pincers	Chain Gloves	Slows target by 25%; Knockback
Cleglaw's Tooth	Long Sword	50% deadly strike; 30% bonus to attack rating

Complete Set Attributes: 35% crushing blow, 6% mana stolen per hit, +50 defense.

DEATH'S DISGUISE (3 ITEMS)

Item Name	Type	Individual Item Effect
Death's Guard	Sash	Cannot be frozen; +20 defense
Death's Hand	Leather Gloves	Poison length reduced by 75%; Poison resist +50%
Death's Touch	War Sword	4% life stolen per hit; Enhanced damage

Complete Set Attributes: 40% bonus to attack rating, All resistances +25, +10 minimum damage.

CHAPTER 4: THE LISTS

SARU'S TRIM (3 ITEMS)

Item Name	Type	Individual Item Effect
Hsaru's Iron Fist	Buckler	Damage reduced by 2 +10 Strength
Hsaru's Iron Heel	Chain Boots	Fast run/walk Fire resist +25%
Hsaru's Iron Stay	Belt	Cold resist +20% +20 Life

Complete Set Attributes: Cannot be Frozen, Lightning resist +25%, +5 maximum damage.

INFERNAL TOOLS (3 ITEMS)

Item Name	Type	Individual Item Effect
Infernal Buckle	Heavy Belt	+25 defense; +20 Life
Infernal Cranium	Cap	20% damage taken goes to mana; All resistances +10
Infernal Torch	Grim Wand	+1 Necromancer skills; +8 min damage

Complete Set Attributes: 20% open wounds, 20% bonus to attack rating, Necromancer skills.

IRATHA'S FINERY (4 ITEMS)

Item Name	Type	Individual Item Effect
Iratha's Coil	Crown	Lightning resist +30%; Fire resist +30%
Iratha's Collar	Amulet	Poison length reduced by 75%; Poison resist +30%
Iratha's Cord	Heavy Belt	+25 defense; +5 min damage
Iratha's Cuff	Light Gauntlets	Half freeze duration; Cold resist +30%

Complete Set Attributes: 10% to maximum poison resist, 10% to maximum cold resist, 10% to maximum lightning resist, 10% to maximum fire resist, All resistances +20%, +15 Dexterity.

ISENHART'S ARMORY (4 ITEMS)

Item Name	Type	Individual Item Effect
Isenhart's Case	Breast Plate	Magic damage reduced by 2; +40 defense
Isenhart's Horns	Full Helm	Damage reduced by 2; +6 Dexterity
Isenhart's Lightband	Broad Sword	+3 light radius; +10 min damage
Isenhart's Parry	Gothic Shield	Attacker takes 4 lightning damage; +40 defense

Complete Set Attributes: 35% bonus to attack rating, 5% life stolen per hit, All resistances +20.

MILABREGA'S REGALIA (4 ITEMS)

Item Name	Type	Individual Item Effect
Milabrega's Diadem	Crown	+15 Mana; +15 Life
Milabrega's Orb	Kite Shield	+25 defense; +20% chance of getting a magic item
Milabrega's Robe	Ancient Armor	Damage reduced by 2; Attacker takes damage of 3
Milabrega's Rod	War Scepter	+1 Paladin skills; Enhanced damage

Complete Set Attributes: +2 Paladin skills, +2 light radius, 8% life stolen per hit, Poison resist 15%.

SIGON'S COMPLETE STEEL (6 ITEMS)

Item Name	Type	Individual Item Effect
Sigon's Gage	Gauntlets	+20 attack rating; +10 Strength
Sigon's Guard	Tower Shield	Increased block; +1 all skills
Sigon's Sabot	Greaves	Faster run/walk; Cold resist +40%
Sigon's Shelter	Gothic Plate	Enhanced defense; Lightning resist +30%
Sigon's Visor	Great Helm	+3 light radius; +30 Mana
Sigon's Wrap	Plated Belt	Fire resist +20%; +20 Life

Complete Set Attributes: Damage reduced by 7, adds 12-24 fire damage, attacker takes 12 damage.

TANCRED'S BATTLEGEAR (5 ITEMS)

Item Name	Type	Individual Item Effect
Tancred's Crowbill	Military Pick	Enhanced damage; +75 attack rating
Tancred's Hobnails	Boots	Heal stamina plus 25%; +10 Dexterity
Tancred's Skull	Bone Helm	Enhanced damage; +40 attack rating
Tancred's Spine	Full Plate Armor	+40 Life; +15 Strength
Tancred's Weird	Amulet	Damage reduced by 2; Magic damage reduced by 1

Complete Set Attributes: Slows target by 35%, 5% mana stolen per hit, All resistances +10, 75% extra gold from monsters.

VIDALA'S RIG (4 ITEMS)

Item Name	Type	Individual Item Effect
Vidala's Ambush	Leather Armor	+50 defense; +11 Dexterity
Vidala's Barb	Long Battle Bow	Adds 1-20 lightning damage
Vidala's Fetlock	Light Plated Boots	Fastest run/walk; +150 max Stamina
Vidala's Snare	Amulet	Cold resist +20%; +15 Life

Complete Set Attributes: Piercing attack, Freezes target, Enhanced damage.

SOCKETED ITEMS

These items have sockets built into them that can hold gems. By placing gems in these items, you can add special abilities and create your own specific magic item. The names of Socketed items appear gray when you move your mouse over them, so you should have no trouble identifying one. When you place a gem into one of the sockets you'll gain magical properties. Below is a list of all of the various gems (and their effects) that you can place into Socketed items.

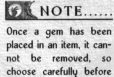

NOTE......

Once a gem has been placed in an item, it cannot be removed, so choose carefully before you drop a gem in!

RUBY

Gem	Weapon Effect	Shield Effect	Helm Effect
Chipped Ruby	+3-4 Fire Damage	+10-12% Resist Fire	+6-8 to Maximum Life
Flawed Ruby	+3-5 Fire Damage	+13-16% Resist Fire	+9-11 to Maximum Life
Ruby	+4-5 Fire Damage	+17-20% Resist Fire	+12-15 to Maximum Life
Flawless Ruby	+5-6 Fire Damage	+21-25% Resist Fire	+16-20 to Maximum Life
Perfect Ruby	+6-10 Fire Damage	+26-30% Resist Fire	+21-25 to Maximum Life

SAPPHIRE

Gem	Weapon Effect	Shield Effect	Helm Effect
Chipped Sapphire	+1-3 Cold damage (1 sec)	+10-12% Resist Cold	+6-8 to maximum Mana
Flawed Sapphire	+2-3 Cold damage (1.5 sec)	+13-16% Resist Cold	+9-11 to maximum Mana
Sapphire	+2-4 Cold damage (2 sec)	+17-20% Resist Cold	+12-15 to maximum Mana
Flawless Sapphire	+3-5 Cold damage (2.5 sec)	+21-25% Resist Cold	+16-20 to maximum Mana
Perfect Sapphire	+3-7 Cold damage (3 sec)	+26-30% Resist Cold	+21-25 to maximum Mana

TOPAZ

Gem	Weapon Effect	Shield Effect	Helm Effect
Chipped Topaz	+1-6 Lightning Damage	+10-12% Resist Lightning	+7-9% Chance to Find Magic Items
Flawed Topaz	+1-7 Lightning Damage	+13-16% Resist Lightning	+11-13% Chance to Find Magic Items
Topaz	+1-8 Lightning Damage	+17-20% Resist Lightning	+14-17% Chance to Find Magic Items
Flawless Topaz	+1-10 Lightning Damage	+21-25% Resist Lightning	+18-20% Chance to Find Magic Items
Perfect Topaz	+1-15 Lightning Damage	+26-30% Resist Lightning	+21-25% Chance to Find Magic Items

WEAPONS & ARMOR

EMERALD

Gem	Weapon Effect	Shield Effect	Helm Effect
Chipped Emerald	+2 Poison damage (3 sec)	+10-12% Resist Poison	+3 to Dexterity
Flawed Emerald	+3 Poison damage (3 sec)	+13-16% Resist Poison	+4 to Dexterity
Emerald	+4 Poison damage (3 sec)	+17-20% Resist Poison	+5-6 to Dexterity
Flawless Emerald	+4 Poison damage (3 sec)	+21-25% Resist Poison	+7-8 to Dexterity
Perfect Emerald	+5 Poison damage (3 sec)	+26-30% Resist Poison	+9-10 to Dexterity

NOTE......

For weapons with multiple emeralds, the time over which the poison damage is applied is cumulative. That is, 2 Emeralds poison over 6 seconds and 3 Emeralds over 9 seconds.

AMETHYST

Gem	Weapon Effect	Shield Effect	Helm Effect
Chipped Amethyst	+15-19 to Attack Rating	+5-6 to Defense	+3 to Strength
Flawed Amethyst	+20-29 to Attack Rating	+7-8 to Defense	+4 to Strength
Amethyst	+30-39 to Attack Rating	+9-10 to Defense	+5-6 to Strength
Flawless Amethyst	+40-49 to Attack Rating	+11-13 to Defense	+7-8 to Strength
Perfect Amethyst	+50-60 to Attack Rating	+15-17 to Defense	+9-10 to Strength

DIAMONDS

Gem	Weapon Effect	Shield Effect	Helm Effect
Chipped Diamond	Damage is 125-129% of normal against undead	+5-6% to all resistances	+10 to attack rating
Flawed Diamond	Damage is 130-135% of normal against undead	+7-8% to all resistances	+15 to attack rating
Diamond	Damage is 136-145% of normal against undead	+9-11% to all resistances	+20 to attack rating
Flawless Diamond	Damage is 146-155% of normal against undead	+12-15% to all resistances	+25 to attack rating
Perfect Diamond	Damage is 156-170% of normalagainst undead	+16-20% to all resistances	+30 to attack Rating

SKULLS

Gem	Weapon Effect	Shield Effect	Helm Effect
Chipped Skull	Steals 2% Life, Steals 1% Mana	Attacker takes 2 Damage	Replenish Life +2, Regenerate Mana 8%
Flawed Skull	Steals 2% Life, Steals 2% Mana	Attacker takes 3 Damage	Replenish Life +3, Regenerate Mana 8%
Skull	Steals 3% Life, Steals 2% Mana	Attacker takes 4 Damage	Replenish Life +3, Regenerate Mana 12%
Flawless Skull	Steals 3% Life, Steals 3% Mana	Attacker takes 5 Damage	Replenish Life +4, Regenerate Mana 12%
Perfect Skull	Steals 4% Life, Hit Steals 3% Mana	Attacker takes 6-7 Damage	Replenishes Life +4-5, Regenerate Mana 16-20%

CHAPTER 4: THE LISTS

Chapter 5
Multiplayer

Multiplayer

The original *Diablo* game presented a multiplayer experience that was unique in the world of computer games. Indeed, *Diablo* encouraged players to cooperate, trade, and depend on each other to gain the most from the game. It has always been possible to simply kill each other, but the most profitable way to play in a multiplayer *Diablo* game is to help your fellow adventurer. With the assistance of your friends you can find more weapons, armor, spells, and potions than you could on your own, and you can gang-up on the toughest monsters using tactics that would make a seasoned war general proud.

Diablo II follows this tradition very closely. Although it is *possible* to play the game simply to kill other players, it is most beneficial to cooperate in quests and follow the game as it unfolds. As with its predecessor, you can collect experience, items, and wealth in greater quantity as a group than as a single player.

For many fans of the game, Multiplayer Diablo II is where it's at.

Diablo II is an extremely engrossing and compelling single-player game that can capture its audience for literally hundreds of hours of gameplay. As if the massive and captivating single-player gameplay isn't enough, the inclusion of a complex and rich multiplayer format for *Diablo II* makes it a game that will be played by fans around the world for years to come. This chapter covers some of the intricacies of multiplayer action. The game manual covers the basics of getting connected to Battle.net and TCP/IP connections, so this chapter spends more time looking at real-life Battle.net multiplayer tactics—many of them gathered from insiders at Blizzard Entertainment!

Battle.Net

Battle.net launched in 1997 with the release of *Diablo* (the predecessor to this game). Since its inception, Battle.net has registered literally millions of users, and there are as many as 70,000 distinct players logging on to the service *on a daily basis*! Battle.net has truly set the standard for gaming-only services. Remarkably, Battle.net is entirely free of charge for all users, bringing the world of games like *Diablo*, *WarCraft*, *StarCraft*, and now *Diablo II* to millions of players who (through Battle.net's magic) can find an unlimited number of new adversaries or allies every time they log on!

Battle.net is a great place to meet and play Diablo II with people from around the planet.

Indeed, with a single click you can log on to Battle.net and do battle against Diablo with other players (up to eight), or even choose to battle *against* other players. Battle.net also gives you the opportunity to chat, trade items, set up your own games, or join games created by other adventurers. For *Diablo II*, Battle.net includes some cool new features such as Hardcore characters. These new features are discussed in detail in the manual, but we'll still touch on them in this chapter just to make sure that you are getting everything you can out of multiplayer *Diablo II*.

NOTE......

Diablo II Battle.net Realm characters are a little different than characters from the original **Diablo**. Information about Realm characters is now stored on the Battle.net server instead of your local hard disk drive. This makes it impossible to cheat by manually editing a character—protection that helps most players who prefer to build a **Diablo** character the old fashioned way. The big advantage to using **Diablo II** characters on Battle.net is that they are available to you from any computer connected to the internet—so you can play the same character at home and at work.

LADDER

The Ladder system provides a great way to see just how you stack up against the best *Diablo II* players in the world. *Diablo II* and Battle.net offer this service, which rates both regular and Hardcore characters. The Ladder system is based on experience, and applies to only one Realm—each Realm ranks and lists only the top-ranked players, so you'll have to be on your toes to make the cut on one of the ladders. When it comes to Hardcore players, they're listed on their ladders even if they die, but can still be removed from the ladder if other players exceed their experience level and bump them off.

The Ladder system in Diablo II keeps track of the top players in each Realm.

TRADING

The trading screen is a secure place to conduct business.

Trading in *Diablo II* must occur within the boundaries of a town; it cannot occur anywhere else outside of a player dropping an item that you may want to pick up. The Trading feature in *Diablo II* is a way for you to 'officially' trade with another player in a sanctioned way that protect both players from cheating or other less than honorabl activities. Any time you wish to make a trade on a partic ularly valuable item or you want to be sure that an unre lated player doesn't hop in and pick up an item you're dropping for someone else, use the secure trading method to be absolutely safe. It ma take a little more time to portal back to a town, but if you're dealing with high-price items, it's worth it.

PARTIES

When you join a multiplayer game, you can select other players in the game to form a team. When in a party, you and the other members of the team will work together with the common goal of getting through the quests in *Diablo II*. You will share common goals, as well as experience with other party members during the course of your adventure. The method that *Diablo II* uses to share experience amongst many players of different levels is complicated, but suffice it to say that a level 3 character will not be receiving gobs of experience just by hanging around with level 25 characters. Indeed there is somewhat of a sliding scale (based on the levels of the party members) tha manages the disbursement of experience. The higher your level, the bigger is your share of experience. Gold, on the other hand, is divided up equally among the members o the party with any gold that doesn't divide equally into the party number going to the character that picked the gold up. Members of your party appear as allies along the top of your screen.

HOSTILITY

Keep in mind that when you become hostile toward someone, any skeletons, Valkyries, Golems, or Mercenaries will also immediately become hostile toward your enemies (and vice versa). To go hostile with another player, you must be in town, and if you used a town portal to get there, your portal will disappear. Also, you cannot use a town portal of a player against whom you are hostile.

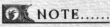

NOTE......

When you ally with another player, you can see a small picture of your teammate and a read-out of their hit points. This allows you keep track of how everyone is doing and rush to the aid of someone who gets too busy to send a message for help.

MAP

The map displayed over the game screen shows you the location of the other players in the game when they are nearby. Each player's marker is labeled with their character name. Additional markers are displayed for any NPCs that are fighting for you or your teammates. When you team up with more than one Necromancer, you can expect the map display to be crowded!

Members of your party appear as allies along the top of your screen.

Remember that when you are hostile toward someone, you will have more than one enemy if they have summoned minions or mercenaries under their command.

The Automap shows where each of your party members is (if they're close enough to you).

CHAT

The chat feature of *Diablo II* multiplayer games works much the same as in the original *Diablo*. You can press the Enter key to bring up a prompt, then type in a message to send to everyone. *Diablo II* also lets you select players from whom to block messages received or sent, which is a good way to filter out distractions from other players not in your area. Refer to the manual for details on Chatting.

Chatting is important in Diablo II because it's the primary method of communication for you and your party.

BATTLE.NET

Multiplayer Tactics

NOTE......

One of the problems with staying in the pack is that you must share the spoils of victory with whoever else is fighting in the same screen. It's sometimes frustrating when you come up against a particularly fierce opponent, finally manage to kill it, and then miss picking up the magic item it dropped because your teammate grabbed it first. Because it is more effective to play closely together, sharing is recommended.

Diablo II has much more open space than the original game (in the original *Diablo*, the dungeon hallways and doors were sometimes too narrow for more than one player to fight monsters at a time), so staying together is more practical. In fact, staying together can be very beneficial. Many skills, especially most Paladin auras and some Barbarian yells, will affect the party members as long as they are within range of the skill's effect. Even the Necromancer with his many skeletons will not feel crowded in most of the areas in *Diablo II*. Indeed, for the most

More space means that managing larger parties is easier in Diablo II.

part there's plenty of room to move around and attack parties of monsters from different angles.

In order to keep comrades happy and your inventory full, it is a good practice to venture into *Diablo II* multiplayer games in small groups. You can select a central spot to collect unwanted items if you want. You should also try to work in the same general area—when someone needs help, they won't want to wait for you to find a Waypoint and jog around looking for them.

TIPS FROM THE EXPERTS

NOTE......

There are plenty of tips relating to many of the skills' multiplayer attributes in Chapter 2: The Characters where each skill is examined in detail.

This section provides a collection of great tips straight from the mouths of the Blizzard QA (Quality Assurance) department. Keep in mind that these folks have literally already being playing *Diablo II* for months (and in some cases, years) even at the time of this writing (before *Diablo II*'s official release). These tips are well worth reading over because they come from the masters themselves! Each member of the QA department is mentioned by name above each tip so you know where each kernel of knowledge originated.

DAVE FRIED

The Paladin's Auras are critical for party play in multiplayer Diablo II.

The Paladin: This is one of the best characters to party with. All of his aura skills have a radius that shows how far a fellow party member can be from the Paladin and still be under its effects. A group consisting of multiple Paladins can be very effective if they each specialize in a different aura. Holy Bolt has the ability to heal other party members. Simply select Holy Bolt as your right-click (Command + left-click on the Mac) skill, target a party member, and then right-click (Command + left-click) on them to fire healing bolts of energy.

The Sorceress: Area effect spells are of prime importance with the Sorceress. You can often turn the tide of a large battle by using Frost Nova to slow the enemies.

The Barbarian: This character's Warcries are often overlooked in lieu of the direct damage skills. However, it is important to remember that when grouped with others, teamwork is critical and Warcries can have a huge impact. You can use Shout to increase the defense of party members within the range of its effects.

The Amazon: When playing the Amazon, remember that ranged attacks are her specialty. It's often better to stand back from combat while others get into melee range of the enemies, and then fire from a distance into the crowd. Remember that missiles will not harm allies, even if you aim directly at them.

Josh Kurtz

When playing as a Sorceress in a group, one of your best spells is the Frost Nova. Run into a group of monsters, let the Frost Nova fly, and then retreat. Watch your melee buddies walk through the frozen creatures with ease.

The Town Portal scroll is essential. If a group sticks together, you can make one player the keeper of the Town Portals.

Also, I cannot stress enough the importance of the Town Portal scroll, or how effectively these can be used by a full group. Make sure someone has a full supply of Town Portal scrolls so that when you get in trouble they can open one up and allow everyone in the party to get to safety. The whole team can run through, get fully healed and mana restored in town, and be back in the fray fairly swiftly. It's like a full rejuvenation potion for the whole team, just make sure the person who casts it is the last one back from town or the portal will close! Always have Town Portal assigned to a hot key to make invoking this scroll quicker.

Make sure your melee fighter is carrying as many health potions as possible. This character is the one who takes the brunt of the attacks by leading the charge into battle—the Barbarian is a good choice because he is much better at absorbing damage than the Sorceress or the Necromancer—so make sure he stays alive.

Conner Brandt

Golem, Amplify Damage, and Corpse Explosion are a great combination against large groups of monsters in big multiplayer games. Necromancers working in concert can be deadly when using combinations of these skills.

PETE UNDERWOOD

Thorns is a powerful aura that, when used with a Necromancer's minions, is an awesome weapon.

Paladins and Necromancers using Zeal and Amplif Damage in a group are a force to be reckoned with. Aura such as Thorns in conjunction with a Necromancer's mir ions is also an incredibly potent combination.

A Paladin with Holy Fire or Holy Shock can draw th attention of the monsters to him while remaining ou of melee range. Other characters may then attack thos monsters with ranged weapons. These skills provide great 'distract and damage' combination.

JOHN LAGRAVE

NOTE......

The difficulty of a multi-player game is dependent on how many players are participating. For example, a six-player game will fea-ture monsters that are much tougher to defeat than a two-player game. This scaling of difficulty is a great feature that ensures that playing through **Diablo II** will be challenging enough even if there's a large party working in unison.

Barbarians grouped together should each specialize in a different weapon clas (one with Sword Mastery, one with Axe Mastery, etc.). This way, when it comes t weapons that the enemies give up, they can divide the loot and conquer their enemie more effectively without squabbling over who gets the unique item.

The Sorceress is the character you need in every party. Static Field can weaken even th toughest opponents quickly, allowing the melee class characters to mop up (rememb that Static Field reduces the enemy's hit points by one-third). This is especially impo tant in large multiplayer games because Diablo's minions are that much tougher. Th importance of Hirelings/Mercenaries should also not be overlooked; they can provid distraction, or even the backup to turn the tide of the battle.

DEREK SIMMONS

Stick Together. The more players that are in the game, the tougher the monster become—regardless of where the players are. Sticking together as a unit is the best wa to survive and conquer your enemies. Diablo's minions will have a difficult time defea ing a party of adventurers who support each other with auras, missile fire, and heavy armor.

CARLOS GUERRERO

Rancid Gas potions are very effective for taking out large groups of monsters in the Blood Moor, Cold Plains, or Stony Field. The key is to get the monsters to chase you and bunch into large groups, then simply throw a potion at them and they will all take substantial (if not fatal) poi-son damage, thus quickly boosting your (and your party's) experience points.

Using Rancid Gas potions giv you the same effect as poison Early in the game they provid an excellent means for killing several enemies while racking up experience points.

Appendix

CHARACTER
SKILLS TABLES

AMAZON BOW & CROSSBOW SKILLS

Skill	Attribute	Level 1	Level 2	Level 3	Level 4	Level 5	Level 6	Level 7	Level 8	Level 9	Level 10	Level 11	Level 12	Level 13	Level 14	Level 15	Level 16	Level 17	Level 18	Level 19	Level 20
Magic Arrow	Mana Cost	1.5	1.3	1.2	1.1	1.0	.8	.7	.6	.5	.3	.2	.1	0	0	0	0	0	0	0	0
	Damage Mod.	0	+1	+2	+3	+4	+5	+6	+7	+8	+9	+10	+11	+12	+13	+14	+15	+16	+17	+18	+19
Fire Arrow	Mana Cost	3	3.2	3.5	3.7	4	4.2	4.5	4.7	5	5.2	5.5	5.7	6	6.2	6.5	6.7	7	7.2	7.5	7.7
	Fire Damage	1-4	3-6	5-8	7-10	9-12	11-14	13-16	15-18	17-20	19-22	21-24	23-26	25-28	27-30	29-32	31-34	33-36	35-38	37-40	39-42
Cold Arrow	Mana Cost	3	3.2	3.5	3.7	4	4.2	4.5	4.7	5	5.2	5.5	5.7	6	6.2	6.5	6.7	7	7.2	7.5	7.7
	Cold Damage	3	5	7	9	11	13	15	17	19	21	23	25	27	29	31	33	35	37	39	41
	Cold Length (secs)	4	5.2	6.4	7.6	8.8	10	11.2	12.4	13.6	14.8	16	17.2	18.4	19.6	20.8	22	23.2	24.4	25.6	26.8
Multiple Shot	Mana Cost	4	5	6	7	8	9	10	11	12	13	14	15	16	17	18	19	20	21	22	23
	# of Arrows	2	3	4	5	6	7	8	9	10	11	12	13	14	15	16	17	18	19	20	21
Exploding Arrow	Mana Cost	5	5.5	6	6.5	7	7.5	8	8.5	9	9.5	10	10.5	11	11.5	12	12	13	13	14	14
	Fire Damage	2-4	7-9	12-14	17-19	22-24	27-29	32-34	37-39	42-44	47-49	52-54	57-59	62-64	67-69	72-74	77-79	82-84	87-89	92-94	97-99
Guided Arrow	Mana Cost	7	6.5	6	5.5	5	4.5	4	3.5	3	2.5	2	1.5	1	1	1	1	1	1	1	1
	Damage Mod +%	0	5%	10%	15%	20%	25%	30%	35%	40%	45%	50%	55%	60%	65%	70%	75%	80%	85%	90%	95%
Ice Arrow	Mana Cost	4	4.2	4.5	4.7	5	5.2	5.5	5.7	6	6.2	6.5	6.7	7	7.2	7.5	7.7	8	8.2	8.5	8.7
	Freeze in Sec.	2	2.2	2.4	2.6	2.8	3	3.2	3.4	3.6	3.8	4	4.2	4.4	4.6	4.8	5	5.2	5.4	5.6	5.8
	Cold Damage	6-10	10-14	14-18	18-22	22-26	26-30	30-34	34-38	38-42	42-46	46-50	50-54	54-58	58-62	62-66	66-70	70-74	74-78	78-82	82-86
Strafe cost 11	Attacks up to	5	7	9	11	13	15	17	19	21	23	25	27	29	31	33	35	37	39	41	43
	Damage Mod +%	5%	10%	15%	20%	25%	30%	35%	40%	45%	50%	55%	60%	65%	70%	75%	80%	85%	90%	95%	100%
Immolation Arrow	Mana Cost	6	7	8	9	10	11	12	13	14	15	16	17	18	19	20	21	22	23	24	25
	Explosion Damage	4-10	10-16	16-22	22-28	28-34	34-40	40-46	46-52	52-58	58-64	64-70	70-76	76-82	82-88	88-94	94-100	100-106	106-112	112-118	118-124
	Fire Duration Seconds	4.6	5.6	6.6	7.6	8.6	9.6	10.6	11.6	12.6	13.6	14.6	15.6	16.6	17.6	18.6	19.6	20.6	21.6	22.6	23.6
	Avg Fire Damage	8-10	14-16	19-22	25-28	31-33	37-39	43-45	49-51	55-57	60-63	66-69	72-75	78-80	84-86	90-92	96-98	101-104	107-110	113-116	119-121
Freezing Arrow	Mana Cost	9	10	11	12	13	14	15	16	17	18	19	20	21	22	23	24	25	26	27	28
Duration 2 secs	Damage Modifier	6-10	12-16	18-22	24-28	30-34	36-40	42-46	48-52	54-58	60-64	66-70	72-76	78-82	84-88	90-94	96-100	102-106	108-112	114-118	120-124

AMAZON JAVELIN & SPEAR SKILLS

Skill	Attribute	Level 1	Level 2	Level 3	Level 4	Level 5	Level 6	Level 7	Level 8	Level 9	Level 10	Level 11	Level 12	Level 13	Level 14	Level 15	Level 16	Level 17	Level 18	Level 19	Level 20
Jab	Mana Cost	2	2.2	2.5	2.7	3	3.2	3.5	3.7	4	4.2	4.5	4.7	5	5.2	5.5	5.7	6	6.2	6.5	6.7
	Attack Rating bonus	+10	+15	+20	+25	+30	+35	+40	+45	+50	+55	+60	+65	+70	+75	+80	+85	+90	+95	+100	+105
	Damage Mod [%]	-15	-12	-9	-6	-3	0	+3	+6	+9	+12	+15	+18	+21	+24	+27	+30	+33	+36	+39	+42
Power Strike	Mana Cost	2	2.2	2.5	2.7	3	3.2	3.5	3.7	4	4.2	4.5	4.7	5	5.2	5.5	5.7	6	6.2	6.5	6.7
	Attack Mod.	10	15	20	25	30	35	40	45	50	55	60	65	70	75	80	85	90	95	100	105
Poison Javelin	Damage	1-8	4-11	7-14	10-17	13-20	16-23	19-26	22-29	25-32	28-35	31-38	34-41	37-44	40-47	43-50	46-53	49-56	52-59	55-62	58-65
	Mana Cost	4	4.2	4.5	4.7	5	5.2	5.5	5.7	6	6.2	6.5	6.7	7	7.2	7.5	7.7	8	8.2	8.5	8.7
Over 3 sec.	Poison Damage	9-14	14-18	18-23	23-28	28-32	32-39	37-42	42-46	46-51	51-56	56-60	60-65	65-70	70-75	75-79	79-84	84-89	89-93	93-98	98-103
Impale	Attack Mod. %	25	32	39	46	53	60	67	74	81	88	95	102	109	116	123	130	137	144	151	158
cost: 3	Wpn Durability %	50	51	52	53	54	55	56	57	58	59	60	61	62	63	64	65	66	67	68	69
Lightning Bolt	Damage Mod.	1-40	1-48	1-56	1-64	1-72	1-80	1-88	1-96	1-104	1-112	1-120	1-128	1-136	1-144	1-152	1-160	1-168	1-176	1-184	1-192
	Mana Cost	6	6.2	6.5	6.7	7	7.2	7.5	7.7	8	8.2	8.5	8.7	9	9.2	9.5	9.7	10	10.2	10.5	10.7
Plague Javelin	Mana Cost	7	8	9	10	11	12	13	14	15	16	17	18	19	20	21	22	23	24	25	26
Over 3 sec.	Poison Damage	9-14	14-18	18-23	23-28	28-32	32-39	37-42	42-46	46-51	51-56	56-60	60-65	65-70	70-75	75-79	79-84	84-89	89-93	93-98	98-103
Charged Strike	Damage Mod.	1-15	6-20	11-25	16-30	21-35	26-40	31-45	36-50	41-55	46-60	51-65	56-70	61-75	66-80	71-85	76-90	81-95	86-100	91-105	96-110
	Mana Cost	4	4.2	4.5	4.7	5	5.2	5.5	5.7	6	6.2	6.5	6.7	7	7.2	7.5	7.7	8	8.2	8.5	8.7
Fend	Attack Mod. +%	10	15	20	25	30	35	40	45	50	55	60	65	70	75	80	85	90	95	100	105
cost: 5	Damage Mod. +%	25	28	31	34	37	40	43	46	49	52	55	58	61	64	67	70	73	76	79	82
Lightning Strike	Mana Cost	9	9.5	10	10.5	11	11.5	12	12	13	13	14	14	15	15	16	16	17	17	18	18
	Lightning x Mod. +%	25	28	31	34	37	40	43	46	49	52	55	58	61	64	67	70	73	76	79	82
	Number of Bolts	2	3	4	5	6	7	8	9	10	11	12	13	14	15	16	17	18	19	20	21
Lightning	Lightning Damage	5-25	15-35	25-45	35-55	45-65	55-75	65-85	75-95	85-105	95-115	105-125	115-135	125-145	135-155	145-165	155-175	165-185	175-195	185-205	195-215
Lightning Fury	Mana Cost	10	10.5	11	11.5	12	12	13	13	14	14	15	15	16	16	17	17	18	18	19	19
	Lightning Bolt Dmg	1-40	1-44	1-48	1-52	1-56	1-60	1-64	1-68	1-72	1-76	1-80	1-84	1-88	1-92	1-96	1-100	1-104	1-108	1-112	1-116
	Number of Bolts	2	3	4	5	6	7	8	9	10	11	12	13	14	15	16	17	18	19	20	21
	Lightning Damage	1-40	11-50	21-60	31-70	41-80	51-90	61-100	71-110	81-120	91-130	101-140	111-150	121-160	131-170	141-180	151-190	161-200	171-210	181-220	191-230

AMAZON PASSIVE & MAGIC SKILLS

Skill	Attribute	Level 1	Level 2	Level 3	Level 4	Level 5	Level 6	Level 7	Level 8	Level 9	Level 10	Level 11	Level 12	Level 13	Level 14	Level 15	Level 16	Level 17	Level 18	Level 19	Level 20
Inner Sight Mana cost: 5	Duration (sec.)	8	12	16	20	24	28	32	36	40	44	48	52	56	60	64	68	72	76	80	84
	Enemy Defense -	46	50	54	57	60	62	63	64	66	67	68	69	70	70	71	72	72	72	73	73
	Radius 13.3 yds																				
Critical Strike (Passive)	Chance to do 2x Dam	16	25	32	38	42	46	49	51	54	56	58	59	61	62	63	65	65	66	67	68
Dodge (Passive)	Chance to Dodge Melee	18	24	29	34	37	40	42	44	46	47	49	50	51	52	52	54	54	55	55	56
Slow Missiles	Radius (yards) 13.3	13.3																			
Mana Cost: 5	Duration (sec.)	12	18	24	30	36	42	48	54	60	66	72	78	84	90	96	102	108	114	120	126
Attacks Slowed Enemy Ranged 33%																					
Avoid (Passive)	Chance to Dodge Missile	24	31	36	41	45	48	50	52	54	55	57	58	60	61	61	63	63	64	64	65
Penetrate (Passive)	% Bonus to AR for Ranged Attacks	35	45	55	65	75	85	95	105	115	125	135	145	155	165	175	185	195	205	215	225
Decoy	Duration	10	15	20	25	30	35	40	45	50	55	60	65	70	75	80	85	90	95	100	105
Duplicate Draws Fire	Mana Cost	19	18	17	16	15	14	13	12	11	10	9	8	7	6	5	4	3	2	1	1
Evade (Passive)	Chance to Dodge any attack	18	24	29	34	37	40	42	44	46	47	49	50	51	52	52	54	55	55	55	56
Valkyrie	Hit Points	317	453	528	604	679	755	830	906	981	1057	1132	1208	1283	1359	1434	1510	1585	1661	1736	1812
Mana cost: 25	% Damage	25	25	50	75	100	125	150	175	200	225	250	275	300	325	350	375	400	425	450	475
	% Attack	25	25	50	75	100	125	150	175	200	225	250	275	300	325	350	375	400	425	450	475
	% Defense Bonus	25	35	50	75	100	125	150	175	200	225	250	275	300	325	350	375	400	425	450	475
Pierce (Passive)	Chance Missiles pass through Target	16	20	24	27	30	32	33	34	36	37	38	39	40	40	41	42	42	42	43	43

BARBARIAN WARCRIES

	Level 1	Level 2	Level 3	Level 4	Level 5	Level 6	Level 7	Level 8	Level 9	Level 10	Level 11	Level 12	Level 13	Level 14	Level 15	Level 16	Level 17	Level 18	Level 19	Level 20
Howl																				
Enemy runs (yds)	16	19.3	22.6	26	29.3	32.6	36	39.3	42.6	46	49.3	52.6	56	59.3	62.6	66	69.3	72.6	76	79.3
Mana Cost: 4																				
Enemy runs (secs)	3	4	5	6	7	8	9	10	11	12	13	14	15	16	17	18	19	20	21	22
Find Health Potion (MC: 2)																				
Chance to find	15%	27%	36%	44%	50%	55%	59%	62%	66%	68%	71%	73%	75%	77%	78%	80%	81%	82%	83%	84%
Taunt																				
Target's Dam Decrease	5%	7%	9%	11%	13%	15%	17%	19%	21%	23%	25%	27%	29%	31%	33%	35%	37%	39%	41%	43%
Mana Cost: 3																				
Target's AR Decrease	5%	7%	9%	11%	13%	15%	17%	19%	21%	23%	25%	27%	29%	31%	33%	35%	37%	39%	41%	43%
Shout																				
Defense Bonus	100%	110%	120%	130%	140%	150%	160%	170%	180%	190%	200%	210%	220%	230%	240%	250%	260%	270%	280%	290%
Mana Cost: 6																				
Duration (secs)	16	18	20	22	24	26	28	30	32	34	36	38	40	42	44	46	48	50	52	54
Find Item (MC: 7)																				
Chance to find	14%	21%	26%	31%	35%	38%	40%	42%	44%	45%	47%	48%	50%	51%	51%	53%	53%	54%	54%	55%
Battlecry																				
Duration (Secs)	12	14.4	16.8	19.2	21.6	24	26.4	28.8	31.2	33.6	36	38.4	40.8	43.2	45.6	48	50.4	52.8	55.2	57.6
Mana Cost: 5																				
Defense Mod -%	50	52	54	56	58	60	62	64	66	68	70	72	74	76	78	80	82	84	86	88
Damage Mod -%	25	26	27	28	29	30	31	32	33	34	35	36	37	38	39	40	41	42	43	44
Battle Orders																				
Duration (secs)	30	36	42	48	54	60	66	72	78	84	90	96	102	108	114	120	126	132	138	144
Mana Cost: 7																				
Max Stam/ HP/Mana Increase	40%	44%	47%	50%	52%	54%	55%	56%	58%	58%	59%	60%	61%	61%	62%	63%	63%	63%	64%	64%
Grim Ward																				
Duration 40																				
Mana Cost: 4																				
Radius	2	2.6	3.3	4	4.6	5.3	6	6.6	7.3	8	8.6	9.3	10	10.6	11.3	12	12.6	13.3	14	14.6
War Cry																				
Mana Cost	17	18	19	20	21	22	23	24	25	26	27	28	29	30	31	32	33	34	35	36
Damage	15-20	20-25	25-30	30-35	35-40	40-45	45-50	50-55	55-60	60-65	65-70	70-75	75-80	80-85	85-90	90-95	95-100	100-105	105-110	110-115
Stun Length (secs)	1	1.2	1.4	1.6	1.8	2	2.2	2.4	2.6	2.8	3	3.2	3.4	3.6	3.8	4	4.2	4.4	4.6	4.8
Battle Command																				
Duration (secs)	12	16	20	24	28	32	36	40	44	48	52	56	60	64	68	72	76	80	84	88
Mana Cost: 11																				

BARBARIAN COMBAT MASTERIES

		Level 1	Level 2	Level 3	Level 4	Level 5	Level 6	Level 7	Level 8	Level 9	Level 10	Level 11	Level 12	Level 13	Level 14	Level 15	Level 16	Level 17	Level 18	Level 19	Level 20
Sword Mastery	Damage Mod +%	28	33	38	43	48	53	58	63	68	73	78	83	88	93	98	103	108	113	118	123
	Attack Mod +%	28	36	44	52	60	68	76	84	92	100	108	116	124	132	140	148	156	164	172	180
Axe Mastery	Damage Mod +%	28	33	38	43	48	53	58	63	68	73	78	83	88	93	98	103	108	113	118	123
	Attack Mod +%	28	36	44	52	60	68	76	84	92	100	108	116	124	132	140	148	156	164	172	180
Mace Mastery	Damage Mod +%	28	36	44	52	60	68	76	84	92	100	108	116	124	132	140	148	156	164	172	180
	Attack Mod +%	28	36	44	52	60	68	76	84	92	100	108	116	124	132	140	148	156	164	172	180
Spear Mastery	Damage Mod +%	30	35	40	45	50	55	60	65	70	75	80	85	90	95	100	105	110	115	120	125
	Attack Mod +%	30	38	46	54	62	70	78	86	94	102	110	118	126	134	142	150	158	166	174	182
Throwing Mastery	Damage Mod +%	30	35	40	45	50	55	60	65	70	75	80	85	90	95	100	105	110	115	120	125
	Attack Mod +%	30	38	46	54	62	70	78	86	94	102	110	118	126	134	142	150	158	166	174	182
Polearm Mastery	Damage Mod +%	30	35	40	45	50	55	60	65	70	75	80	85	90	95	100	105	110	115	120	125
	Attack Mod +%	30	38	46	54	62	70	78	86	94	102	110	118	126	134	142	150	158	166	174	182
Increased Stamina	Stamina Bonus %	30	45	60	75	90	105	120	135	150	165	180	195	210	225	240	255	270	285	300	315
Iron Skin	Increase DR	30%	40%	50%	60%	70%	80%	90%	100%	110%	120%	130%	140%	150%	160%	170%	180%	190%	200%	210%	220%
Increased Speed	Walk/Run Speed Bonus %	13	18	22	25	28	30	32	33	35	36	37	38	39	40	40	41	41	42	42	43
Natural Resistance	Increase all Resistances	12%	21%	28%	35%	40%	44%	47%	49%	52%	54%	56%	58%	60%	61%	62%	64%	64%	65%	66%	67%

BARBARIAN COMBAT SKILLS

		Level 1	Level 2	Level 3	Level 4	Level 5	Level 6	Level 7	Level 8	Level 9	Level 10	Level 11	Level 12	Level 13	Level 14	Level 15	Level 16	Level 17	Level 18	Level 19	Level 20
Bash	Add'l Damage	+1	+2	+3	+4	+5	+6	+7	+8	+9	+10	+11	+12	+13	+14	+15	+16	+17	+18	+19	+20
Mana Cost: 2	Damage Mod +%	50	55	60	65	70	75	80	85	90	95	100	105	110	115	120	125	130	135	140	145
	Attack Mod +%	20	25	30	35	40	45	50	55	60	65	70	75	80	85	90	95	100	105	110	115
Leap Mana Cost: 2	Radius (Yards)	4.6	7.3	8.6	10	11.3	12	12.6	13.3	14	14	14.6	14.6	15.3	16	16	16	16.6	16.6	16.6	16.6
Double Swing Mana Cost: 2	Attack Mod +%	15	20	25	30	35	40	45	50	55	60	65	70	75	80	85	90	95	100	105	110
Stun	Attack Mod +%	15	20	25	30	35	40	45	50	55	60	65	70	75	80	85	90	95	100	105	110
Mana Cost: 2	Duration (secs)	1.2	1.4	1.6	1.8	2.0	2.2	2.4	2.6	2.8	3.0	3.2	3.4	3.6	3.8	4.0	4.2	4.4	4.6	4.8	5.0
Double Throw Mana Cost: 2	Attack Mod +%	20	30	40	50	60	70	80	90	100	110	120	130	140	150	160	170	180	190	200	210
Leap Attack	Radius (yards)	4.6	7.3	8.6	10	11.3	12.	12.6	13.3	14	14	14.6	14.6	15.3	16	16	16	16.6	16.6	16.6	16.6
Mana Cost: 9	Damage Mod +%	100	130	160	190	220	250	280	310	340	370	400	430	460	490	520	550	580	610	640	670
Concentrate	Defense Mod +%	20	30	40	50	60	70	80	90	100	110	120	130	140	150	160	170	180	190	200	210
Mana Cost: 2	Attack Mod +%	25	30	35	40	45	50	55	60	65	70	75	80	85	90	95	100	105	110	115	120
Frenzy	Duration (secs)	2	3	4	5	6	7	8	9	10	11	12	13	14	15	16	17	18	19	20	21
Mana Cost: 2	Attack Mod +%	10	20	30	40	50	60	70	80	90	100	110	120	130	140	150	160	170	180	190	200
Whirlwind	Mana Cost	25	27	29	31	33	35	37	39	41	43	45	47	49	51	53	55	57	59	61	63
	Damage Mod %	-50	-35	-20	-5	+10	+25	+40	+55	+70	+85	+100	+115	+130	+145	+160	+175	+190	+205	+220	+235
	Attack Mod +%	25	30	35	40	45	50	55	60	65	70	75	80	85	90	95	100	105	110	115	120
Berserk	Attack Mod +%	56	72	88	104	120	136	152	168	184	200	216	232	248	264	280	296	312	328	344	360
Mana Cost: 5	Magic Damage +%	56	66	76	86	96	106	116	126	136	146	156	166	176	186	196	206	216	226	236	246
	Duration (secs)	2.7	2.4	2.2	2.1	2.0	1.9	1.8	1.7	1.6	1.6	1.6	1.5	1.5	1.4	1.4	1.4	1.4	1.3	1.3	1.3

NECROMANCER POISON & BONE SPELLS

		Level 1	Level 2	Level 3	Level 4	Level 5	Level 6	Level 7	Level 8	Level 9	Level 10	Level 11	Level 12	Level 13	Level 14	Level 15	Level 16	Level 17	Level 18	Level 19	Level 20
Teeth	Mana Cost	3	3.5	4	4.5	5	5.5	6	6.5	7	7.5	8	8.5	9	9.5	10	10.5	11	11.5	12	12
	Damage	2-4	3-5	4-6	5-7	6-8	7-9	8-10	9-11	10-12	11-13	12-14	13-15	14-16	15-17	16-18	17-19	18-20	19-21	20-22	21-23
	# of Teeth	2	3	4	5	6	7	8	9	10	11	12	13	14	15	16	17	18	19	20	21
Bone Armor	Dam Shield	20	30	40	50	60	70	80	90	100	110	120	130	140	150	160	170	180	190	200	210
	Mana Cost	11	12	13	14	15	16	17	18	19	20	21	22	23	24	25	26	27	28	29	30
Poison Dagger	Mana Cost	3	3.2	3.5	3.7	4.0	4.2	4.5	4.7	5.0	5.2	5.5	5.7	6.0	6.2	6.5	6.7	7.0	7.2	7.5	7.7
	Poison Dam	7-15	10-20	14-26	18-33	23-40	29-48	35-56	41-65	49-75	57-85	65-95	74-106	84-118	94-131	105-144	116-157	128-171	141-186	154-201	168-217
	Duration [sec]	4	5	6	7	8	9	10	11	12	13	14	15	16	17	18	19	20	21	22	23
	AR Bonus	15%	25%	35%	45%	55%	65%	75%	85%	95%	105%	115%	125%	135%	145%	155%	165%	175%	185%	195%	205%
Corpse Explosion	Mana Cost	15	16	17	18	19	20	21	22	23	24	25	26	27	28	29	30	31	32	33	34
	Radius (yds)	2.6	3.3	4	4.6	5.3	6	6.6	7.3	8	8.6	9.3	10	10.6	11.3	12	12.6	13.3	14	14.6	15.3
	60-100% of Corpse Hit points																				
Bone Wall	Hit Points	19	23	28	33	38	42	47	52	57	61	66	71	76	80	85	90	95	99	104	109
	Mana Cost 17: Duration [sec] 48																				
Bone Spear	Damage	16-24	24-32	32-40	40-48	48-56	56-64	64-72	72-80	80-88	88-96	96-104	104-112	112-120	120-128	128-136	136-144	144-152	152-160	160-168	168-176
	Mana Cost	7	7.2	7.5	7.7	8	8.2	8.5	8.7	9	9.2	9.5	9.7	10	10.2	10.5	10.7	11	11.2	11.5	11.7
Poison Explosion	Poison Dam	25-50	30-60	35-70	40-80	45-90	50-100	55-110	60-120	65-130	70-140	75-150	80-160	85-170	90-180	95-190	100-200	105-210	110-220	115-230	120-240
Mana Cost: 8	Duration [sec]	4	4.8	5.6	6.4	7.2	8	8.8	9.6	10.4	11.2	12	12.8	13.6	14.4	15.2	16	16.8	17.6	18.4	19.2
Bone Prison	Mana Cost	27	25	23	21	19	17	15	13	11	9	7	5	3	1	1	1	1	1	1	1
	Hit Points	19	23	28	33	38	42	47	52	57	61	66	71	76	80	85	90	95	99	104	109
	Duration: 48 seconds																				
Poison Nova	Poison Dam	50-75	55-82	60-90	65-97	70-105	75-112	80-120	85-127	90-135	95-142	100-150	105-157	110-165	115-172	120-180	125-187	130-195	135-202	140-210	145-217
Mana Cost: 25	Duration [sec]	8	8.8	9.6	10.4	11.2	12	12.8	13.6	14.4	15.2	16	16.8	17.6	18.4	19.2	20	20.8	21.6	22.4	23.2
Bone Spirit	Mana Cost	12	12	13	13	14	14	15	15	16	16	17	17	18	18	19	19	20	20	21	21
	Damage	20-30	38-48	52-62	68-78	84-94	100-110	116-126	132-142	148-158	164-174	180-190	196-206	212-222	228-238	244-254	260-270	276-286	292-302	308-318	324-334
	Chases Target																				

NECROMANCER SUMMONING & CONTROL SPELLS

Spell	Attribute	Level 1	Level 2	Level 3	Level 4	Level 5	Level 6	Level 7	Level 8	Level 9	Level 10	Level 11	Level 12	Level 13	Level 14	Level 15	Level 16	Level 17	Level 18	Level 19	Level 20
Raise Skeleton	# of Skeletons	1	2	3	4	5	6	7	8	9	10	11	12	13	14	15	16	17	18	19	20
	Mana Cost	6	7	8	9	10	11	12	13	14	15	16	17	18	19	20	21	22	23	24	25
	Hit Points: 21; Damage 1-2																				
Skeleton Mastery	Skeleton HP	+7	+14	+21	+28	+35	+42	+49	+56	+63	+70	+77	+84	+91	+98	+105	+112	+119	+126	+133	+140
	Skeleton Dam	+2	+4	+6	+8	+10	+12	+14	+16	+18	+20	+22	+24	+26	+28	+30	+32	+34	+36	+38	+40
	Monster HP %	+7%	14%	21%	28%	35%	42%	49%	56%	63%	70%	77%	84%	91%	98%	105%	112%	119%	126%	133%	140%
	Monster Dam %	+2%	4%	6%	8%	10%	12%	14%	16%	18%	20%	22%	24%	26%	28%	30%	32%	34%	36%	38%	40%
Clay Golem	Mana Cost	15	18	21	24	27	30	33	36	39	42	45	48	51	54	57	60	63	66	69	72
Heal themselves automatically	Damage	2-5	2-6	3-8	4-10	4-12	5-13	6-15	6-17	7-19	8-20	9-22	9-24	10-26	11-27	11-29	12-31	13-33	13-34	14-36	15-38
	Hitpoints	100	135	170	205	240	275	310	345	380	415	450	485	520	555	590	625	660	695	730	765
Golem Mastery	Hitpoints	+20%	40%	60%	80%	100%	120%	140%	160%	180%	200%	220%	240%	260%	280%	300%	320%	340%	360%	380%	400%
	Velocity increase	+6%	10%	14%	17%	20%	22%	23%	24%	26%	27%	28%	29%	30%	30%	31%	32%	32%	32%	33%	33%
Raise Skeletal Mage	# of Mages	1	2	3	4	5	6	7	8	9	10	11	12	13	14	15	16	17	18	19	20
	Mana Cost	8	9	10	11	12	13	14	15	16	17	18	19	20	21	22	23	24	25	26	27
	Hitpoints	61																			
Blood Golem	Mana Cost	25	29	33	37	41	45	49	53	57	61	65	69	73	77	81	85	89	93	97	101
	Damage	6-16	8-21	10-27	12-32	14-38	16-44	18-49	20-55	22-60	24-66	27-72	29-77	31-83	33-88	35-94	37-100	39-105	41-111	43-116	45-122
	Hitpoints	201																			
	Heal, Convert damage to life	31	32	33	34	35	35	35	36	36	36	37	37	37	37	37	38	38	38	38	38
Summon Resist	Resist All %	28%	34%	39%	44%	47%	50%	52%	54%	56%	57%	59%	60%	61%	62%	62%	64%	64%	65%	65%	66%
Iron Golem	Mana Cost	35																			
	Damage	7-19																			
	Hitpoints	367																			
Thorns	Mana Cost	50	60	70	80	90	100	110	120	130	140	150	160	170	180	190	200	210	220	230	240
	Damage	0%	150%	165%	180%	195%	210%	225%	240%	255%	270%	285%	300%	315%	330%	345%	360%	375%	390%	405%	420%
Fire Golem (Hit Points: 375)	Mana Cost																				
	Damage	10-27	12-33	15-40	17-47	20-54	22-60	25-67	27-74	30-81	32-87	35-94	37-101	40-108	42-114	45-121	47-128	50-135	52-141	55-148	57-155
	Absorbs Fire Damage to HP	36%	45%	52%	58%	62%	66%	69%	71%	74%	76%	78%	79%	81%	82%	83%	85%	85%	86%	87%	88%
Revive	Mana Cost	45																			
	# of monsters	1	2	3	4	5	6	7	8	9	10	11	12	13	14	15	16	17	18	19	20
	HP (Orig Monster %)	200%	220%	240%	260%	280%	300%	320%	340%	360%	380%	400%	420%	440%	460%	480%	500%	520%	540%	560%	580%

NECROMANCER CURSES

		Level 1	Level 2	Level 3	Level 4	Level 5	Level 6	Level 7	Level 8	Level 9	Level 10	Level 11	Level 12	Level 13	Level 14	Level 15	Level 16	Level 17	Level 18	Level 19	Level 20
Amplify Damage	Radius (yards)	2	2.6	3.3	4	4.6	5.3	6	6.6	7.3	8	8.6	9.3	10	10.6	11.3	12	12.6	13.3	14	14.6
Mana Cost: 4	Damage taken +100%	8	11	14	17	20	23	26	29	32	35	38	41	44	47	50	53	56	59	62	65
Dim Vision *Reduces Enemy Vision*	Radius (yards)	2.6	3.3	4	4.6	5.3	6	6.6	7.3	8	8.6	9.3	10	10.6	11.3	12	12.6	13.3	14	14.6	15.3
Mana Cost: 9	Duration (sec.)	7	9	11	13	15	17	19	21	23	25	27	29	31	33	35	37	39	41	43	45
Weaken	Radius (yards)	6	6.6	7.3	8	8.6	9.3	10	10.6	11.3	12	12.6	13.3	14	14.6	15.3	16	16.6	17.3	18	18.6
Mana Cost: 4 *Target's Damage -33%*	Duration (sec.)	14	16.4	18.8	21.2	23.6	26	28.4	30.8	33.2	35.6	38	40.4	42.8	45.2	47.6	50	52.4	54.8	57.2	59.6
Iron Maiden	% Dam Returned	200	225	250	275	300	325	350	375	400	425	450	475	500	525	550	575	600	625	650	675
Mana Cost: 5	Radius (yards)	4.6																			
Terror	Radius (yards)	2.6																			
Mana Cost: 7 *Enemies run in Fear for duration of curse*	Duration (sec.)	8	9	10	11	12	13	14	15	16	17	18	19	20	21	22	23	24	25	26	27
Confuse	Radius (yards)	4	4.6	5.3	6	6.6	7.3	8	8.6	9.3	10	10.6	11.3	12	12.6	13.3	14	14.6	15.3	16	16.6
Mana Cost: 13 *Cursed Attack Random Targets*	Duration (sec.)	10	12	14	16	18	20	22	24	26	28	30	32	34	36	38	40	42	44	46	48
Life Tap	Radius (yards)	2.6	3.3	4	4.6	5.3	6	6.6	7.3	8	8.6	9.3	10	10.6	11.3	12	12.6	13.3	14	14.6	15.3
Mana Cost: 9	Duration (sec.)	16	18.4	20.8	23.2	25.6	28	30.4	32.8	35.2	37.6	40	42.4	44.8	47.2	49.6	52	54.4	56.8	59.2	61.6
"When Cursed are Damaged, Attacker gets Healed 50% of Attack Damage"																					
Attract *Radius: 6 yards*																					
Mana Cost: 17 *Cursed becomes Target of all nearby Monsters*	Duration (sec.)	12	15.6	19.2	22.8	26.4	30	33.6	37.2	40.8	44.4	48	51.6	55.2	58.8	62.4	66	69.6	73.2	76.8	80.4
Decrepify	Radius (yards)	2.6	3.3	4	4.6	5.3	6	6.6	7.3	8	8.6	9.3	10	10.6	11.3	12	12.6	13.3	14	14.6	15.3
Mana Cost: 11	Duration (sec.)	2	2.2	2.4	2.6	2.8	3	3.2	3.4	3.6	3.8	4	4.2	4.4	4.6	4.8	5	5.2	5.4	5.6	5.8
Lower Resist	Radius (yards)	4.6	5.3	6	6.6	7.3	8	8.6	9.3	10	10.6	11.3	12	12.6	13.3	14	14.6	15.3	16	16.6	17.3
Mana Cost: 22	Duration (sec.)	20	22	24	26	28	30	32	34	36	38	40	42	44	46	48	50	52	54	56	58
	Resist All -%	31	37	41	44	47	49	51	52	54	55	56	57	58	59	60	61	61	61	62	62

PALADIN DEFENSIVE AURAS

		Level 1	Level 2	Level 3	Level 4	Level 5	Level 6	Level 7	Level 8	Level 9	Level 10	Level 11	Level 12	Level 13	Level 14	Level 15	Level 16	Level 17	Level 18	Level 19	Level 20
Prayer	Radius (yards)	7.3	8.6	10	11.3	12.6	14	15.3	16.6	18	19.3	20.6	22	23.3	24.6	26	27.3	28.6	30	31.3	32.6
	Healing	2	3	4	5	6	7	8	9	10	11	12	13	14	15	16	17	18	19	20	21
Resist Fire	Mana Cost	1	1.1	1.3	1.5	1.7	1.9	2.1	2.3	2.5	2.6	2.8	3	3.2	3.4	3.6	3.8	4	4.1	4.3	4.5
	Radius (yards)	7.3	8.6	10	11.3	12.6	14	15.3	16.6	18	19.3	20.6	22	23.3	24.6	26	27.3	28.6	30	31.3	32.6
	Resist Fire +%	54	58	60	63	65	66	67	68	69	70	71	71	72	73	73	74	74	74	74	75
Defiance	Radius (yards)	7.3	8.6	10	11.3	12.6	14	15.3	16.6	18	19.3	20.6	22	23.3	24.6	26	27.3	28.6	30	31.3	32.6
	Defense Mod. +%	70	80	90	100	110	120	130	140	150	160	170	180	190	200	210	220	230	240	250	260
Resist Cold	Radius (yards)	7.3	8.6	10	11.3	12.6	14	15.3	16.6	18	19.3	20.6	22	23.3	24.6	26	27.3	28.6	30	31.3	32.6
	Resist Cold	54	58	60	63	65	66	67	68	69	70	71	71	72	73	73	74	74	74	74	75
Cleansing	Radius (yards)	7.3	8.6	10	11.3	12.6	14	15.3	16.6	18	19.3	20.6	22	23.3	24.6	26	27.3	28.6	30	31.3	32.6
	Duration Reduction	39	46	51	56	60	63	65	67	69	70	72	73	75	76	76	78	78	79	79	80
Resist Lightning	Radius (yards)	7.3	8.6	10	11.3	12.6	14	15.3	16.6	18	19.3	20.6	22	23.3	24.6	26	27.3	28.6	30	31.3	32.6
	Resist Lightning	54	58	60	63	65	66	67	68	69	70	71	71	72	73	73	74	74	74	74	75
Vigor	Radius (yards)	10	12	14	16	18	20	22	24	26	28	30	32	34	36	38	40	42	44	46	48
	Walk/Run Speed +%	13	18	22	25	28	30	32	33	35	36	37	38	39	40	40	41	41	42	42	43
	Max Stam Increase +%	50	75	100	125	150	175	200	225	250	275	300	325	350	375	400	425	450	475	500	525
	Incr Stam Recovery +%	50	75	100	125	150	175	200	225	250	275	300	325	350	375	400	425	450	475	500	525
Meditation	Radius (yards)	7.3	8.6	10	11.3	12.6	14	15.3	16.6	18	19.3	20.6	22	23.3	24.6	26	27.3	28.6	30	31.3	32.6
	Mana Recovery +%	65	80	95	110	125	140	155	170	185	200	215	230	245	260	275	290	305	320	335	350
Redemption	Radius (yards)	7.3	7.3	7.3	7.3	7.3	7.3	7.3	7.3	7.3	7.3	7.3	7.3	7.3	7.3	7.3	7.3	7.3	7.3	7.3	7.3
	Chance to Redeem %	23	34	42	49	55	59	63	65	69	71	73	75	77	79	80	82	82	83	84	85
	HP/Mana Recovery (pts)	25	30	35	40	45	50	55	60	65	70	75	80	85	90	95	100	105	110	115	120
Salvation	Radius (yards)	7.3	8.6	10	11.3	12.6	14	15.3	16.6	18	19.3	20.6	22	23.3	24.6	26	27.3	28.6	30	31.3	32.6
	Resist All	54	58	60	63	65	66	67	68	69	70	71	71	72	73	73	74	74	74	74	75

PALADIN OFFENSIVE AURAS

		Level 1	Level 2	Level 3	Level 4	Level 5	Level 6	Level 7	Level 8	Level 9	Level 10	Level 11	Level 12	Level 13	Level 14	Level 15	Level 16	Level 17	Level 18	Level 19	Level 20
Might	Radius (yards)	7.3	8.6	10	11.3	12.6	14	15.3	16.6	18	19.3	20.6	22	23.3	24.6	26	27.3	28.6	30	31.3	32.6
	Damage Mod +%	40	50	60	70	80	90	100	110	120	130	140	150	160	170	180	190	200	210	220	230
Holy Fire	Radius (yards)	4	4.6	5.3	6	6.6	7.3	8	8.6	9.3	10	10.6	11.3	12	12.6	13.3	14	14.6	15.3	16	16.6
	Fire Damage	1-3	1.5-3.5	2.5-4.5	3-5	4-6	4.5-6.5	5.5-7.5	6-8	7-9	7.5-9.5	8.5-10.5	9-11	10-12	10.5-12.5	11.5-13.5	12-14	13-15	13.5-15.5	14.5-16.5	15-17
Thorns	Radius (yards)	7.3	8.6	10	11.3	12.6	14	15.3	16.6	18	19.3	20.6	22	23.3	24.6	26	27.3	28.6	30	31.3	32.6
	Damage Return +%	250	290	330	370	410	450	490	530	570	610	650	690	730	770	810	850	890	930	970	1010
Blessed Aim	Radius (yards)	7.3	8.6	10	11.3	12.6	14	15.3	16.6	18	19.3	20.6	22	23.3	24.6	26	27.3	28.6	30	31.3	32.6
	Attack x Return +%	75	90	105	120	135	150	165	180	195	210	225	240	255	270	285	300	315	330	345	360
Concentration	Uninterrupt Chance	20	20	20	20	20	20	20	20	20	20	20	20	20	20	20	20	20	20	20	20
	Damage +%	60	75	90	105	120	135	150	165	180	195	210	225	240	255	270	285	300	315	330	345
Holy Freeze	Radius (yards)	4	4.6	5.3	6	6.6	7.3	8	8.6	9.3	10	10.6	11.3	12	12.6	13.3	14	14.6	15.3	16	16.6
	Slowed by %	30	34	37	40	42	44	45	46	48	48	49	50	51	51	52	53	53	53	54	54
Holy Shock	Radius (yards)	3.3	4	4.6	5.3	6	6.6	7.3	8	8.6	9.3	10	10.6	11.3	12	12.6	13.3	14	14.6	15.3	16
	Lightning Damage	1-5	2-6	4-8	5-9	7-11	8-12	10-14	11-15	13-17	14-18	16-20	17-21	19-23	20-24	22-26	23-27	25-29	26-30	28-32	29-33
Sanctuary	Radius (yards)	3.3	4	4.6	5.3	6	6.6	7.3	8	8.6	9.3	10	10.6	11.3	12	12.6	13.3	14	14.6	15.3	16
	Magic Damage	8-16	12-20	16-24	20-28	24-32	28-36	32-40	36-44	40-48	44-52	48-56	52-60	56-64	60-68	64-72	68-76	72-80	76-84	80-88	84-92
Fanaticism	Radius (yards)	7.3	7.3	7.3	7.3	7.3	7.3	7.3	7.3	7.3	7.3	7.3	7.3	7.3	7.3	7.3	7.3	7.3	7.3	7.3	7.3
	Attack x Mod +%	8-16	12-20	16-24	20-28	24-32	28-36	32-40	36-44	40-48	44-52	48-56	52-60	56-64	60-68	64-72	68-76	72-80	76-84	80-88	84-92
Conviction	Attack Mod +%	40	45	50	55	60	65	70	75	80	85	90	95	100	105	110	115	120	125	130	135
	Radius (yards)	6	6.6	7.3	8	8.6	9.3	10	10.6	11.3	12	12.6	13.3	14	14.6	15.3	16	16.6	17.3	18	18.6
	Defense Mod -%	8-16	12-20	16-24	20-28	24-32	28-36	32-40	36-44	40-48	44-52	48-56	52-60	56-64	60-68	64-72	68-76	72-80	76-84	80-88	84-92
	Maximum Resist -%	26	32	36	39	42	44	46	47	49	50	51	52	53	54	55	56	56	56	57	57

PALADIN COMBAT SKILLS

Skill	Attribute	Level 1	Level 2	Level 3	Level 4	Level 5	Level 6	Level 7	Level 8	Level 9	Level 10	Level 11	Level 12	Level 13	Level 14	Level 15	Level 16	Level 17	Level 18	Level 19	Level 20
Sacrifice	Attack Rating Mod +%	20	25	30	35	40	45	50	55	60	65	70	75	80	85	90	95	100	105	110	115
Damage to Self: 8%	Damage +%	180	192	204	216	228	240	252	264	276	288	300	312	324	336	348	360	372	384	396	408
Smite	Damage Mod +%	15	30	45	60	75	90	105	120	135	150	165	180	195	210	225	240	255	270	285	300
Mana Cost: 2	Stun [sec.]	0.6	0.8	1.0	1.2	1.4	1.6	1.8	2.0	2.2	2.4	2.6	2.8	3.0	3.2	3.4	3.6	3.8	4.0	4.2	4.4
Holy Bolt	Magic Damage	8-16	14-22	20-28	26-34	32-40	38-46	44-52	50-58	56-64	62-70	68-76	74-82	80-88	86-94	92-100	98-106	104-112	110-118	116-124	122-130
	Healing	1-6	3-8	5-10	7-12	9-14	11-16	13-18	15-20	17-22	19-24	21-26	23-28	25-30	27-32	29-34	31-36	33-38	35-40	37-42	39-44
	Mana Cost	4	4.2	4.5	4.7	5	5.2	5.5	5.7	6	6.2	6.5	6.7	7	7.2	7.5	7.7	8	8.2	8.5	8.7
Zeal	Attack Mod +%	10	15	20	25	30	35	40	45	50	55	60	65	70	75	80	85	90	95	100	105
Mana Cost: 2	Number of Hits	2	3	4	5	6	7	8	9	10	11	12	13	14	15	16	17	18	19	20	21
Charge Mana Cost: 9	Damage Mod +%	100	125	150	175	200	225	250	275	300	325	350	375	400	425	450	475	500	525	550	575
Vengeance	Mana Cost	4	4.5	5	5.5	6	6.5	7	7.5	8	8.5	9	9.5	10	10.5	11	11.5	12	12	13	13
	Cold Length	1.2	1.8	2.4	3.0	3.6	4.2	4.8	5.4	6.0	6.6	7.2	7.8	8.4	9.0	9.6	10.2	10.8	11.4	12.0	12.6
Attack Mod +20%	Elem Damage +%	35	40	45	50	55	60	65	70	75	80	85	90	95	100	105	110	115	120	125	130
Blessed Hammer	Damage Mod +%	12-16	20-24	28-32	36-40	44-48	52-56	60-64	68-72	76-80	84-88	92-96	100-104	108-112	116-120	124-128	132-136	140-144	148-152	156-160	164-168
Mana Cost: 35	Mana Cost	5	5.2	5.5	5.7	6	6.2	6.5	6.7	7	7.2	7.5	7.7	8	8.2	8.5	8.7	9	9.2	9.5	9.7
Conversion	Chance to Convert %	11	20	27	33	37	41	44	46	49	51	53	54	56	57	58	60	60	61	62	63
Mana Cost: 4	Duration [sec.]	20	30	40	50	60	70	80	90	100	110	120	130	140	150	160	170	180	190	200	210
Holy Shield	Duration [sec.]	30	40	50	60	70	80	90	100	110	120	130	140	150	160	170	180	190	200	210	220
Mana Cost: 35	Defense Mod +%	25	55	70	70	85	100	115	130	145	160	175	190	205	220	235	250	265	280	295	310
	Chance to Block +%	8	10	12	13	15	16	16	17	18	18	19	19	20	20	20	21	21	21	21	21
Fist of the Heavens	Holy Bolt Dmg	1-16	1-22	1-28	1-34	1-40	1-46	1-52	1-58	1-64	1-70	1-76	1-82	1-88	1-94	1-100	1-106	1-112	1-118	1-124	1-130
	Lightning Damage	1-40	9-48	17-56	25-64	33-72	41-80	49-88	57-96	65-104	73-112	81-120	89-128	97-136	105-144	113-152	121-160	129-168	137-176	145-184	153-192
	Mana Cost	25	27	29	31	33	35	37	39	41	43	45	47	49	51	53	55	57	59	61	63

SORCERESS COLD SPELLS

Spell	Stat	Level 1	Level 2	Level 3	Level 4	Level 5	Level 6	Level 7	Level 8	Level 9	Level 10	Level 11	Level 12	Level 13	Level 14	Level 15	Level 16	Level 17	Level 18	Level 19	Level 20
Ice Bolt (Mana Cost: 3)	Damage	3-5	4-6	5-7	6-8	7-9	8-10	9-11	10-12	11-13	12-14	13-15	14-16	15-17	16-18	17-19	18-20	19-21	20-22	21-23	22-24
	Cold Length (secs)	6	7.4	8.8	10.2	11.6	13	14.4	15.8	17.2	18.6	20	21.4	22.8	24.2	25.6	27	28.4	29.8	31.2	32.6
Frozen Armor (Mana Cost: 7)	Defense Bonus %	30	35	40	45	50	55	60	65	70	75	80	85	90	95	100	105	110	115	120	125
	Duration (secs)	120	132	144	156	168	180	192	204	216	228	240	252	264	276	288	300	312	324	336	348
Frost Nova	Freeze Length (secs)	1.2	1.3	1.4	1.5	1.6	1.8	1.9	2	2.1	2.2	2.4	2.5	2.6	2.7	2.8	3	3.1	3.2	3.3	3.4
	Mana Cost	9	11	13	15	17	19	21	23	25	27	29	31	33	35	37	39	41	43	45	47
	Cold Damage	2-4	4-6	6-8	8-10	10-12	12-14	14-16	16-18	18-20	20-22	22-24	24-26	26-28	28-30	30-32	32-34	34-36	36-38	38-40	40-42
Ice Blast (Mana Cost 11)	Cold Length (secs)	8	9	10	11	12	13	14	15	16	17	18	19	20	21	22	23	24	25	26	27
	Mana Cost	6	6.5	7	7.5	8	8.5	9	9.5	10	10.5	11	11.5	12	12	13	13	14	14	15	15
	Damage	10	17	24	31	38	45	52	59	66	73	80	87	94	101	108	115	122	129	136	143
	Freeze Length (secs)	3	3.2	3.4	3.6	3.8	4	4.2	4.4	4.6	4.8	5	5.2	5.4	5.6	5.8	6	6.2	6.4	6.6	6.8
Shiver Armor (Cold Length: 4 secs)	Defense Bonus %	45%	51%	57%	63%	69%	75%	81%	87%	93%	99%	105%	111%	117%	123%	129%	135%	141%	147%	153%	159%
	Mana Cost	6-8	8-10	10-12	12-14	14-16	16-18	18-20	20-22	22-24	24-26	26-28	28-30	30-32	32-34	34-36	36-38	38-40	40-42	42-44	44-46
	Duration (secs)	120	132	144	156	168	180	192	204	216	228	240	252	264	276	288	300	312	324	336	348
Glacial Spike	Mana Cost	10	10.5	11	11.5	12	12	13	13	14	14	15	15	16	16	17	17	18	18	19	19
	Damage	16-24	23-31	30-38	37-45	44-52	51-59	58-66	65-73	72-80	79-87	86-94	93-101	100-108	107-115	114-122	121-129	128-136	135-143	142-150	149-157
	Freeze Length (secs)	2	2.1	2.2	2.3	2.4	2.6	2.7	2.8	2.9	3	3.2	3.3	3.4	3.5	3.6	3.8	3.9	4	4.1	4.2
Blizzard	Mana Cost	23	24	25	26	27	28	29	30	31	32	33	34	35	36	37	38	39	40	41	42
	Damage (per sec)	32-35	38-41	44-47	50-53	56-59	62-65	68-71	74-77	80-83	86-89	92-95	98-101	104-107	110-113	116-119	122-125	128-131	134-137	140-143	146-149
	Duration (secs)	144	150	156	162	168	174	180	186	192	198	204	210	216	222	228	234	240	246	252	258
Chilling Armor (Mana Cost: 17)	Defense Bonus %	45	50	55	60	65	70	75	80	85	90	95	100	105	110	115	120	125	130	135	140
	Duration (secs)	120	132	144	156	168	180	192	204	216	228	240	252	264	276	288	300	312	324	336	348
Frozen Orb	Mana Cost	25	27	29	31	33	35	37	39	41	43	45	47	49	51	53	55	57	59	61	65
	Damage	16-24	20-28	24-32	28-36	32-40	36-44	40-48	44-52	48-56	52-60	56-64	60-68	64-72	68-76	72-80	76-84	80-88	84-92	88-96	92-100
Cold Mastery (Enemy)	Cold Length (secs)																				

SORCERESS LIGHTNING SPELLS

Spell	Attribute	Level 1	Level 2	Level 3	Level 4	Level 5	Level 6	Level 7	Level 8	Level 9	Level 10	Level 11	Level 12	Level 13	Level 14	Level 15	Level 16	Level 17	Level 18	Level 19	Level 20
Charged Bolt	Damage	2-4	2-4	3-5	3-5	4-6	4-6	5-7	5-7	6-8	6-8	7-9	7-9	8-10	8-10	9-11	9-11	10-12	10-12	11-13	11-13
	# of Bolts	3	4	5	6	7	8	9	10	11	12	13	14	15	16	17	18	19	20	21	22
	Mana Cost	3	3.5	4	4.5	5	5.5	6	6.5	7	7.5	8	8.5	9	9.5	10	10.5	11	11.5	12	12
Static Field	Damage	reduces creature's current life points by 33%																			
Mana Cost: 9	Radius (yards)	3.3	4	4.6	5.3	6	6.6	7.3	8	8.6	9.3	10	10.6	11.3	12	12.6	13.3	14	14.6	15.3	16
	Mana Cost	7	7	7	7	7	7	7	7	7	7	7	7	7	7	7	7	7	7	7	7
Telekinesis	Damage	1-2	2-3	3-4	4-5	5-6	6-7	7-8	8-9	9-10	10-11	11-12	12-13	13-14	14-15	15-16	16-17	17-18	18-19	19-20	20-21
	Mana Cost	7	7	7	7	7	7	7	7	7	7	7	7	7	7	7	7	7	7	7	7
Nova	Damage	1-20	8-27	15-34	22-41	29-48	36-55	43-62	50-69	57-76	64-83	71-90	78-97	85-104	92-111	99-118	106-125	113-132	120-139	127-146	134-153
	Mana Cost	15	16	17	18	19	20	21	22	23	24	25	26	27	28	29	30	31	32	33	34
Lightning	Damage	1-40	1-48	1-56	1-64	1-72	1-80	1-88	1-96	1-104	1-112	1-120	1-128	1-136	1-144	1-152	1-160	1-168	1-176	1-184	1-192
	Mana Cost	8	8.5	9	9.5	10	10.5	11	11.5	12	12	13	13	14	14	15	15	16	16	17	17
Chain Lightning	Damage	1-32	7-38	13-44	19-50	25-56	31-62	37-68	43-74	49-80	55-86	61-92	67-98	73-104	79-110	85-116	91-122	97-128	103-134	109-140	115-146
Hits: 5	Mana Cost	9	10	11	12	13	14	15	16	17	18	19	20	21	22	23	24	25	26	27	28
Teleport	Mana Cost	24	23	22	21	20	19	18	17	16	15	14	13	12	11	10	9	8	7	6	5
Thunder Storm	Mana Cost	19	19	19	19	19	19	19	19	19	19	19	19	19	19	19	19	19	19	19	19
	Damage	1-100	11-110	21-120	31-130	41-140	51-150	61-160	71-170	81-180	91-190	101-200	111-210	121-220	131-230	141-240	151-250	161-260	171-270	181-280	191-290
	Duration (sec.)	32	40	48	56	64	72	80	88	96	104	112	120	128	136	144	152	160	168	176	184
Energy Shield	Absorbs % Damage	15	23	30	35	40	43	46	48	51	52	54	56	57	58	59	61	61	62	63	63
Mana Cost: 5	Duration (secs)	144	192	240	288	336	384	432	480	528	576	624	672	720	768	816	864	912	960	1008	1056
Lightning Mastery	Lightning Costs Reduced	15%	23%	30%	35%	40%	43%	46%	48%	51%	52%	54%	56%	57%	58%	59%	61%	61%	62%	63%	63%

SORCERESS FIRE SPELLS

	Level 1	Level 2	Level 3	Level 4	Level 5	Level 6	Level 7	Level 8	Level 9	Level 10	Level 11	Level 12	Level 13	Level 14	Level 15	Level 16	Level 17	Level 18	Level 19	Level 20
Fire Bolt — Mana Cost 2·5																				
Damage	3-6	4-7	6-9	7-10	9-12	10-13	12-15	13-16	15-18	16-19	18-21	19-22	21-24	22-25	24-27	25-28	27-30	28-31	30-33	31-34
Percent	30	42	54	66	78	90	102	114	126	138	150	162	174	186	198	210	222	234	246	258
Warmth																				
Mana Cost	7	7	8	9	10	10	11	12	13	14	14	15	16	17	17	18	19	20	21	21
Inferno																				
Damage 3 (per sec)	12-25	21-34	31-43	40-53	50-62	59-71	68-81	78-90	87-100	96-109	106-118	115-128	125-137	134-146	143-146	153-165	162-175	171-184	181-193	190-20
Range (yards)	3-3	3-3	4	4-6	5-3	5-3	6	6-6	7-3	7-3	8	8-6	9-3	9-3	10	10-6	11-3	11-3	12	12-6
Blaze																				
Mana Cost	11	11-5	12	12	13	13	14	14	15	15	16	16	17	17	18	18	19	19	20	20
Damage (per sec)	18-37	28-46	37-56	46-65	56-75	65-84	75-93	84-103	93-112	103-121	112-131	121-140	131-150	140-159	150-168	159-178	168-187	178-196	187-206	196-215
Duration (secs)	4-6	5-6	6-6	7-6	8-6	9-6	10-6	11-6	12-6	13-6	14-6	15-6	16-6	17-6	18-6	19-6	20-6	21-6	22-6	23-6
Fireball — Radius: 2 yds																				
Mana Cost	5	5-5	6	6-5	7	7-5	8	8-5	9	9-5	10	10-5	11	11-5	12	12-5	13	13-5	14	14
Damage	6-14	13-21	20-28	27-35	34-42	41-49	48-56	55-63	62-70	69-77	76-84	85-91	90-98	97-105	104-112	111-119	118-126	125-133	132-140	139-147
Fire Wall																				
Mana Cost	22	24	26	28	30	32	34	36	38	40	42	44	46	48	50	52	54	56	58	60
Damage (secs)	4-6	5-6	6-6	7-6	8-6	9-6	10-6	11-6	12-6	13-6	14-6	15-6	16-6	17-6	18-6	19-6	20-6	21-6	22-6	23-6
Radius (yds)	4	6	7	8	10	11	12	14	15	16	18	19	20	22	23	24	26	27	28	30
Duration (secs)	4-6	5-6	6-6	7-6	8-6	9-6	10-6	11-6	12-6	13-6	14-6	15-6	16-6	17-6	18-6	19-6	20-6	21-6	22-6	23-6
Enchant																				
Mana Cost	25	30	35	40	45	50	55	60	65	70	75	80	85	90	95	100	105	110	115	120
Damage	8-10	9-11	10-12	11-13	12-14	13-15	14-16	15-17	16-18	17-19	18-20	19-21	20-22	21-23	22-24	23-25	24-26	25-27	26-28	27-29
Duration (secs)	144	168	192	216	240	264	288	312	336	360	384	408	432	456	480	504	528	552	576	600
Meteor — Radius: 4 yards																				
Mana Cost	17	18	19	20	21	22	23	24	25	26	27	28	29	30	31	32	33	34	35	36
Damage	40-50	52-62	64-74	76-86	88-98	100-110	112-122	124-134	136-146	148-158	160-170	172-182	184-194	196-206	208-218	220-230	232-242	244-254	256-266	268-278
Fire Damage (per sec)	16-21	23-28	30-35	37-42	44-49	51-56	58-63	65-70	72-77	79-84	86-91	93-98	100-105	107-112	114-119	121-126	128-133	135-140	142-147	150-154
Fire Mastery																				
Fire Damage Increase	18%	32%	43%	52%	60%	66%	70%	74%	79%	81%	85%	87%	90%	92%	93%	96%	97%	98%	99%	100%
Hydra																				
Mana Cost	21	23	25	27	29	31	33	35	37	39	41	43	45	47	49	51	53	55	57	59
Damage	11-23	15-27	19-31	23-35	27-39	31-43	35-47	39-51	43-55	47-59	51-63	55-67	59-71	63-75	67-79	71-83	75-87	79-91	83-95	87-99
Duration (secs)	12	13	14	15	16	17	18	19	20	21	22	23	24	25	26	27	28	29	30	31

Index

A

Akara, 131
Alkor, 148
Amazon, 18
    multiplayer, 201
    skill sets, 42–61
Andariel, 175
antidote potions, 14
Arcane Sancturary quest, 145
armor, 12, 181–182
    magic, 182–186
    rare, 186–189
Armor shrine, 15
Asheara, 148
Atma, 140

B

baboon demon, 161
Barbarian, 19
    multiplayer, 201
    skill sets, 98–112
bat demon, 167
Battle.Net, 197–199
Battlemaid Sabrina, 177
Beetleburst, 176
belt, 13
bestiary
    monsters, champion, 174
    monsters, standard, 158–173
    monsters, super unique, 175–178
big head, 159
Bishibosh, 175
Blackened Temple quest, 153–154
Blade of the Old Religion quest, 149–150
blood hawk, 159
Bloodwitch, the Wild, 176
blunderbore, 169

Boneash, 176
Bonebreak, 175
Bremm Sparkfist, 178
Cairn Stones quest, 134–136

C

cantor, 170
character classes, 18–19
character development, 20
characters, major characters, 10
Charsi, 131
chat, multiplayer, 199
choking gas potions, 14
claw viper, 163
Cold skill set, Sorceress, 91–97
Coldcrow, 175
Coldworm the Burrower, 176
Combat shrine, 15
Combat skill set
    Barbarian, 98–103
Paladin, 62–68
Corpsefire, 176
corrupt archer, 168
corrupt rogue, 161
Countess, 175
Creeping Feature, 177
Dark Elder, 177

D-E

Deckard Cain, 131, 140, 155
Den of Evil quest, 132
difficulty levels, 16
Drognan, 140

Elzix, 140
Ephasto the Amorer, 178
evil spiders, 166

Experience shrine, 15
Exploding potions, 14
Exploding Shrine, 15
Fallen Angel quest, 156

F

Fallen shaman, 162
Fallen, The, 160
Fangskin, 176
Fara, 140
Fetish, 168
Fetish shaman, 172
Finger mage, 172
Fire Eye, 176
Fire shrine, 15
Flame Spike the Crawler, 176
Forgotten Tower quest, 136–137
Frog, 170
Geglash, 140

G

Geleb Flamefinger, 178
Gem Shrine, 15
Gheed, 131
Goatmen, 162
Golden Bird quest, 149
Grand Vizier of Chaos, 178
Greater mummy, 165
Griez, 140
Griswold, 175
Guardian quest, 154–155
Halbu, 155
Hardcore mode, multiplayer, 197
Harrowing, 155–156
Healing potions, 14

Health shrine, 15
Hellforce quest, 156–157
Horadric Cube recipes, 12
Horadric Staff quest, 142–144
Hralti, 148

I

Icehawk Riftwing, 177
Infector of Souls, 178
Infernal Gate, 148–154
inventory, 11–12
Ismail Vilehand, 177

J-K

Jamella, 155
Jechyn, 140

Kaelan, 140
Kasha, 131
Khalim's Will quest, 150–152

Laddering system, multiplayer, 198
Lam Esen's Tome quest, 153
Lightning skill set, Sorceress, 86–91
Lut Gholein, 140
Lysander, 140

Maffer Drangonhand, 178
magic
    armor, 182–186
    poison and bone, Necromancer, 21–28
mana potions, 14
Mana recharge shrine, 15
Mana shrine, 15
maps, multiplayer, 199
Masteries skill set, Barbarian, 104–107
megademon, 173
mercenaries
    Infernal Cafe, 148–149
    Rogue Encampment, 131
    Secret of Vizjerei, 140
Meshif, 148
Monster shrine, 15
monsters, 158–178
mosquito demon, 166
mouse cursor, 12
multiplayer information, 196–202
mummy, 165

Necromancer, 19, 21–41

Oemus, 148
Offensive Auras skill set, Paladin, 68–73
oil potions, 14

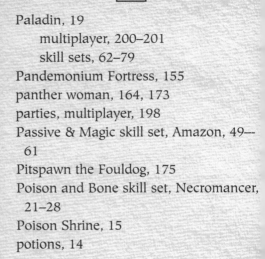

Paladin, 19
    multiplayer, 200–201
    skill sets, 62–79
Pandemonium Fortress, 155
panther woman, 164, 173
parties, multiplayer, 198
Passive & Magic skill set, Amazon, 49–61
Pitspawn the Fouldog, 175
Poison and Bone skill set, Necromancer, 21–28
Poison Shrine, 15
potions, 14

quests, 132–154

Radament, 176
Radament's Lair quest, 141–142
Rakanishu, 175
rancid gas potions, 14
Recharge shrine, 15
Refill shrine, 15
regurgitator, 172
rejuvination potions, 14
Resist Cold shrine, 15
Resist Fire shrine, 15
Resist Lightning shrine, 15
Resist Poison shrine, 15
Rogue Encampment, 131–140

S

and leaper, 163
and maggot, 163
and maggot young, 169
and raider, 160
carab demon, 164
crolls, 13
Secret of the Vizjerei, 140–148
ets, weapons, 189–193
Seven Tombs quest, 147–148
hrines, 15
Sister's Burial quest, 133–134
Sisters to the Slaughter quest, 138–140
keleton, 158
keleton archer, 169
keleton mage, 171
kill sets, 19
    Amazon, 42–61
    Barbarian, 98–112
    Necromancer, 21–41
    Paladin, 62–79
    Sorceress, 80–97
kill shrine, 15
mith, 176
ocketed weapons, 193–194
orceress, 19
    multiplayer, 201
    skill sets, 80–97
pike fiend, 162
szark the Burning, 177
tamina potions, 14
tamina shrine, 15
tormtree, 177
trangling gas potions, 14
ummoner, 177
ummoner quest, 146–147
warm, 164
ainted Sun quest, 144

T

tentacle, 171
tentaclehead, 171
thawing potions, 14
thorned hulk, 167
Tools of the Trade quest, 137–138
Toorc Icefist, 178
trading, multiplayer, 198
Treehead Woodfist, 175
Tyrael, 155

U–V

undead horror, 173

vampires, 167
vulture demon, 165
Warcries skill set, Barbarian, 107–112

W–Z

Warriv, 131, 140
weapons, 12
    armor, 179–181
    magic, 182–186
    rare, 186–189
    sets, 189–193
    socketed, 193–194
    standard, 179–181
wendigo, 160
WillOWisp, 166
Witch Doctor Endugu, 177
wraith, 161
Wyand Voidfinger, 178

zealot, 170
zombie, 159

Where Gamers Go to Know

PC

PlayStation 2

Dreamcast

PlayStation

N64

Reviews | Previews | Demos

Patches | Hints | News

Movies | Features | Forums

The best library of online Game Guides on the planet - more than 100 titles available!

w w w . g a m e s p o t . c o m